# NATIONHOOD, EXECUTIVE POWER AND THE AUSTRALIAN CONSTITUTION

The first comprehensive study of the nature and scope of the nationhood power, this book brings a fresh perspective to the scholarship on the powers of the executive branch in Australia.

The question of when the Federal Executive Government can act without the authorisation of the Parliament is contested and highly topical in Australia. In recent judicial decisions, Australian courts have suggested that statutory authorisation may not be required where the Federal Executive Government is exercising the nationhood power; that is, the implied executive power derived from the character and status of the Commonwealth as the national government.

The Federal Executive Government has relied on this power to implement controversial spending programmes respond to national emergencies and exclude non-citizens from Australia. Together, the chapters in this book analyse and evaluate judicial observations about the operation of the nationhood power in these different contexts and the limits that apply to it.

While the focus of this book is on the nationhood power, it also addresses broader issues concerning the relationship between the legislative and executive branches in parliamentary systems of government. This book makes an important contribution to the literature on executive power and will appeal to constitutional lawyers, scholars and practitioners and those who are involved in the administration of government.

**Volume 12 in the series Hart Studies in Constitutional Law**

**Hart Studies in Constitutional Law**

**Volume 1** The House of Lords 1911–2011: A Century of Non-Reform
*Chris Ballinger*

**Volume 2** Parliament and the Law
*Edited by Alexander Horne, Gavin Drewry and Dawn Oliver*

**Volume 3** Law in Politics, Politics in Law
*Edited by David Feldman*

**Volume 4** Parliamentary Sovereignty in the UK Constitution
*Michael Gordon*

**Volume 5** Parliament: Legislation and Accountability
*Edited by Alexander Horne and Andrew Le Sueur*

**Volume 6** The Codes of the Constitution
*Andrew Blick*

**Volume 7** Essays on the History of Parliamentary Procedure: In Honour of Thomas Erskine May
*Edited by Paul Evans*

**Volume 8** Parliament and the Law
*Edited by Alexander Horne and Gavin Drewry*

**Volume 9** Stretching the Constitution
*Andrew Blick*

**Volume 10** The New Labour Constitution: Twenty Years On
*Edited by Michael Gordon and Adam Tucker*

**Volume 11** Parliament and the Law
*Edited by Alexander Horne, Louise Thompson and Ben Yong*

**Volume 12** Nationhood, Executive Power and the Australian Constitution
*Peta Stephenson*

# Nationhood, Executive Power and the Australian Constitution

Peta Stephenson

• HART •
OXFORD • LONDON • NEW YORK • NEW DELHI • SYDNEY

HART PUBLISHING
Bloomsbury Publishing Plc
Kemp House, Chawley Park, Cumnor Hill, Oxford, OX2 9PH, UK
1385 Broadway, New York, NY 10018, USA
29 Earlsfort Terrace, Dublin 2, Ireland

HART PUBLISHING, the Hart/Stag logo, BLOOMSBURY and the Diana logo are trademarks of Bloomsbury Publishing Plc

First published in Great Britain 2022



A catalogue record for this book is available from the British Library.

Library of Congress Cataloging-in-Publication data

Names: Stephenson, Peta, author.

Title: Nationhood, executive power, and the Australian Constitution / Peta Stephenson.

Description: Oxford, UK ; New York, NY : Hart Publishing, an imprint of Bloomsbury Publishing, 2022. | Series: Hart studies in constitutional law; volume 12 | Includes bibliographical references and index.

Identifiers: LCCN 2022022068 (print) | LCCN 2022022069 (ebook) | ISBN 9781509942329 (hardback) | ISBN 9781509942367 (paperback) | ISBN 9781509942343 (pdf) | ISBN 9781509942336 (Epub)

Subjects: LCSH: Executive power–Australia. | Federal government—Australia. | Legislative bodies—Australia. | Nationalism—Australia. | Constitutional law—Australia.

Classification: LCC KU2200 .S74 2022 (print) | LCC KU2200 (ebook) | DDC 342.94/06—dc23/eng/20220630

LC record available at https://lccn.loc.gov/2022022068

LC ebook record available at https://lccn.loc.gov/2022022069

ISBN: HB: 978-1-50994-232-9
ePDF: 978-1-50994-234-3
ePub: 978-1-50994-233-6

Typeset by Compuscript Ltd, Shannon

# FOREWORD

Sir Garfield Barwick, in the *AAP Case*, described the powers 'inherent in the fact of nationhood' as including the 'power to explore, whether it be foreign lands or seas or in areas of scientific knowledge or technology'.[1] Beyond the pith helmets and telescopes that this observation conjures up, there remains an underlying question of why exploration is something inherent to the national level of government and why it is not something that States, through their universities and research institutions could not adequately engage in.

While exploration is an outlier in later descriptions of the scope of the nationhood power, it is relevant to the nationhood power in a different way. Just as an explorer might search for the source of the Nile, so one might search, most likely in vain, for a clear source of the nationhood power. We know that it falls within that vague expanse of the executive power, but that still does not tell us its original source. At best we can identify it only by what it is not. It is not sourced in the prerogative power derived from the historical power of Kings. It is not sourced in the democratic mandate of Parliament. It is not sourced in the legal personality of the Crown, from which executive capacities are drawn. Instead, we must be satisfied by descriptions of the nationhood power as an 'inherent' or 'implied' power. This is not far from identifying it by reference to 'the vibe of the Constitution', or perhaps more alarmingly, those matters that 'befit the national government of the federation', as the Commonwealth Government once unsuccessfully claimed.[2]

Why does the lack of clarity about the source of this power matter? The source of a power helps identify the principles that provide its foundation and the limits that circumscribe it. For example, the regal historical origins of the prerogative reveal its undemocratic nature, the yoke that harnesses it to historical instances and its modern-day subordination to exercises of legislative power. Without such foundational knowledge in relation to the nationhood power, we remain explorers, seeking signs from infrequent High Court judgments and making educated guesses about where they lead.

This book by Dr Peta Stephenson is the best map or guide to the nationhood power that we, as explorers, could hope for. It meticulously pieces together all the clues left by the High Court in its few attempts to elucidate the operation of the nationhood power. It is not an opinionated work, but rather, one that is objective and rational. It allows the reader to reach their own conclusion and set their

[1] *Victoria v Commonwealth and Hayden* (1975) 134 CLR 338, 362.
[2] *Williams v Commonwealth* (2014) 252 CLR 416, [70].

own path, but it provides the comfort of guidance and the knowledge that one has surveyed all the available knowledge before embarking on further exploration.

There is still much to be explored. For example, if spending on a matter does not require statutory authorisation when it falls within the scope of a prerogative power, is such spending also authorised without statutory authorisation if it falls within the nationhood power? This question was left unsettled in the *Williams* cases.

To what extent do the limits that apply to the prerogative also affect the nationhood power? If a prerogative is displaced by legislation, is a nationhood power that covers the same subject matter as the prerogative, such as a power to deal with an emergency, displaced to the same extent by that legislation?

Does the executive nationhood power displace the prerogative in the same way that statute does? If so, what if the nationhood power is both wider than the prerogative it is displacing (eg because the nationhood power is not constrained by historical evidence of its existence and scope) and narrower (eg because it must meet the federal limits imposed in Mason J's test from the *AAP* case)? Can remnants of the prerogative survive to the extent that they exceed the scope of the nationhood power?

What if a prerogative may be exercised at both the State and Commonwealth levels, but the Commonwealth prerogative has been displaced by the nationhood power? Are the equivalent State prerogative and Commonwealth nationhood powers subject to the same or different limitations and how might this affect their operation?

Matters become far more complex once the incidental power in s 51(xxxix) is thrown into the equation, converting the nationhood power into a legislative one. The scope of the incidental power is itself unsettled. Does the fact that the law must be 'incidental to the execution' of the executive power limit it to a narrow category of law or can it give full legislative effect to the executive nationhood power? Must a proportionality test be applied to ascertain the relationship between the incidental legislative power and the nationhood executive power to which it is giving effect? If so, on what basis? Is it because the nationhood power is purposive in nature or is proportionality the test for all instances of the exercise of the incidental power? If a proportionality test applies, is it a structured proportionality test and how would it operate in relation to the nationhood power?

More testing still is the potentially curious consequence of the movement from non-statutory executive power to legislative power and then to a statutory executive power. For example, if the nationhood power, as an executive power, is then given statutory effect by the incidental power, can this statute confer statutory executive power on ministers or officials that then displaces the non-statutory nationhood power that was its original source? If so, how is such legislation amended in the future? An example might be an exercise of the nationhood power to authorise the use of the Australian Defence Forces to provide civilian aid during a natural disaster or pandemic. If the incidental power were used to give effect to legislation which conferred statutory executive power in a comprehensive manner to deal with the provision of civilian aid during such emergencies, would it displace the nationhood executive power with respect to civilian aid, and if so, is there any non-statutory executive power left to support the exercise of the incidental power to amend the statute? Unlike in the *Kartinyeri* case,[3] when there was a substantive head of power to support the primary law, including its future repeal or amendment, greater conceptual difficulty arises where the legislative power was only ever incidental to a non-statutory executive power that has since been displaced. Perhaps due to the vexing nature of such a conundrum the Commonwealth has so far chosen not to legislate to govern this subject.

This book does not indulge in all these mind-bending dilemmas. Instead, it methodically and lucidly prepares the groundwork for any such exploration, analysing the relevant cases and drawing together the different strands of the High Court's jurisprudence (and that of the Federal Court, in cases such as the *Tampa* case[4]). In Part I it situates the nationhood power within the broader executive power, outlining the distinctions that the High Court has drawn from the prerogative and the capacities of the Crown. This provides the foundation for addressing some of the perplexing problems outlined above that turn on the relationship between the nationhood power, the prerogatives and the Crown's capacities.

Part II provides a detailed survey of the development of the High Court's jurisprudence on the nationhood power. It sparks current interest by delving deeply into two highly political controversies. The first is the use of the Australian Defence Forces to provide civil aid during non-violent emergencies, such as natural disasters and pandemics. The second concerns border protection and the power to exclude aliens from Australia, including their removal for processing in offshore locations.

Part III then focuses on the limitations on the nationhood power. It mines the High Court's jurisprudence to extract the different elements of federalism which have been used to limit the exercise of the nationhood power. This is a difficult exercise, as federalism holds a fraught relationship with the nationhood power. On the one hand, the nationhood power was established as a means of ensuring that the Commonwealth Government could exercise powers that had not been explicitly allocated to it in the federal distribution of powers by the Constitution. It is said to fill a 'lacuna' in that distribution of powers. Yet, on the other hand, the High Court has taken care not to be seen to be overturning that distribution of powers as determined by the Constitution. So the nationhood power must simultaneously expand the powers of the Commonwealth while not limiting or having a deleterious impact upon the powers of the States. Hence, we see the awkward assessments of whether an exercise of the nationhood power would result in 'competition' with the States.

[3] *Kartinyeri v Commonwealth* (1998) 195 CLR 337.
[4] *Ruddock v Vadarlis* (2001) 110 FCR 491.

The mysteries of the nationhood power are manifold. This book does not purport to unravel them, but rather to prepare the ground for future exploration. It fulfils this role splendidly, with the right mix of attention to detail and astute observations, conveyed with merciful clarity. It lays the groundwork for future development and analysis, including, hopefully, from the author, Dr Stephenson, who is a rising star in the field of constitutional law.

Anne Twomey
*University of Sydney*
*13 July 2022*

# ACKNOWLEDGEMENTS

This book is derived from my doctoral thesis: *Measuring the Metes and Bounds of Commonwealth Executive Power: Nationhood and Section 61 of the Constitution*, which I completed at the University of Queensland in 2018. There are many people who have, in various ways, assisted me in writing this book whom I wish to acknowledge here.

First, I am indebted to my supervisors, Jonathan Crowe and Nicholas Aroney, for their encouragement, support and guidance over the course of this project.

I sincerely thank HP Lee and Thomas Poole for examining my thesis and for providing thoughtful comments and suggestions that have been immensely helpful in transforming the thesis into a book. I also thank the two anonymous reviewers for their very useful feedback during the publishing process.

There are many colleagues who have generously spared their time and expertise to assist me with this project, by reading my work and discussing my ideas with me, for which I am very grateful. In particular, I thank Anne Twomey, George Williams, Gabrielle Appleby, Michael White, Murray Wesson and Benjamin Saunders. I also thank Teagan Matthews for her research assistance.

Special thanks are due to Andrew Lynch for the opportunity to participate in the Great Australian Dissents Workshop in 2015 and to contribute a chapter to the subsequent edited collection, which explored Mason J's judgment in *Victoria v Commonwealth and Hayden* (1975) 134 CLR 338. In that regard, I would like to express my gratitude to the Hon Sir Anthony Mason AC KBE GBM QC for taking the time to read that chapter and discuss it with me.

My thanks go to Hart Publishing for the opportunity to publish this book. In particular, I thank Kate Whetter for her enthusiasm about the project, as well as Rosemarie Mearns, Linda Staniford and Carolyn Fox for their editorial assistance.

I am very grateful for the love and support of my friends and family. I thank Sarah-Jane Bennett and Natalie Alexander for their encouragement and friendship. I especially thank my dad, Tom, for his unwavering confidence in me and his support of my academic endeavours over many years.

Finally, I thank my best friend and partner, Ben. The completion of this book would not have been possible without his love, support and good humour.

Some of the material in this book has been published in the following works and has been reproduced with the permission of the publishers: 'Nationhood and Section 61 of the Constitution' (2018) 43 *University of Western Australia Law Review* 149; 'Justice Mason in the *Australian Assistance Plan Case* (1975): Nationhood, Federalism and Commonwealth Executive Power' in Andrew Lynch (ed), *Great Australian Dissents* (Cambridge University Press, 2016) 169; 'Statutory

Displacement of the Prerogative in Australia' in Janina Boughey and Lisa Burton Crawford (eds), *Interpreting Executive Power* (Federation Press, 2020) 203; 'The Relationship between the Royal Prerogative and Statute in Australia' (2021) 44 *Melbourne University Law Review* 1001.

Peta Stephenson
*Brisbane*
*March 2022*

# CONTENTS

## PART II
## THE SCOPE OF THE NATIONHOOD POWER

PART III
LIMITATIONS ON THE NATIONHOOD POWER

# TABLE OF CASES

# TABLE OF LEGISLATION

**Australia**

**New South Wales**



**Queensland**



**South Australia**



**Tasmania**



**Victoria**



**Western Australia**



**Australian Capital Territory**

### Northern Territory



### United Kingdom



### United States



### International

# PART I

# Executive Power in Australia

# 1

# Introduction

> Australia has grown into nationhood. With the march of history the Australian colonies are now the Australian nation. The words of the Constitution must be read with that in mind and to meet, as they arise, the national needs of the 'one indissoluble Federal Commonwealth' under the Crown.
>
> Sir Victor Windeyer, 1969[1]

In Australia, the executive power of the Commonwealth is described, but not defined, in s 61 of the Constitution.[2] Section 61 provides:

> The executive power of the Commonwealth is vested in the Queen and is exercisable by the Governor-General as the Queen's representative, and extends to the execution and maintenance of this Constitution, and of the laws of the Commonwealth.

It is generally understood that the meaning of 'executive power' in s 61 is informed by constitutional history and the common law, and encompasses many of the powers that were enjoyed by the British Crown at the time of Australia's federation.[3] There are, however, significant differences between the constitutional settings which exist in Australia and the United Kingdom. As such, it cannot be assumed that the executive power conferred by s 61 is coextensive with British executive power.[4] Rather, the nature and scope of the 'executive power of the Commonwealth' must be determined by construing the text of s 61 in its constitutional context.[5]

[1] *Bonser v La Macchia* (1969) 122 CLR 177, 223. Reproduced with permission of Thomson Reuters (Professional) Australia Limited, legal.thomsonreuters.com.au.

[2] *Plaintiff M68/2015 v Minister for Immigration and Border Protection* (2016) 257 CLR 42, 96 [129] (Gageler J). See also KM Hayne, 'Government Contracts and Public Law' (2017) 41 *Melbourne University Law Review* 155, 173.

[3] C Saunders, 'The Concept of the Crown' (2015) 38 *Melbourne University Law Review* 873, 888.

[4] *Williams v Commonwealth [No 2]* (2014) 252 CLR 416, 469 [81]–[83] (French CJ, Hayne, Kiefel, Bell and Keane JJ). See also L Burton Crawford, *The Rule of Law and the Australian Constitution* (Annandale, The Federation Press, 2017) 167.

[5] *Re Ditfort; Ex parte Deputy Commissioner of Taxation* (1988) 19 FCR 347, 369 (Gummow J); *Ruddock v Vadarlis* (2001) 110 FCR 491, 540 [183], 542 [191] (French CJ) (*Tampa case*); *Pape v Federal Commissioner of Taxation* (2009) 238 CLR 1, 60 [127] (French CJ), 83 [215] (Gummow, Crennan and Bell JJ).

This approach to interpreting s 61 was adopted by the High Court of Australia in a series of recent decisions, the most significant of which include *Pape v Federal Commissioner of Taxation*,[6] *Williams v Commonwealth [No 1]*[7] and *Williams v Commonwealth [No 2]*.[8] These cases have developed our understanding of the nature and scope of Commonwealth executive power.[9] They clarify that s 61, understood in its constitutional context, is the primary source of Commonwealth executive power in Australia, but that its content can be ascertained by reference to different 'categories' of power.[10]

In addition to the executive powers that are conferred directly on the Executive Government by provisions of the Australian Constitution[11] and by statute, the High Court has recognised that the 'executive power of the Commonwealth' in s 61 derives some of its content from the common law or 'non-statutory' powers of the Crown that are appropriate to the Commonwealth.[12] In a classification that has received judicial endorsement in Australia, Sir William Blackstone divided these powers into two categories, namely, the 'prerogative' and the other capacities enjoyed by the Crown in common with legal persons.[13]

According to Blackstone, the term 'prerogative' could only be applied 'to those rights and capacities which the king enjoys alone, in contradistinction to others'.[14] It is generally accepted that by vesting the executive power in the Queen,[15] s 61 encompasses 'such of the prerogatives of the Crown as are properly attributable to the Commonwealth'.[16] The prerogative remains an important source of authority for government action in Australia. The power to declare war and peace,[17] enter

[6] *Pape* (n 5).

[7] *Williams v Commonwealth [No 1]* (2012) 248 CLR 156.

[8] *Williams v Commonwealth [No 2]* (n 4).

[9] Other significant decisions include *Cadia Holdings Pty Ltd v New South Wales* (2010) 242 CLR 195; *CPCF v Minister for Immigration and Border Protection* (2015) 255 CLR 514; *Plaintiff M68* (n 2).

[10] See especially *Pape* (n 5) 60 [126]–[127] (French CJ); *Williams [No 1]* (n 7) 184–85 [22] (French CJ), 342 [484]–[485] (Crennan J).

[11] See, eg, powers to prorogue the Parliament and dissolve the House of Representatives (ss 5 and 28); issue writs for general elections (s 32); recommend money votes (s 56); assent to proposed laws (s 58); appoint ministers (ss 62, 64), civil servants (s 67) and judges (s 72); and command the naval and military forces of the Commonwealth (s 68).

[12] *Barton v Commonwealth* (1974) 131 CLR 477, 498 (Mason J). See also *Williams [No 1]* (n 7) 189 [30] (French CJ).

[13] W Blackstone, *Commentaries on the Laws of England*, Book I, 1st edn (Oxford, Oxford University Press, 2016) 155 [232]. See also *Davis v Commonwealth* (1988) 166 CLR 79, 107–09 (Brennan J); *Williams [No 1]* (n 7) 185–86 [25] (French CJ), 344 [488] (Crennan J); *Plaintiff M68* (n 2) 97–99 [132]–[136] (Gageler J). AV Dicey, on the other hand, defined the prerogative as 'the residue of discretionary or arbitrary authority, which at any given time is legally left in the hands of the Crown' in AV Dicey, *Introduction to the Study of the Law of the Constitution*, 10th edn (London, MacMillan, 1959) 424.

[14] Blackstone (n 13) 155 [232].

[15] *Federal Commissioner of Taxation v Official Liquidator of E O Farley Ltd (in liq)* (1940) 63 CLR 278, 304 (Dixon J); *Barton* (n 12) 498 (Mason J); *Cadia* (n 9) 226 [86] (Gummow, Hayne, Heydon and Crennan JJ); *Williams [No 1]* (n 7) 185 [24] (French CJ). See also G Winterton, *Parliament, the Executive and the Governor-General: A Constitutional Analysis* (Carlton, Melbourne University Press, 1983) 50.

[16] *Williams [No 1]* (n 7) 180 [22] (French CJ).

[17] *Farey v Burvett* (1916) 21 CLR 433, 452 (Isaacs J).

into international treaties and conduct foreign affairs,[18] request the extradition of fugitives from foreign states,[19] call out the military to maintain internal security,[20] and exclude non-citizens from Australia[21] are all executive acts that are understood as falling within the prerogative.

The 'capacities', on the other hand, were those powers attributable to the legal personality of the Crown that it shared in common with its subjects.[22] In Australia, the Commonwealth as a polity enjoys certain capacities that are derived from its legal personality, including the capacity to enter into contracts and spend money.[23] The capacities of the Commonwealth are not, however, as extensive as those enjoyed by natural persons.[24] In *Williams v Commonwealth [No 1]* the High Court held that, when interpreted in its constitutional context, s 61 conferred a limited power to contract and spend on the Commonwealth, which was constrained by the federal distribution of powers effected by the Constitution,[25] and the principles of representative and responsible government that required parliamentary scrutiny of the expenditure of public money.[26] As such, in Australia, many executive contracts and expenditure in the Commonwealth's sphere must now be supported by valid legislation.

The High Court has also recognised that s 61 of the Constitution encompasses power derived from 'the character and status of the Commonwealth as the national government'.[27] This power, which has been described as the 'nationhood power'

[18] *R v Burgess; Ex parte Henry* (1936) 55 CLR 608, 635–36 (Latham CJ), 681 (Evatt and McTiernan JJ); *Koowarta v Bjelke-Petersen* (1982) 153 CLR 168, 193 (Gibbs CJ).

[19] *Barton* (n 12) 485 (Barwick CJ), 498–99 (Mason J), 505–06 (Jacobs J); *Oates v Attorney-General (Cth)* (2003) 214 CLR 496, 511 [37] (Gleeson CJ, McHugh, Gummow, Kirby, Hayne and Heydon JJ).

[20] See *R v Secretary of State for the Home Department; Ex parte Northumbria Police Authority* [1989] 1 QB 26, 44 (Croom-Johnson LJ), 45–46 (Purchas LJ), 58–59 (Nourse LJ). In Australia, the exercise of this power would be subject to s 119 of the Australian Constitution. It is unclear whether, and to what extent, this prerogative has survived the enactment of Part IIIAAA of the *Defence Act 1903* (Cth), which sets out a comprehensive regime for the deployment of the Australian Defence Force when it is called out to protect the States against domestic violence or to protect Commonwealth interests. This question has not yet received judicial consideration. See the discussion in Chapter 4.

[21] See *Tampa case* (n 5). Note that Black CJ (in dissent) held that the existence of a prerogative power to exclude aliens was 'uncertain' and had, in any event, been abrogated by Commonwealth legislation: at 495–501 [9]–[29], 508 [64]. See also *CPCF* (n 9) 596–98 [261]–[269], 599 [271], 600 [277] (Kiefel J). See the discussion in Chapter 5.

[22] Blackstone (n 13) 155 [232].

[23] *Williams [No 1]* (n 7) 184 [21] (French CJ), 237 [154] (Gummow and Bell JJ), 253–54 [204] (Hayne J), 342 [484] (Crennan J).

[24] *Williams [No 1]* (n 7) 193 [38] (French CJ), 237–38 [154]–[155] (Gummow and Bell JJ), 253–54 [204] (Hayne J), 352–53 [518]–[524] (Crennan J), 373–74 [595] (Kiefel J). See also *Plaintiff M68* (n 2) 101 [145] (Gageler J).

[25] ibid 192–93 [37] (French CJ), 218 [89] (Gummow and Bell JJ), 248–52 [192]–[199] (Hayne J), 353 [522] (Crennan J), 370 [581], 372 [586]–[590] (Kiefel J).

[26] ibid 236 [151] (Gummow and Bell JJ), 241 [173], 258–59 [216] (Hayne J), 351–52 [516], [519] (Crennan J), 368–69 [577] (Kiefel J).

[27] *Victoria v Commonwealth and Hayden* (1975) 134 CLR 338, 397 (Mason J) (*AAP case*); *Davis* (n 13) 94 (Mason CJ, Deane and Gaudron JJ); *R v Duncan; Ex parte Australian Iron & Steel Pty Ltd* (1983) 158 CLR 535, 560 (Mason J); *R v Hughes* (2000) 202 CLR 535, 554–55 [38] (Gleeson CJ,

in the Australian case law[28] and academic commentary,[29] is captured by Mason J's formulation of it in the important and influential decision in *Victoria v Commonwealth and Hayden* ('*AAP case*'):

> [T]here is to be deduced from the existence and character of the Commonwealth as a national government and from the presence of ss 51(xxxix) and 61 a capacity to engage in enterprises and activities peculiarly adapted to the government of a nation and which cannot otherwise be carried on for the benefit of the nation.[30]

For convenience, this book will refer to this formula as the 'peculiarly adapted' test. Without attempting to define the scope of the nationhood power in the *AAP case*, Mason J suggested that it provided the constitutional basis for national scientific research, including the establishment of the Commonwealth Scientific and Industrial Research Organisation (CSIRO)[31] and Commonwealth expenditure on 'inquiries, investigation and advocacy in relation to matters affecting public health'.[32] These examples were not exhaustive and Mason J accepted that the 'functions appropriate and adapted to a national government will vary from time to time'.[33]

While Mason J contemplated that a potentially wide range of executive activities could enliven the nationhood power, he cautioned that its scope was not

Gaudron, McHugh, Gummow, Hayne and Callinan JJ); *Pape* (n 5) 60–61 [128], 63 [133] (French CJ), 87–88 [228], 91–92 [248] (Gummow, Crennan and Bell JJ); *Williams [No 1]* (n 7) 184–85 [22], 191 [34], 216–17 [83] (French CJ), 342 [485] (Crennan J), 370 [583] (Kiefel J).

[28] See, eg, *Williams [No 2]* (n 4) 454 [23] (French CJ, Hayne, Kiefel, Bell and Keane JJ); *CPCF* (n 9) 568 [150] (Hayne and Bell JJ), 596 [260] (Kiefel J). For some time, however, Australian courts did not refer to this power as the 'nationhood power' despite it being a popular description in academic commentary. This has contributed to the uncertainty as to the nature and scope of this power. See further A Twomey, 'Pushing the Boundaries of Executive Power: *Pape*, the Prerogative and Nationhood Powers' (2010) 34 *Melbourne University Law Review* 313, 317–18.

[29] See, eg, Twomey, 'Pushing the Boundaries' (n 28); A Twomey, 'The French Court, the Nature of the Executive Power and its Reconciliation with the Expenditure Power' in H Jackson (ed), *Essays in Honour of Chief Justice French* (Alexandria, Federation Press, 2019) 27; C Saunders, 'Separation of Legislative and Executive Power' in C Saunders and A Stone (eds), *The Oxford Handbook of the Australian Constitution* (Oxford, Oxford University Press, 2018) 617; Winterton, *Parliament, the Executive and the Governor-General* (n 15) 40–44; P Gerangelos, 'The Executive Power of the Commonwealth of Australia: Section 61 of the Commonwealth Constitution, "Nationhood" and the Future of the Prerogative' (2012) 12 *Oxford University Commonwealth Law Journal* 97; N Condylis, 'Debating the Nature and Ambit of the Commonwealth's Non-Statutory Executive Power' (2015) 39 *Melbourne University Law Review* 385, 389, 399, 426–28; J Stellios, *Zines's The High Court and the Constitution*, 6th edn (Annandale, Federation Press, 2015) 447–56; P Stephenson, 'Nationhood and Section 61 of the Constitution' (2018) 43 *University of Western Australia Law Review* 149; P Stephenson, Justice Mason in the Australian Assistance Plan Case (1975): Nationhood, Federalism and Commonwealth Executive Power in A Lynch (ed), *Great Australian Dissents* (Cambridge, Cambridge University Press, 2016) 169; G Williams, S Brennan and A Lynch, *Blackshield and Williams Australian Constitutional Law and Theory: Commentary and Materials*, 7th edn (Annandale, Federation Press, 2018) 379–97; J Kirk, 'Constitutional Implications (I): Nature, Legitimacy, Classification, Examples' (2000) 24 *Melbourne University Law Review* 645, 669–71; A Hanna, 'Nationhood Power and Judicial Review: A Bridge Too Far' (2015) 39 *University of Western Australia Law Review* 327.

[30] *AAP case* (n 27) 397.

[31] ibid.

[32] ibid.

[33] ibid.

unlimited. The nationhood power could not be exercised to effect a 'radical transformation' of the federal constitutional structure.[34] Justice Mason explained that the mere fact that an enterprise or activity could be 'conveniently formulated and administered by the national government'[35] was not sufficient to render it 'peculiarly adapted' to the national government and within the scope of the nationhood power.

In the decades since the *AAP case* was decided, the Commonwealth Government has relied on the nationhood power to: support executive action undertaken to commemorate events of national significance;[36] implement controversial spending programmes[37] and intergovernmental agreements;[38] respond to national emergencies, including a national fiscal emergency;[39] maintain internal security;[40] and prevent non-citizens from entering Australia.[41] This is not, however, an exhaustive list and the full range of Commonwealth initiatives, enterprises and activities that might fall within the scope of the nationhood power has not yet been settled.

Furthermore, in some cases, the nationhood power was given legislative expression by the operation of the express incidental power in s 51(xxxix) of the Constitution.[42] Section 51(xxxix) confers power on the Commonwealth Parliament to make laws with respect to 'matters incidental to the execution of any power vested by this Constitution … in the government of the Commonwealth'. As such, where executive action is supported by the nationhood power, the Commonwealth Parliament may enact legislation to facilitate the exercise of that power under s 51(xxxix). This raises additional questions about the matters that are 'incidental' to the exercise of the nationhood power.

While the High Court has made it clear that the Commonwealth cannot decide for itself what 'befits' its status as the national government, academic commentators[43] and a number of justices of the High Court[44] have expressed

[34] ibid 398.

[35] ibid.

[36] *Davis* (n 13).

[37] *Pape* (n 5). Note that the High Court did not accept the Commonwealth's submissions that the nationhood power provided the constitutional basis for the spending on the National School Chaplaincy Program in *Williams [No 1]* (n 7) and *Williams [No 2]* (n 4).

[38] *Duncan* (n 27) 560 (Mason J).

[39] *Pape* (n 5).

[40] *R v Sharkey* (1949) 79 CLR 121; *Burns v Ransley* (1949) 79 CLR 101; *Australian Communist Party v Commonwealth* (1951) 83 CLR 1.

[41] *Tampa case* (n 5) 542 [191], 543 [193] (French J, Beaumont J agreeing at 514 [95]).

[42] See, eg, *Commonwealth v Tasmania* (1983) 158 CLR 1 ('*Tasmanian Dam Case*'); *Davis* (n 13); *Pape* (n 5).

[43] See especially Twomey, 'Pushing the Boundaries' (n 28); Stellios (n 29) 453–56; G Winterton, 'The Relationship between Commonwealth Legislative and Executive Power' (2004) 25 *Adelaide Law Review* 21, 33–36.

[44] See, eg, *AAP case* (n 27) 362 (Barwick CJ), 392 (Mason J); *Pape* (n 5) 122–23 [352]–[354] (Hayne and Kiefel JJ, in dissent), 193 [551]–[552] (Heydon J, in dissent). See also the observations made extra-curially by M Gordon, 'Communist Party Case: Core Themes and Legacy' (Speech Delivered at the Centre for Comparative Constitutional Studies Constitutional Law Conference, Melbourne, 23 July 2021) 42–43; W Gummow, 'Unity' in C Saunders and A Stone (eds), *The Oxford Handbook of the Australian Constitution* (Oxford, Oxford University Press, 2018) 405, 422–24.

concern about the ongoing uncertainty that surrounds the source, nature and scope of the nationhood power. Adding to this uncertainty is the lack of clarity in Australia as to whether the nationhood power is to be understood as a separate source or 'category' of non-statutory executive power, or whether 'the character and status of the Commonwealth as the national government' is merely a factor that is relevant to the High Court's consideration of whether the non-statutory executive powers can be exercised by the Commonwealth, rather than the States. There are conflicting judicial statements in the case law about the relationship between the nationhood power and the other categories of executive power that are encompassed by s 61 of the Constitution.

Hence, the aim of this book is to provide an account of the nature and scope of the nationhood power. This requires an examination of the development of the nationhood power in the Australian constitutional jurisprudence. The book considers the types of executive action that have been accepted by Australian courts as being supported by the nationhood power. It also examines whether there are limits to the nationhood power and seeks to identify what those limits are.

## I. The Scope of this Book

As the preceding discussion suggests, this book is a doctrinal analysis of Australian case law. It analyses and evaluates decisions made by Australian courts about the nature and scope of the nationhood power in different contexts. It undertakes a comprehensive analysis of the relevant case law in order to identify themes or trends in the High Court's approach to interpreting the nationhood power. This has not been a straightforward task. While there are relatively few decided cases in the area, opinions have differed among individual justices of the Court about the interrelated questions of the source, nature and scope of the nationhood power. Furthermore, there is a lack of judicial consensus about the use of the terminology of the 'nationhood power', which, as mentioned above, has made its way into the Court's judgments relatively recently. This lack of consistency has made it difficult to discern clear statements of legal principle from these decisions and has contributed to the confusion in this area.

There are several issues that are potentially relevant to a study of the relationship between nationhood and the Australian Constitution which cannot be explored within the confines of this book. In particular, the book does not undertake an independent historical analysis of the events that led to Australia's attainment of nationhood or a detailed consideration of the political and constitutional history of Australia and the United Kingdom.[45] While it does examine judicial observations

[45] See generally WJ Hudson and MP Sharp, *Australian Independence: Colony to Reluctant Kingdom* (Carlton, Melbourne University Press, 1988); L Zines, 'The Growth of Australian Nationhood and its Effect on the Powers of the Commonwealth' in L Zines (ed), *Commentaries on the Australian*

made about the constitutional significance of Australia's attainment of nationhood for the Court's interpretation of s 61 of the Constitution, this book does not purport to explore the concept of nationhood in political theory.[46] That is because 'the nationhood power' is simply a shorthand description of the implied executive power derived from the character and status of the Commonwealth as a national government. While it is important to have some understanding of the events that led to Australia's attainment of 'nationhood', which the Court has understood as being synonymous with Australia's acquisition of independence in the exercise of its legislative, executive and judicial power, it is not necessary to define the concept of nationhood in this book.

This book is not a comparative study of executive power, but it does address broader issues about the relationship between the legislative and executive branches in a parliamentary system of government that are not unique to Australia. For example, in 2017 the Supreme Court of the United Kingdom handed down its decision in *R (Miller) v Secretary of State for Exiting the European Union*.[47] The Supreme Court found that British Ministers could not rely on the prerogative to give notice to the European Council of the United Kingdom's intention to withdraw from the European Union without statutory authorisation. As *Miller* demonstrated, questions regarding when the executive branch of government can act without the approval or authorisation of the Parliament, and when legislation will be held to have abrogated or displaced the prerogative, are contested and complex ones. This book provides an Australian perspective on these issues by considering how Australian courts have adapted common law principles, such as the rules governing the abrogation or displacement of the prerogative, to the Australian constitutional context.

As this book is not a general study of the executive branch of government in Australia, it does not examine the exercise of reserve powers by the

*Constitution: A Tribute to Geoffrey Sawer* (Sydney, Butterworths, 1977) 15; G Winterton, 'The Acquisition of Independence in R French, G Lindell and C Saunders' (eds), *Reflections on the Australian Constitution* (Annandale, Federation Press, 2003) 33–36; G Lindell, 'Further Reflections on the Date of the Acquisition of Australia's Independence' in R French, G Lindell and C Saunders (eds), *Reflections on the Australian Constitution* (Annandale, Federation Press, 2003) 52; A Twomey, '*Sue v Hill* – The Evolution of Australian Independence' in A Stone and G Williams (eds), *The High Court at the Crossroads: Essays in Constitutional Law* (Leichhardt, Federation Press, 2000) 102–03; A Twomey, *The Chameleon Crown: The Queen and Her Australian Governors* (Annandale, Federation Press, 2006); A Twomey, 'Independence' in C Saunders and A Stone (eds), *The Oxford Handbook of the Australian Constitution* (Oxford, Oxford University Press, 2018) 96. For a discussion of the relationship between nationhood and popular sovereignty see, eg, G Duke, 'Popular Sovereignty and the Nationhood Power' (2017) 45 *Federal Law Review* 415; BB Saunders and SP Kennedy, 'Popular Sovereignty, "the People" and the Australian Constitution: A Historical Reassessment' (2019) 30 *Public Law Review* 36.

[46] See, eg, SD Krasner, *Sovereignty: Organized Hypocrisy* (Princeton, Princeton University Press, 1999); SD Krasner (ed), *Problematic Sovereignty: Contested Rules and Political Possibilities* (New York, Columbia University Press, 2001); H Kalmo and Q Skinner (eds), *Sovereignty in Fragments: The Past, Present and Future of a Contested Concept* (Cambridge, Cambridge University Press, 2010).

[47] *R (Miller) v Secretary of State for Exiting the European Union* [2017] UKSC 5; [2018] AC 61.

Governor-General[48] or the 1975 constitutional crisis in Australia.[49] The focus of this book is on the inherent or 'non-statutory' executive powers that comprise the 'executive power of the Commonwealth' in s 61. As such, it does not consider the scope of the powers conferred on the Commonwealth Executive by specific provisions of the Constitution or by statute. Nor does it consider issues of administrative law, including questions concerning the justiciability or judicial review of executive action, as this book is situated squarely in the field of Australian constitutional law.[50]

While this book analyses and evaluates the reasoning employed by the High Court to 'unearth' or 'uncover' the implied nationhood power, its central task is to examine the nature and scope of the nationhood power and identify the limits that apply to it. This book does not, therefore, extensively analyse or critique the wisdom of Australian courts in confirming the existence of this power, nor does it engage in the wider debate about constitutional implications and the circumstances in which they may legitimately be recognised by the High Court.[51]

[48] See A Twomey, *The Veiled Sceptre: Reserve Powers of Heads of State in Westminster Systems* (Port Melbourne, Cambridge University Press, 2018).

[49] See, eg, G Sawer, *Federation Under Strain: Australia 1972–1975* (Carlton, Melbourne University Press, 1977); C Howard and C Saunders, 'The Blocking of the Budget and Dismissal of the Government' in G Evans (ed), *Labor and the Constitution 1972–1975: Essays and Commentaries on the Constitutional Controversies of the Whitlam Years* (Richmond, Heinemann Educational Australia, 1977) 251; LJM Cooray, *Conventions, the Australian Constitution and the Future* (Sydney, Legal Books, 1979) 106–58; G Winterton, '1975: The Dismissal of the Whitlam Government' in G Winterton and HP Lee (eds), *Australian Constitutional Landmarks* (Port Melbourne, Cambridge University Press, 2003) 229; J Hocking, *The Dismissal Dossier Updated Edition: Everything You Were Never Meant to Know about November 1975* (Carlton, Melbourne University Press, 2016); J Hocking, *The Palace Letters: The Queen, the Governor-General and the Plot to Dismiss Gough Whitlam* (Brunswick, Scribe Publishing, 2020).

[50] See especially A Sapienza, 'Judicial Review of Non-Statutory Executive Action: Australia and the United Kingdom Reunited?' (2018) 43 *University of Western Australia Law Review* 67; A Sapienza, 'Interpreting the Limits of Non-Statutory Executive Action: What Role for Grounds of Judicial Review?' in J Boughey and L Burton Crawford (eds), *Interpreting Executive Power* (Alexandria, Federation Press, 2020) 222; A Sapienza, *Judicial Review of Non-Statutory Executive Action* (Alexandria, Federation Press, 2020). See also F Wheeler, 'Judicial Review of Prerogative Power in Australia: Issues and Prospects' (1992) 14 *Sydney Law Review* 432; C Horan, 'Judicial Review of Non-Statutory Executive Powers' (2003) 31 *Federal Law Review* 551; Hanna (n 29).

[51] See, eg, HP Lee, 'The Australian High Court and Implied Fundamental Guarantees' [1993] *Public Law* 606; J Goldsworthy, 'Implications in Language, Law and the Constitution' in G Lindell (ed), *Future Directions in Australian Constitutional Law: Essays in Honour of Professor Leslie Zines* (Sydney, Federation Press, 1994) 150; J Goldsworthy, 'The High Court, Implied Rights and Constitutional Implications' (1995) 39 *Quadrant* 46; J Kirk, 'Constitutional Implications from Representative Democracy' (1995) 23 *Federal Law Review* 37; Kirk, 'Constitutional Implications (I)' (n 29); J Kirk, 'Constitutional Implications (II): Doctrines of Equality and Democracy' (2001) 25 *Melbourne University Law Review* 24; M Detmold, 'The New Constitutional Law' (1994) 16 *Sydney Law Review* 228; N Aroney, 'A Seductive Plausibility: Freedom of Speech in the Constitution' (1995) 18 *University of Queensland Law Journal* 249; S Donaghue, 'The Clamour of Silent Constitutional Principles' (1996) 24 *Federal Law Review* 133; J Goldsworthy, 'Constitutional Implications and Freedom of Political Speech: A Reply to Stephen Donaghue' (1997) 32 *Monash University Law Review* 362; HP Lee, 'The Implied Freedom of Political Communication' in HP Lee and G Winterton (eds), *Australian Constitutional Landmarks* (Cambridge, Cambridge University Press, 2003) 383; P Emerton, 'Political Freedoms and Entitlements in the *Australian Constitution* – An Example of Referential Intentions Yielding

Finally, the subject of this book is the nationhood power, which arises under s 61 of the Australian Constitution and has been held capable of supporting certain types of executive action undertaken by the Commonwealth Government. As such, it does not engage in an analysis of the source and scope of the executive power of the governments of the Australian States. While it is possible that the decision of the High Court in *Williams [No 1]* could have implications for the scope of the executive capacities of the State governments to enter into contracts and spend money,[52] it is not possible to fully explore these issues within the confines of this book.

## II. Overview and Structure of the Book

This book is divided into three parts. Part I begins with this chapter, which has introduced the nationhood power as the subject of this book. Chapter 2 examines the executive power of the Commonwealth in more detail, which will underpin and inform the analysis of the nationhood power in subsequent chapters. It provides an overview of the different categories of executive power that comprise s 61. Chapter 2 also examines recent judicial decisions that have effected a change in the interpretation of s 61 by overturning long-held assumptions about when the Commonwealth Executive Government can act in the absence of statutory authorisation. Chapter 2 concludes by setting out a conceptual framework for determining the scope of the executive power of the Commonwealth that will be adopted and applied in this book.

Part II of the book analyses and evaluates judicial observations about the scope of the nationhood power. Chapter 3 traces the development of the nationhood power in the Australian constitutional jurisprudence. It considers a series of cases where the nationhood power was relied on by the Commonwealth Government to carry out national enterprises or activities, including controversial spending programmes. It concentrates on the influential decision of the High Court in the *AAP case*, where Mason J declared that the Commonwealth has 'a capacity to engage in enterprises and activities peculiarly adapted to the government of a nation and which cannot otherwise be carried on for the benefit of the nation'.[53]

Unintended Legal Consequences' (2010) 38 *Federal Law Review* 169; J Goldsworthy, 'Constitutional Implications Revisited' (2011) 30 *University of Queensland Law Journal* 9; N Aroney, 'Towards the "Best Explanation" of the Constitution: Text, Structure, History and Principle in *Roach v Electoral Commissioner*' (2011) 30 *University of Queensland Law Journal* 145.

[52] See further Hayne (n 2); Sapienza, 'Judicial Review of Non-Statutory Executive Action' (n 50) 38–39; K Foley, 'What Is the Relevance of *Williams* and *Plaintiff M61* for the Exercise of State Executive Power?' (2013) 36 *University of Western Australia Law Review* 234; S Bateman, 'Constitutional Dimensions of State Executive Power: An Analysis of the Power to Contract and Spend' (2015) 26 *Public Law Review* 255.

[53] *AAP case* (n 27) 397.

The chapter then examines how the 'peculiarly adapted' test has been applied to determine the scope of the nationhood power in subsequent decisions.

Chapter 4 considers the scope of the nationhood power to support the use of the Australian Defence Force (ADF) to deal with internal security and national emergencies. It considers the constitutional and statutory powers of the Commonwealth Executive Government to use the ADF within Australia for the purpose of protecting Commonwealth interests or the States and Territories against domestic violence. It also examines the recent utilisation of the ADF to provide assistance in relation to the devastating 2019–20 'Black Summer' bushfires and the COVID-19 pandemic. As these operations were not authorised by legislation, the chapter considers the non-statutory executive powers that were relied on by the Commonwealth Executive Government and whether the nationhood power could provide the constitutional basis for executive action of this nature.

Chapter 5 examines the exercise of the nationhood power in the immigration and border protection context. In particular, it critically analyses the reasoning employed by the majority of the Full Court of the Federal Court of Australia in the important and influential decision in *Ruddock v Vadarlis* ('*Tampa case*').[54] In the *Tampa case* the nationhood power was held to provide the constitutional basis for coercive executive action undertaken by the Commonwealth in the absence of statutory authorisation, including the exclusion, expulsion and detention of non-citizens. It is demonstrated that the decision of the majority in the *Tampa case* sits uncomfortably with the weight of authority on the nature and scope of the nationhood power, examined in the preceding chapters of this book. The chapter concludes by examining the relationship between the executive power and the *Migration Act 1958* (Cth).

The analysis of the Australian case law undertaken in Part II of the book reveals that Australian courts have recognised that there are limitations on the nationhood power, which are examined in Part III. Chapter 6 demonstrates that the High Court has ascertained the limits on the nationhood power by reference to the federal character of the Commonwealth. It explores how the principle of federalism has been employed by the High Court to constrain the scope of the nationhood power. It also considers the broader conception of federalism that has underpinned the reasoning of the High Court in cases concerning the nationhood power. The book concludes in Chapter 7 by drawing together the analysis from the preceding chapters to present an account of the scope of the nationhood power that sheds fresh light on the types of executive action that can be supported by the nationhood power and, more generally, the circumstances in which the Executive Government can act in the absence of statutory authorisation in Australia.

[54] *Tampa case* (n 5).

# 2

# The Executive Power of the Commonwealth

> The executive power of the Commonwealth is vested in the Queen and is exercisable by the Governor-General as the Queen's representative, and extends to the execution and maintenance of this Constitution, and of the laws of the Commonwealth.
>
> Australian Constitution, s 61

Chapter 1 introduced the relationship between s 61 of the Constitution as the source of Commonwealth executive power in Australia, and the categories of power which inform its content. It also introduced the nationhood power. This chapter examines the executive power of the Commonwealth in more detail, in order to lay the foundations for the consideration of the nature and scope of the nationhood power in subsequent chapters. The chapter begins with an examination of s 61 of the Constitution and its drafting history. It then considers the categories of power that are understood as falling within the scope of s 61, with a particular focus on the 'inherent' or 'non-statutory' executive powers. The chapter concludes by introducing a framework of analysis for determining the scope of the executive power of the Commonwealth. This framework draws a useful distinction between the 'depth' and 'breadth' of executive power and will be adopted and applied in this book.

## I. Section 61 of the Australian Constitution

Section 61 is the principal provision dealing with Commonwealth executive power in the Australian Constitution. Section 61 is the first provision in Chapter II, which is entitled 'The Executive Government'. It vests 'the executive power of the Commonwealth' in the Queen and states that it is exercisable by the Governor-General as the Queen's representative. Owing to its origins in British legal and political tradition, s 61 can only be understood if it is interpreted in light of the principle and conventions of responsible government, as they operate in Australia.[1] As such, while s 61 identifies the Queen as the formal repository of

[1] See also C Saunders, 'Separation of Legislative and Executive Power' in C Saunders and A Stone (eds), *The Oxford Handbook of the Australian Constitution* (Oxford, Oxford University Press, 2018).

Commonwealth executive power, and states that it is exercisable by the Governor-General as the Queen's representative, by convention this power is exercised on the advice of Ministers who are responsible to the lower, representative House of Parliament.

Partial expression of the principle of responsible government can be found in the provisions of Chapter II of the Constitution. Section 62 states that there is a Federal Executive Council 'to advise the Governor-General in the government of the Commonwealth'. Section 64 of the Constitution provides that the 'Queen's Ministers of State', who are appointed by the Governor-General to administer 'departments of State of the Commonwealth', are to be members of the Federal Executive Council and must sit in the Commonwealth Parliament. The result is that the executive power of the Commonwealth is 'functionally' exercised by Ministers and by other officers of the Executive government.[2]

The 'third declaration'[3] of s 61 states that the executive power 'extends to the execution and maintenance of this Constitution, and of the laws of the Commonwealth'. While s 61 'marks the external boundaries'[4] of Commonwealth executive power, it does not define what 'executive power' is.[5] Furthermore, s 61 does not clarify the areas of responsibility that are allocated to the Commonwealth Executive by the Constitution. In this respect, the provision stands in contrast to ss 51 and 52 of the Constitution, which specify the subject matters with respect to which the Commonwealth Parliament can legislate.[6]

The drafting history of s 61 reveals that this was a deliberate choice on the part of the framers of the Australian Constitution. The first draft of the provision which had been included in the 1891 draft Constitution stated:

> The authority of the Executive Government of the Commonwealth shall extend to all matters over which the legislative powers of the Commonwealth may be exercised, excepting only matters, being within the legislative powers of any State, with respect to which the Legislature of that State for the time-being exercises such powers and the Federal Parliament has not exercised its powers.[7]

However, the draft clause was subsequently amended to provide that 'the Executive power and authority of the Commonwealth shall extend to the execution of the

[2] Australian Constitution, s 67; *Plaintiff M68/2015 v Minister for Immigration and Border Protection* (2016) 257 CLR 42, 95–96 [128] (Gageler J).

[3] *Commonwealth v Colonial Combing, Spinning and Weaving Co Ltd* (1922) 31 CLR 421, 437–38, 439, 440–41 (Isaacs J) (Wool Tops case).

[4] ibid 437.

[5] ibid. See also *Plaintiff M68* (n 2) 96 [129] (Gageler J); *Davis v Commonwealth* (1988) 166 CLR 79, 92 (Mason CJ, Deane and Gaudron JJ) quoted in *Pape v Federal Commissioner of Taxation* (2009) 238 CLR 1, 62 [131] (French CJ) and *Williams v Commonwealth [No 1]* (2012) 248 CLR 156, 372 [588] (Kiefel J).

[6] See also G Appleby and S McDonald, 'Looking at the Executive Power through the High Court's New Spectacles' (2013) 35 *Sydney Law Review* 253, 254.

[7] First Proof Submitted to the Constitutional Committee, 26 March 1891, cl 8 reprinted in J Williams, *The Australian Constitution: A Documentary History* (Carlton, Melbourne University Press, 2005) 178.

provisions of this Constitution, and the Laws of the Commonwealth'.[8] The rationale for the change was to remove a limitation on the executive power and instead provide a 'positive statement' of what the executive power of the Commonwealth was to be.[9] In moving the amendment, Sir Samuel Griffith had expressed the somewhat 'optimistic'[10] view that 'the amendment covers all that is meant by the clause, and is quite free from ambiguity'.[11]

The drafting history of s 61, then, suggests that the framers of the Australian Constitution were concerned to divide executive power between the new national government and the governments of the respective States. Indeed, it was assumed for a long time after federation that the executive power of the Commonwealth was coextensive with Commonwealth legislative power, and extended to the subject matters in ss 51, 52 and 122 of the Constitution.[12] As is shown below, the High Court of Australia overturned that assumption in the decision of *Williams v Commonwealth [No 1]*.[13]

It is also apparent from the drafting history of s 61 that the framers of the Australian Constitution elected not to provide an exhaustive definition of executive power. Professor Peter Gerangelos and Professor Anne Twomey have suggested that this was due, in part, to 'provincial sensitivities'.[14] The framers wanted to avoid giving any impression of 'a lack of constitutional refinement'[15] by setting out the content of executive power and the attendant conventions of responsible government in a written constitutional instrument. The framers also anticipated that the executive power would adapt to changing conditions and evolve as the Commonwealth of Australia acquired independence. This was acknowledged in the '*Vondel* opinion', which was signed by Alfred Deakin in his capacity as Commonwealth Attorney-General. Any attempt at exhaustively defining the scope of the executive power of the Commonwealth in the Constitution would have, in Deakin's view, 'involved a risk of undue, and perhaps unintentional, limitation of the executive power'.[16]

[8] Official Report of the National Australasian Convention Debates, Sydney, 6 April 1891, 777–78 (Sir Samuel Griffith) ('Convention Debates').

[9] ibid.

[10] M Crommelin, 'The Executive' in Gregory Craven (ed), *The Convention Debates 1891–1898: Commentaries, Indices and Guide* (Sydney, Legal Books, 1986) 127, 131.

[11] Convention Debates (n 8) 778.

[12] G Winterton, *Parliament, the Executive and the Governor-General: A Constitutional Analysis* (Carlton, Melbourne University Press, 1983) 30. Leslie Zines described them as 'riding in tandem' in L Zines, *The High Court and the Constitution*, 5th edn (Annandale, Federation Press, 2008) 347.

[13] *Williams [No 1]* (n 5).

[14] P Gerangelos, 'The Executive' in N Aroney, P Gerangelos, J Stellios and SL Murray, *The Constitution of the Commonwealth of Australia: History, Principle and Interpretation* (Port Melbourne, Cambridge University Press, 2015) 411; A Twomey, 'The French Court, the Nature of the Executive Power and its Reconciliation with the Expenditure Power' in H Jackson (ed), *Essays in Honour of Chief Justice French* (Alexandria, Federation Press, 2019) 41.

[15] Gerangelos (n 14) 411. See also Winterton (n 12) 3.

[16] A Deakin, 'Channel of Communication with Imperial Government: Position of Consuls: Executive Power of Commonwealth Constitution' in P Brazil and B Mitchell (eds), *Opinions of Attorneys-General of the Commonwealth of Australia*, vol 1 (Canberra, Australian Government Publishing Service, 1981) 130.

Therefore, while the Australian Constitution 'describes'[17] the executive power of the Commonwealth and provides for its exercise in s 61, the preceding discussion has demonstrated that the text of the provision and its drafting history does not tell us very much about its nature and scope. In Australia, it is generally understood that the executive power of the Commonwealth can be ascertained by reference to different 'categories' of power. The next section of this chapter examines each of these categories of power and where the nationhood power fits among them.

## II. Sources of Commonwealth Executive Power

The precise scope of the executive power of the Commonwealth has not been definitively settled. The High Court has, however, identified different 'categories' of executive power that reflect their original source, and are understood as falling within s 61 of the Constitution.[18] These categories include powers conferred directly on the Commonwealth Executive by specific provisions of the Australian Constitution; powers that are conferred by statute; powers derived from the royal prerogative as are attributable to the Commonwealth; and the capacities of the Commonwealth derived from its legal personality. The High Court has also recognised that the Commonwealth enjoys inherent executive power derived from its character and status as the national government. This 'nationhood power' is the subject of this book; however, it is helpful to introduce it in this chapter as a category of Commonwealth executive power.

### A. The Australian Constitution

The text of s 61 indicates that the executive power of the Commonwealth includes the power to 'execute' the Constitution. In the *Wool Tops case* Chief Justice Knox and Gavan Duffy J considered that the phrase 'execution … of this Constitution' in s 61 meant 'the doing of something immediately prescribed or authorized by the Constitution without the intervention of Federal legislation'.[19]

In that regard, there are a number of provisions in the Australian Constitution which vest specific powers in the Governor-General and may be understood as being encapsulated by the reference to the 'execution … of this Constitution' in s 61.[20] For example, the Constitution empowers the Governor-General to prorogue

[17] *Plaintiff M68* (n 2) 96 [129] (Gageler J).

[18] See also Twomey, 'The French Court' (n 14) 44–49.

[19] *Australian Communist Party v Commonwealth* (1951) 83 CLR 1, 230 (Williams J) (*Communist Party case*) affirming *Wool Tops case* (n 3) 432 (Knox CJ and Gavan Duffy J).

[20] In accordance with responsible government, these powers are usually exercised on ministerial advice. The specific powers vested in the Governor-General by the Constitution, including the 'reserve powers', are relevant to a general study of the executive branch of government, however it is beyond

the Parliament and dissolve the House of Representatives;[21] issue writs for general elections;[22] recommend money votes;[23] give royal assent to Bills;[24] appoint Ministers,[25] public servants,[26] and federal judges;[27] and exercise command of the naval and military forces of the Commonwealth.[28] As these powers are derived directly from the Constitution, they are capable of being exercised in the absence of statutory authorisation. Furthermore, an important consequence of these powers having a constitutional source is that while the Commonwealth Parliament may enact legislation that regulates the exercise of these powers, it cannot enact legislation to remove them from the Governor-General.[29]

The 'execution … of the Constitution' also encompasses executive powers that are necessary to discharge the duties and obligations conferred on the Commonwealth by particular provisions of the Constitution.[30] For example, s 119 stipulates that the Commonwealth 'shall protect every State against invasion and, on the application of the Executive Government of the State, against domestic violence'. Section 61 is capable of authorising executive action undertaken by the Commonwealth, including the use of the armed forces, to 'execute' its duty under s 119 of the Constitution.[31] While the procedure for calling out the armed forces to protect the States and Territories against domestic violence is now regulated by Part IIIAAA of the *Defence Act 1903* (Cth), Professor George Winterton observed that the Commonwealth Parliament could not enact legislation to circumvent or 'opt out' of this duty, because it has a constitutional source in s 119.[32]

the scope of this book to engage in a detailed exploration of these powers and the constitutional issues that can arise in connection with their exercise. For a comprehensive analysis of the reserve powers see A Twomey, *The Veiled Sceptre: Reserve Powers of Heads of State in Westminster Systems* (Port Melbourne, Cambridge University Press, 2018).

[21] Australian Constitution, ss 5, 28.

[22] ibid s 32.

[23] ibid s 56.

[24] ibid s 58.

[25] ibid ss 62, 64.

[26] ibid s 67.

[27] ibid s 72.

[28] ibid s 68.

[29] G Winterton, 'The Relationship between Commonwealth Legislative and Executive Power' (2004) 25 *Adelaide Law Review* 21, 38–39; Twomey, 'The French Court' (n 14) 44.

[30] For example, s 119 of the Constitution confers a duty on the Commonwealth to protect the States against invasion and, on application, against domestic violence: Winterton, 'The Relationship' (n 29) 25; P Gerangelos, 'Parliament, the Executive, the Governor-General and the Republic: The George Winterton Thesis' in HP Lee and P Gerangelos (eds), *Constitutional Advancement in a Frozen Continent: Essays in Honour of George Winterton* (Annandale, Federation Press, 2009) 189, 193–91; P Stephenson, 'Fertile Ground for Federalism? Internal Security, the States and Section 119 of the *Constitution*' (2015) 43 *Federal Law Review* 289; Twomey, 'The French Court' (n 14) 44–45.

[31] See also ss 61 and 68 of the Constitution. See Winterton, 'The Relationship' (n 29) 25–26; Twomey, 'The French Court' (n 14) 45.

[32] Winterton, 'The Relationship' (n 29) 42.

## B. Statute

The executive power of the Commonwealth in s 61 also includes powers conferred on the Executive by legislation, which clearly fall within the reference to 'the execution and maintenance … of the laws of the Commonwealth'. The reference to the 'laws of the Commonwealth' in s 61 includes statutes and subordinate legislation made by or under the authority of the Parliament, rather than the common law.[33] Legislation that confers executive power must be validly enacted pursuant to an enumerated head of power in ss 51, 52 or 122 of the Constitution, and must not contravene any express or implied constitutional limitations on power.[34] Today, the vast majority of executive powers are conferred and regulated by legislation.[35]

While it is clear from the text of s 61 that the Commonwealth Executive Government enjoys power to execute and maintain the Constitution and the laws enacted by the Commonwealth Parliament, considerable uncertainty remains in Australia about the scope of the powers that can be exercised by the Commonwealth Executive Government in the absence of statutory authorisation. As Twomey has observed, the difficulty in Australia is that 'any structural separation of powers between the Executive and the Parliament is compromised by the inherent requirements of a system of responsible government in which the Executive is derived from, and responsible to, the Parliament'.[36] Australia is also a federation, and so the 'field' over which the executive power operates must reflect the federal division of powers between the Commonwealth and the States.

In addition to those powers conferred on the Commonwealth Executive by specific provisions of the Australian Constitution and by statute, the High Court has recognised that s 61 incorporates the common law powers of the Crown that are appropriate to the position of the Commonwealth as the national government of a federal polity.[37] These powers can be exercised in the absence of statutory authorisation, and as such, are often referred to collectively as 'inherent' or 'non-statutory' executive powers. The non-statutory executive powers include powers derived from the royal prerogative, as are attributable to the Commonwealth and the capacities derived from the Commonwealth's legal personality.[38]

The High Court has also recognised that the Commonwealth Executive enjoys power derived from its character and status as a national government, which is capable of being exercised without statutory authorisation. Important questions about the scope of the 'nationhood power' aspect of Commonwealth executive power have been raised in various contexts, which are examined in subsequent

[33] Winterton, *Parliament* (n 12) 28; Winterton, 'The Relationship' (n 29) 25.

[34] *Plaintiff M68* (n 2) 93 [122] (Gageler J).

[35] See J Boughey and L Burton-Crawford, 'Executive Power in an Age of Statutes' in J Boughey and L Burton-Crawford (eds), *Interpreting Executive Power* (Alexandria, Federation Press, 2020) 1.

[36] Twomey, 'The French Court' (n 14) 41.

[37] *Barton v Commonwealth* (1974) 131 CLR 477, 498 (Mason J).

[38] *Williams [No 1]* (n 5) 184–85 [22], 189 [30] (French CJ).

chapters of this book. It is, however, helpful to introduce the nationhood power here as a 'category' of non-statutory executive power.

## C. The Royal Prerogative

The executive power of the Commonwealth in s 61 of the Constitution includes content derived from the royal prerogative. The royal prerogative refers collectively to the bundle of discretionary rights, powers, privileges and immunities that were enjoyed exclusively by the Monarch in the United Kingdom.[39] The prerogative has been described as 'a relic of a past age',[40] left over from a time when the Monarch was directly involved in the administration of government.[41] These 'powers' were progressively curtailed and distributed among the Parliament, Executive and judiciary in the aftermath of the constitutional struggle of the seventeenth century, as parliamentary democracy and the rule of law developed in the United Kingdom.[42] A defining characteristic of prerogative powers is that they can be exercised independently of parliamentary approval, but their precise nature remains contested.[43]

In his foundational text, *An Introduction to the Study of the Law of the Constitution*, Albert Venn Dicey defined the prerogative as 'the residue of discretionary or arbitrary authority, which at any given time is legally left in the hands of the Crown'.[44] Dicey attributed significance to the fact that the prerogative was exercisable by the Monarch, which in practice meant responsible Ministers, and concluded that 'every act which the executive government can lawfully do without the authority of an Act of parliament is done in virtue of this prerogative'.[45] Dicey's definition emphasises the *residual* nature of the prerogative, which coheres with contemporary understandings of the prerogative as being limited to historically exercised powers.[46] However, Dicey favoured a broader definition of the prerogative in the sense that he understood the term as including all of the common law, or non-statutory, powers of the Crown.[47] This necessarily includes all of the

[39] For a detailed consideration of the royal prerogative in Australia see HV Evatt, *The Royal Prerogative* (North Ryde, Law Book Co, 1987); HE Renfree, *The Executive Power of the Commonwealth of Australia* (Sydney, Legal Books, 1984) 392–94, 415–22.

[40] *Burmah Oil Co (Burma Trading) Ltd v Lord Advocate* [1964] SC (HL) 117; [1965] AC 75, 101 (Lord Reid).

[41] T Poole, 'United Kingdom: The Royal Prerogative' (2010) 8 *International Journal of Constitutional Law* 146, 147.

[42] ibid 146–47; *R (Miller) v Secretary of State for Exiting the European Union* [2017] UKSC 5; [2018] AC 61, [41] (Lord Neuberger with whom Lady Hale, Lord Mance, Lord Kerr, Lord Clarke, Lord Wilson, Lord Sumption and Lord Hodge agreed).

[43] Poole (n 41) 146–47.

[44] AV Dicey, *An Introduction to the Study of the Law of the Constitution*, 10th edn (London, Macmillan, 1959) 424, 424–25.

[45] ibid 425.

[46] See also B Saunders, 'Democracy, Liberty and the Prerogative: The Displacement of Inherent Executive Power by Statute' (2013) 41 *Federal Law Review* 363, 366.

[47] Dicey (n 44) 423.

capacities that the Crown has as a legal person that it shares with its citizens, such as the power to enter into contracts and spend public money, as these capacities were capable of being exercised without statutory authorisation. Dicey's broader conception of the prerogative has received endorsement by the Supreme Court of the United Kingdom, which appears to favour this definition over the competing account of the prerogative put forward by Sir William Blackstone.[48]

In the *Commentaries on the Laws of England 1765–1769* Blackstone used the term 'prerogative' to describe those powers that were unique to the Crown. Blackstone divided the non-statutory executive powers into two categories, namely the prerogatives and capacities of the Crown.[49] Blackstone defined the prerogative as 'that special pre-eminence, which the king hath, over and above all other persons, and out of the ordinary course of the common law, in right of his real dignity' and added that it is

> in its nature singular and eccentrical; that it can only be applied to those rights and capacities which the King enjoys alone, in contradistinction to others, and not to those which he enjoys in common with any of his subjects: for if once any one prerogative of the Crown could be held in common with the subject, it would cease to be prerogative any longer.[50]

Blackstone placed emphasis on the fact that the prerogative was *unique* to the Monarch, in the sense that it was derived from the Monarch's royal authority.[51] Blackstone's distinction recognises the fundamental difference in the nature of the prerogative powers and capacities. According to Blackstone, the prerogative was capable of being exercised in a way that could interfere with, or override, the legal rights and duties of individuals.[52] Indeed, there are examples of prerogative powers being exercised in this way where it is 'inherent in the prerogative power',[53] including the exercise of power to alter the terms of service of civil servants,[54] and the power to destroy property in wartime.[55] Other examples include the power

[48] See, eg, *Attorney-General v De Keyser's Royal Hotel Ltd* [1920] UKHL 1; [1920] AC 508, 526 (Lord Dunedin) ('*De Keyser*'); *Burmah Oil* (n 40) 99 (Lord Reid); *Laker Airways Ltd v Department of Trade* [1976] EWCA Civ 10; [1977] QB 643, 719 (Roskill LJ); *Council of Civil Service Unions v Minister for the Civil Service* [1984] UKHL 9; [1985] AC 374, 398 (Lord Fraser) (*GCHQ case*); *R (Bancoult) v Secretary of State for Foreign and Commonwealth Affairs (No 2)* [2008] UKHL 61; [2009] AC 453, 490 [69] (Lord Bingham); *Miller* (n 42) 139–40 [47]–[48].

[49] W Blackstone, *Commentaries on the Laws of England*, Book I, 1st edn (Oxford, Oxford University Press, 2016) 155 [232].

[50] ibid.

[51] See also B Saunders (n 46) 365.

[52] Blackstone (n 49) cited in *Plaintiff M68* (n 2) 98 [135] (Gageler J). See also *Miller* (n 42) 140–41 [52]–[53], citing as examples the prerogative to decide on and alter terms of service of servants of the Crown: *GCHQ case* (n 48); and prerogative power to destroy property in wartime: *Burmah Oil* (n 40). In some cases, the exercise of a prerogative power cannot affect the legal rights and interests of individuals, unless legislative action is taken to give effect to it. An example is the exercise of the prerogative capacity to enter into a treaty: A Twomey, 'The Prerogative and the Courts in Australia' (2021) 3 *Journal of Commonwealth Law* 55, 59. See also A Sapienza, *Judicial Review of Non-Statutory Executive Action* (Alexandria, Federation Press, 2020) 29–30.

[53] *Miller* (n 42) 140–41 [52].

[54] ibid 140–41 [52]–[53] citing *GCHQ case* (n 48).

[55] *Miller* (n 42) citing *Burmah Oil* (n 40).

to detain enemy aliens during wartime, the power to maintain the peace during an emergency, and the power of mercy to grant a person liberty.[56] Blackstone distinguished those powers in the nature of the prerogative from 'capacities' that were powers that the Crown shared with its citizens. While Dicey and Blackstone's respective conceptions of the prerogative have received judicial endorsement, the High Court of Australia has, in its recent decisions, adopted Blackstone's distinction between the two categories of non-statutory executive power and it will also be adopted in this book.[57] Accordingly, this book uses the term 'prerogative' as Blackstone used it – to describe those powers that were enjoyed exclusively by the Monarch, which have been inherited by the Crown in right of the Commonwealth of Australia.

### *i. The Effect of Australia's Acquisition of Independence on the Exercise of the Prerogative*

The prerogative had formed part of the common law that was received in the Australian colonies at the time of British 'settlement'[58] and was exercisable by local Governors who were agents of the British Government.[59] The Crown was understood at the time to be indivisible, and as such, the prerogative powers existed throughout the British Empire, unless they had been limited or excluded by statute.

Accordingly, when the Australian colonies federated on 1 January 1901, it was understood that by vesting the executive power of the Commonwealth in the Queen, s 61 of the Constitution incorporated many of the prerogative powers of the Crown that were relevant to Australia. There were, however, certain prerogative powers that were not capable of being exercised by the Commonwealth Executive Government at the time of Australia's federation. In particular, the prerogative powers to declare war or peace; negotiate or enter into agreements with foreign countries; receive or appoint diplomatic representatives or foreign ambassadors; or acquire territory[60] remained with the Sovereign and were exercisable on the advice of British Ministers.[61]

[56] Twomey, 'The Prerogative and the Courts' (n 52) 59.

[57] *Davis* (n 5) 107–09 (Brennan J); *Cadia Holdings Pty Ltd v New South Wales* (2010) 242 CLR 195, 223 [75] (Gummow, Hayne, Heydon and Crennan JJ); *Williams [No 1]* (n 5) 186 [25] (French CJ), 343–44 [488] (Crennan J); *Plaintiff M68* (n 2) 97–99 [132]–[136] (Gageler J).

[58] *New South Wales v Commonwealth* (1975) 135 CLR 337, 438 (Stephen J) ('*Seas and Submerged Lands case*'); *Cadia* (n 57) 206 [21] (French CJ). Note that 'settlement' remains a contested political concept in Australia.

[59] See generally Anne Twomey, *The Chameleon Crown: The Queen and Her Australian Governors* (Annandale, Federation Press, 2006); L Zines, 'The Growth of Australian Nationhood and its Effect on the Powers of the Commonwealth' in L Zines (ed) *Commentaries on the Australian Constitution: A Tribute to Geoffrey Sawer* (Sydney, Butterworths, 1977) 1.

[60] See Zines, 'Nationhood' (n 59) 25–27; A Twomey, '*Sue v Hill* – The Evolution of Australian Independence' in A Stone and G Williams (eds), *The High Court at the Crossroads: Essays in Constitutional Law* (Liechhardt, Federation Press, 2000) 77, 80–87; G Winterton, 'The Acquisition of Independence' in R French, G Lindell and C Saunders (eds), *Reflections on the Australian Constitution* (Annandale, Federation Press, 2003) 31, 41–42.

[61] Convention Debates, Sydney, 6 April 1891, 773 (Alfred Deakin).

As a result of changes to conventions following the 1923, 1926 and 1930 Imperial Conferences, these prerogative powers were transferred to the Commonwealth and became exercisable by the Governor-General on the advice of Australian ministers. The Imperial Conference of 1923 recognised the power of the Dominions to enter into bilateral treaties, provided that they did not affect other parts of the British Empire.[62] The 1926 Imperial Conference issued the Balfour Declaration of 1926, which stated that the United Kingdom and the Dominions were

> autonomous Communities within the British Empire, equal in status, in no way subordinate one to another in any aspect of their domestic or external affairs, though united by a common allegiance to the Crown, and freely associated as members of the British Commonwealth of Nations.[63]

The Balfour Declaration granted Australia and the other Dominions independence in the exercise of executive power in relation to domestic and foreign affairs. From 1926, the Commonwealth Executive Government could exercise executive power to negotiate and enter into international treaties and appoint diplomatic representatives for this purpose.[64]

The 1926 Imperial Conference resolved that the Governor-General was no longer an agent or representative of the British Government.[65] However, it was not until the Imperial Conference of 1930 that it was confirmed that the Sovereign acts upon the advice of responsible Dominion Ministers in relation to the appointment of the Governor-General and in the exercise of other powers.[66] Twomey has explained that the effect of the Imperial Conferences was

> to make the Crown divisible, creating a separate Crown for Australia and each of the other Dominions, under which the King acted upon the advice of ministers responsible to the Parliament of the relevant Dominion, rather than the Westminster Parliament.[67]

This change in the status of the Dominions can be attributed to the change of convention, agreed at the Imperial Conferences, concerning who provided advice to the Sovereign in the exercise of their powers.[68] Professor Zines observed, in this respect, that the Commonwealth attained independence in the exercise of executive power, not by amending the text of the Australian Constitution, but 'by the simple device of changing the constitutional convention or practice as to who would give effective advice to "the Crown"'.[69]

[62] A Twomey, 'Independence' in C Saunders and A Stone (eds), *The Oxford Handbook of the Australian Constitution* (Oxford, Oxford University Press, 2018) 107; Twomey, '*Sue v Hill*' (n 60) 83.

[63] United Kingdom, *Imperial Conference, 1926, Summary of Proceedings* (Cmd 2768) 14.

[64] Note that Australia did not actually exercise the power to appoint diplomatic representatives until 1940: Twomey, '*Sue v Hill*' (n 60) 86–87.

[65] ibid. See also Zines, 'Nationhood' (n 59) 28; Winterton, 'Acquisition of Independence' (n 60) 35–36.

[66] Twomey 'Independence' (n 62) 107.

[67] ibid.

[68] These changes only applied at the Commonwealth level and did not affect the States. See further Twomey 'Independence' (n 62) 107.

[69] Zines, 'Commentary' in HV Evatt, *The Royal Prerogative* (North Ryde, Law Book Co, 1987) c1, c3.

In some cases, however, prerogative powers were formally delegated to the Governor-General by the Sovereign under s 2 of the Australian Constitution.[70] Section 2 provides:

> A Governor-General appointed by the Queen shall be Her Majesty's representative in the Commonwealth and shall have and may exercise in the Commonwealth during the Queen's pleasure, but subject to this Constitution, such powers and functions of the Queen as Her Majesty may be pleased to assign to him.

As Australia attained executive independence, s 2 ceased to have any contemporary significance. Section 61 of the Constitution was understood as the primary source of Commonwealth executive power in Australia, encompassing all of the powers that would otherwise have been assigned to the Governor-General under s 2.[71] The constitutional significance of Australia's acquisition of independence, then, was that all of the Crown's prerogative powers that were regarded as appropriate to the Commonwealth were accepted as being incorporated in s 61 of the Constitution and exercisable by the Governor-General on the advice of Australian Ministers.[72]

## *ii. The Prerogative in the Australian Constitutional Context*

Section 61 of the Constitution is understood as comprising 'only such of the prerogatives of the Crown as are properly attributable to the Commonwealth'.[73] The prerogative powers enjoyed by the Commonwealth Executive under s 61 are not coextensive with the prerogative in the United Kingdom.[74] The Australian Constitution also created a different legal system from that which exists in the United Kingdom. As such, in ascertaining whether a prerogative power forms part

[70] For example, the power to declare war was delegated to the Governor-General under s 2 in 1941. This power was exercised to make declarations of war against Finland, Hungary and Romania. Japan was added to the request on 8 December 1941: Twomey, 'The Prerogative and the Courts' (n 52) 60. Zines had observed that the Queen also assigned powers to the Governor-General under s 2 to appoint certain diplomatic officers and consuls in 1954 and ambassadors and high commissioners in 1973. On 8 December 1987 there was an assignment 'related to characters of incorporation'. These assignments were revoked by the Queen, on the advice of the Prime Minister, on 1 December 1987: J Stellios, *Zines's The High Court and the Constitution*, 6th edn (Leichhardt, Federation Press, 2015) 371.

[71] Stellios (n 70) 371; Saunders, 'Separation of Legislative and Executive Power' (n 1) 631.

[72] *R v Burgess; Ex parte Henry* (1936) 55 CLR 608, 643–44 (Latham CJ) endorsed in *Barton* (n 37) 498 (Mason J). See also *Seas and Submerged Lands case* (n 58) 379, 381 (McTiernan J), 503 (Murphy J). Leslie Zines has also made this point in Zines, 'Nationhood' (n 59) 30–31, 42–43; Zines, 'Commentary' (n 69) c3–c4; Stellios (n 70) 371–72.

[73] *Williams v Commonwealth [No 1]* (2012) 248 CLR 156, 186 [25] (French CJ), 343–44 [488] (Crennan J); *Cadia* (n 57) 226 [86] (Gummow, Hayne, Heydon and Crennan JJ). Renfree noted that some prerogative powers were not regarded as being suitable for exercise in Australia and did not form part of the executive power of the Commonwealth or the States, such as prerogatives relating to the revenues of the Duchies and the prerogative relating to the Sovereign as Head of the Established Church of England: Renfree (n 39) 431. Sapienza notes that another example is the prerogative power to legislate for colonies: *Bancoult* (n 48) in Sapienza (n 52) 25.

[74] See also C Saunders, 'The Concept of the Crown' (2015) 38 *Melbourne University Law Review* 873, 891.

of the executive power of the Commonwealth in s 61, regard must be had to the Australian constitutional context.[75]

We have already seen in this chapter that there are certain prerogative-type powers vested in the Governor-General by specific provisions of the Australian Constitution.[76] There are also provisions in the Australian Constitution that have restricted the exercise of particular prerogatives in Australia. For example, s 75 of the Constitution has been held to have curtailed the prerogative immunity of the Crown and its officers from suit in Australia.[77] Many prerogative powers have also been abrogated or displaced by Commonwealth legislation[78] or operate together with a statutory scheme that expressly preserves the prerogative power.[79]

In *Farley's Case* Evatt J classified the Crown prerogatives as falling within three categories.[80] Pursuant to its executive prerogatives, the Commonwealth could take action without the approval or authorisation of the Parliament. Examples of the executive prerogatives include the power to declare war and peace, negotiate and enter into treaties, appoint ambassadors, confer honours, coin money, acquire territory and grant pardons.[81] The Crown was also entitled to the benefit of legal preferences, immunities and exceptions which were denied to its subjects, such as priority in payment of debts.[82] Third, the Crown enjoyed proprietary rights in relation to royal metals, 'treasure trove', and the foreshore, seabed and subsoil within territorial limits.[83]

The principle of federalism is another factor that has affected the scope and exercise of prerogative powers in Australia. Section 61 includes only those prerogative powers that are 'appropriate' to the position of the Commonwealth as the national government of a federal polity. While the Australian Constitution sets out the subject matters over which the legislative power of the Commonwealth can be exercised in ss 51 and 52, it does not address the distribution of prerogative powers between the Commonwealth and State governments. As the majority explained in *Cadia Holdings Pty Ltd v New South Wales*,

> the creation of the federation presented issues still not fully resolved of the allocation between the Commonwealth and States of prerogatives which pre-federation had been

[75] *Williams v Commonwealth [No 2]* (2014) 252 CLR 416, 469 [81]–[83] (French CJ, Hayne, Kiefel, Bell and Keane JJ); Saunders, 'Separation of Legislative and Executive Power' (n 1) 617, 632.

[76] See, eg, the power to convene and prorogue the Parliament (s 5); appoint ministers (s 64), civil servants (s 67) and judges (s 72); and command the naval and military forces of the Commonwealth (s 68). See also Twomey, 'The Prerogative and the Courts' (n 52) 63; Sapienza (n 52) 25.

[77] *Commonwealth v Mewett* (1997) 191 CLR 471.

[78] Sapienza gives the examples of the *Currency Act 1965* (Cth) (prerogative to coin money), *Corporations Act 2001* (Cth) (prerogative to establish corporations) and the *Patents Act 1990* (Cth) (prerogative in relation to issue of patents) in Sapienza (n 52) 26.

[79] See, eg, *Royal Commissions Act 1902* (Cth). See also *Mining Act 1992* (NSW); *Cadia* (n 57).

[80] *Federal Commissioner of Taxation v Official Liquidator of E O Farley Ltd (in liq)* (1940) 63 CLR 278, 320–21 (Evatt J) (*Farley's case*). This classification was first presented in HV Evatt's doctoral thesis, which was subsequently published as Evatt (n 39).

[81] *Farley's case* (n 80) 320–21 (Evatt J); Evatt (n 39) 30–31.

[82] *Farley's case* (n 80) 321 (Evatt J).

[83] ibid.

> divided between the Imperial and colonial governments, and of their adaptation to the division of executive authority in the federal system established by the *Constitution*.[84]

In ascertaining the allocation of the prerogatives between the Commonwealth and the States in *Farley's Case*, Evatt J indicated that they should generally follow the distribution of legislative powers effected by ss 51 and 52 of the Australian Constitution.[85] Accordingly, most of the 'executive prerogatives' were transferred to, and exercised exclusively by, the Commonwealth. Today, they are exercisable by the Governor-General, acting on the advice of Commonwealth Ministers. The preferences and immunities of the Crown, such as the prerogative of mercy, were shared between the Commonwealth and State executives.[86] The States retained the proprietary rights of the Crown,[87] with the exception of rights in respect of the territorial sea, which were vested in the Crown in right of the Commonwealth.[88]

### *iii. Limits on the Prerogative*

While the prerogative can be exercised without the approval or authorisation of the Parliament, it is subject to limitations on its exercise, derived from the common law. Indeed, these limits have been cited by some constitutional scholars in support of confining the scope of Commonwealth executive power to the prerogative.[89] Prerogative powers can lapse due to disuse.[90] The prerogative is also limited to historically exercised powers.[91] While the prerogative can evolve and adapt to changing circumstances, new prerogatives cannot be created.[92]

One of the most important limitations is that the prerogative cannot be used to authorise or enforce the deprivation of liberty of individuals.[93] In *Plaintiff M68/2015 v Minister for Immigration and Border Protection* Gageler J explained this limit as follows:

> The inability of the Executive Government of the Commonwealth to authorise or enforce a deprivation of liberty is not simply the consequence of the absence of any

[84] *Cadia* (n 57) 226 [87] (Gummow, Hayne, Heydon and Crennan JJ).

[85] See, eg, *Farley's case* (n 80) 320 (Evatt J); *Cadia* (n 57) 210 [31] (French CJ).

[86] *Farley's* case (n 80) 322–23 (Evatt J).

[87] ibid. Some doubt has been cast on this assumption following *Cadia* (n 57) 210–11 [30]–[34] (French CJ), 226–27 [87]–[89] (Gummow, Hayne, Heydon and Crennan JJ).

[88] *Seas and Submerged Lands case* (n 58).

[89] George Winterton was the leading proponent of this view in Winterton, *Parliament* (n 12) 31–34, 115–16, 137–39. See also P Gerangelos, 'The Executive Power of the Commonwealth of Australia: Section 61 of the Commonwealth Constitution, "Nationhood" and the Future of the Prerogative' (2012) 12 *Oxford University Commonwealth Law Journal* 97, 122–23.

[90] *Ruddock v Vadarlis* (2001) 110 FCR 491, 498 [19]–[20], 500–01 [29]–[30] (Black CJ) (*Tampa case*). See also Winterton, *Parliament* (n 12) 119–20.

[91] *British Broadcasting Corporation v Johns* [1965] Ch 32, 79 (Diplock LJ).

[92] See eg, *R v Secretary of State for the Home Department; Ex parte Northumbria Police Authority* [1988] 1 All ER 556; [1989] QB 26; Winterton, *Parliament* (n 12) 120–21; G Winterton, 'The Prerogative in Novel Situations' (1983) 99 *Law Quarterly Review* 407, 407–08; Gerangelos, 'The Executive Power of the Commonwealth of Australia' (n 89) 122; Anne Twomey, 'Pushing the Boundaries of Executive Power: Pape, the Prerogative and Nationhood Powers' (2010) 34 *Melbourne University Law Review* 313, 319.

[93] *Ex parte Walsh and Johnson; In re Yates* (1925) 37 CLR 36, 79 (Isaacs J); *Entick v Carrington* (1765) 2 Wils KB 275; 95 ER 807, 817 (Lord Camden CJ).

> prerogative power on the part of the Executive Government to dispense with the operation of the common law. It is the consequence of an inherent constitutional incapacity which is commensurate with the availability, long settled at the time of the establishment of the Commonwealth, of habeas corpus to compel release from any executive detention not affirmatively authorised by statute.[94]

The Executive Government cannot exercise the prerogative to create an offence,[95] raise taxes,[96] or dispense with the operation of the law.[97] Nor can the prerogative be exercised to change statutes or the common law,[98] compel persons to give evidence or produce documents in relation to a government inquiry,[99] or 'create or modify individual domestic rights and obligations by entering into treaties or other agreements'.[100]

As the prerogative originated from the United Kingdom under a system of parliamentary sovereignty, it is susceptible to control by the Parliament.[101] In the leading twentieth-century case on the topic, *Attorney General v De Keyser's Royal Hotel Ltd*,[102] the House of Lords declared that a prerogative of the Crown may be abrogated, curtailed or displaced by a validly enacted statute.[103] It has been described as a 'constitutional principle'[104] and 'inherent in its residual nature'[105] that a prerogative power will be displaced by a statute that confers or directly regulates a power that is equivalent to the prerogative. In these circumstances, the Executive Government derives its authority from the statutory regime, rather than the prerogative, and must observe the conditions, limitations and restrictions placed on the exercise of its power by the Parliament. The statutory abrogation or displacement of the prerogative may occur by express words or by necessary

[94] *Plaintiff M68* (n 2) 105 [159] (Gageler J).

[95] *Davis* (n 5) 112 (Brennan J).

[96] *Wool Tops case* (n 3) 433–34 (Isaacs J).

[97] *A v Hayden* (1984) 156 CLR 532, 580–81 (Brennan J).

[98] *Case of Proclamations* (1610) 12 Co Rep 74; 77 ER 1352, 1353 (Coke CJ). See *Bill of Rights 1688*, 1 Wm & M sess 2, c 2. See also *Miller* (n 42) [25]–[28] (Lord Thomas CJ, Sir Terence Etherton MR and Sales LJ), 159 [122] (Lord Neuberger PSC, Baroness Hale DPSC, Lords Mance, Kerr, Clarke, Wilson, Sumption and Hodge JJSC). Twomey has suggested that this proposition may not be entirely accurate because the exercise of the prerogative may affect the *application* of the common law: see A Twomey, '*Miller* and the Prerogative' in M Elliott, J Williams and AL Young (eds), *The UK Constitution after Miller: Brexit and Beyond* (Oxford, Hart Publishing, 2018) 69, 73–76.

[99] *McGuinness v Attorney-General (Vic)* (1940) 63 CLR 73, 83 (Latham CJ), 91 (Starke J), 98–99 (Dixon J) cited in *Tampa case* (n 90) 501 [31] (Black CJ).

[100] *Victoria v Commonwealth* (1996) 187 CLR 416, 480–82 (Brennan CJ, Toohey, Gaudron, McHugh and Gummow JJ).

[101] *Miller* (n 42) 75 [25] (Lord Thomas CJ, Sir Terence Etherton MR and Sales LJ), 139 [48] (Lord Neuberger PSC, Baroness Hale DPSC, Lords Mance, Kerr, Clarke, Wilson, Sumption and Hodge JJSC).

[102] *De Keyser* (n 48).

[103] ibid 526 (Lord Dunedin), 539–40 (Lord Atkinson), 554 (Lord Moulton), 561–62 (Lord Sumner), 575 (Lord Parmoor).

[104] ibid 575 (Lord Parmoor).

[105] *Miller* (n 42) 139 [48] (Lord Neuberger PSC, Baroness Hale DPSC, Lords Mance, Kerr, Clarke, Wilson, Sumption and Hodge JJSC).

implication.[106] The *De Keyser* principle has been adopted and applied by courts in Australia, including in cases concerning the nationhood power, and is an important limit on the exercise of the prerogative.[107]

While the proliferation of statutes has prompted some commentators to declare that there is a shrinking field of non-statutory executive power, the royal prerogative remains an important source of authority for government action in Australia. Executive acts such as declaring war and peace;[108] entering into treaties with foreign powers;[109] requesting extradition of fugitives from foreign states;[110] calling out the military to maintain the peace;[111] and excluding non-citizens from entering Australia[112] are all acts that fall within the royal prerogative and within the non-statutory executive power of the Commonwealth that is incorporated in s 61 of the Constitution. Justice Evatt referred to these powers as the 'executive prerogatives' in his tripartite classification in *Farley's Case*. These executive prerogatives, and their relationship with the nationhood power, will be further examined in this book.

## D. Capacities of the Commonwealth Derived from Legal Personality

Section 61 of the Constitution also includes capacities derived from the legal personality of the Commonwealth as a polity. The nature of the common law capacities is

[106] *De Keyser* (n 48) 576 (Lord Parmoor). See also *Laker Airways* (n 48) 719–21 (Roskill LJ); *R v Secretary of State for the Home Department; Ex parte Fire Brigades Union* [1995] 2 AC 513, 552 (Lord Browne-Wilkinson); *Miller* (n 42) 139–40 [48].

[107] *Re Richard Foreman & Sons Pty Ltd; Uther v Federal Commissioner of Taxation (Cth)* (1947) 74 CLR 508, 514 (Latham CJ); *Barton* (n 37) 488 (Barwick CJ), 501 (Mason J); *Brown v West* (1990) 169 CLR 195, 202, 205 (Mason CJ, Brennan, Deane, Dawson and Toohey JJ); *Ling v Commonwealth* (1994) 51 FCR 88, 92 (Gummow, Lee and Hill JJ); *Re Residential Tenancies Tribunal (NSW) and Henderson; Ex parte Defence Housing Authority* (1997) 190 CLR 410, 459 (McHugh J); *Tampa case* (n 90) 501 [33] (Black CJ), 539 [181]–[182] (French J); *Oates v Attorney-General (Cth)* (2003) 214 CLR 496; *Jarratt v Commissioner of Police (NSW)* (2005) 224 CLR 44, 69–70 [85] (McHugh, Gummow and Hayne JJ), 85–85 [129] (Callinan J); *Northern Territory v Arnhem Land Aboriginal Land Trust* (2008) 236 CLR 24, 58 [27] (Gleeson CJ, Gummow, Hayne and Crennan JJ); *Cadia* (n 57) 204 [14] (French CJ), 227 [94] (Gummow, Hayne, Heydon and Crennan JJ); *CPCF v Minister for Immigration and Border Protection* (2015) 255 CLR 514, 600–01 [279] (Kiefel J).

[108] *Farey v Burvett* (1916) 21 CLR 433, 452 (Isaacs J).

[109] *Burgess* (n 72) 635–36 (Latham CJ), 681 (Evatt and McTiernan JJ); *Koowarta v Bjelke-Petersen* (1982) 153 CLR 168, 193 (Gibbs CJ).

[110] *Barton* (n 37) 485 (Barwick CJ), 498–99 (Mason J), 505–06 (Jacobs J); *Oates* (n 107) 511 [37] (Gleeson CJ, McHugh, Gummow, Kirby, Hayne and Heydon JJ).

[111] See *Northumbria Police Authority* (n 92) 44 (Croom-Johnson LJ), 45–46 (Purchas LJ), 58–59 (Nourse LJ). In Australia, the exercise of this power would be subject to s 119 of the Constitution. It is unclear whether, and to what extent, this prerogative has survived the enactment of Part IIIAAA of the *Defence Act 1903* (Cth) ('*Commonwealth Defence Act*'), which sets out a comprehensive regime for the deployment of the Australian Defence Force when it is called out to protect the states against domestic violence or to protect Commonwealth interests. This question has not yet received judicial consideration.

[112] *Tampa case* (n 90) 495–501 [9]–[29] (Black CJ).

fundamentally different from that of the prerogative. This is because the capacities, unlike the prerogative, are derived from the status of the Crown as a legal person, rather than from the Monarch's royal authority. They are not, therefore, confined to a narrow class of historically exercised powers, like the prerogative. They are much wider in scope and can be exercised by the Commonwealth Executive Government to engage in a range of government activities and transactions, including entering into contracts, establishing trusts, and owning property.

Blackstone distinguished the two categories of power on the basis that the capacities were powers that the Crown shared in common with its subjects.[113] Because these powers extend to any act which can also be performed by individuals, and which are not prohibited or otherwise regulated by law, an act done in execution of a capacity is not capable of interfering with the legal rights and duties of individuals.[114] The capacities of the Crown are 'facultative' or permissive in nature, and remain subject to the law.[115]

In *Plaintiff M68*[116] Gageler J summarised the distinction between the prerogative and capacities of the Crown in those terms. His Honour observed that the 'essential difference' between an act done in the execution of prerogative power and an act done in execution of a capacity, is that the former 'is an act which is capable of interfering with [the] legal rights of others' whereas the latter

> involves nothing more than the utilisation of a bare capacity or permission, which can also be described as an ability to act or as a 'faculty'. Such effects as the act might have on legal rights or juridical relations result not from the act being uniquely that of the Executive Government but from the application of the act of the same substantive law as would be applicable in respect of the act had it been done by any other actor.[117]

In the United Kingdom today it is accepted that the Crown is a legal person that can exercise, in the absence of statutory authorisation, powers to contract and spend, hold and dispose of property, create trusts, register a company, enter into partnerships, and sue and be sued, provided that it complies with relevant laws.[118] Historically, it was assumed that the Commonwealth Executive Government in Australia enjoyed similar powers. There were two views about the scope of these powers. On one view, the Federal Executive enjoyed the same unlimited capacity to contract and spend as a natural person.[119] On the other view, it was a commonly held assumption that the Federal Executive could enter into contracts and spend public money without statutory authorisation (save for a parliamentary

[113] Blackstone (n 49) 232.
[114] ibid. See also *Plaintiff M68* (n 2) 98 [135] (Gageler J).
[115] *Plaintiff M68* (n 2) 98 [135] (Gageler J).
[116] *Plaintiff M68* (n 2).
[117] ibid 98 [135] (Gageler J).
[118] BV Harris, 'The "Third Source" of Authority for Government Action Revisited' (2007) 123 *Law Quarterly Review* 225, 635–36. For a detailed discussion of public finance in the United Kingdom and Australia see W Bateman, *Public Finance and Parliamentary Constitutionalism* (Cambridge, Cambridge University Press, 2020).
[119] See E Campbell, 'Commonwealth Contracts' (1970) 44 *Australian Law Journal* 14.

appropriation), provided that the expenditure was for a purpose that fell within an area of Commonwealth responsibility, set out in ss 51, 52 and 122 of the Australian Constitution. This 'common assumption' had underpinned a number of decisions of the High Court.[120] It was widely accepted by constitutional scholars[121] and one judge remarked that it 'should be treated as the law'.[122]

Both of these views were rejected by the High Court in the landmark decision in *Williams v Commonwealth [No 1]*. This case concerned a challenge to the National School Chaplaincy Program (NSCP), which was not established or regulated by legislation. Under this programme the Commonwealth entered into a funding agreement with Scripture Union Queensland for the provision of chaplaincy services to the Darling Heights state school in Queensland. The High Court held that s 61 did not support the Commonwealth entering into the funding agreement, or spending money under it, in the absence of prior statutory authorisation. The High Court held that, when interpreted in its constitutional context, s 61 conferred a power to contract and spend that was limited by the principles of representative and responsible government and which required parliamentary scrutiny of the expenditure of public money[123] and the federal distribution of powers effected by the Constitution.[124]

In *Williams v Commonwealth [No 1]* the majority of the High Court confirmed that it is the Commonwealth of Australia as a polity, rather than the executive, that has legal personality and therefore enjoys the capacities of a legal person, including the capacity to enter into contracts and spend money.[125] These powers were not, however, as extensive as those powers enjoyed by a natural person.[126] The Court regarded it as significant that the Federal Executive spends public funds rather than its 'own' money.[127] In their joint judgment, Gummow and Bell JJ reasoned that the law of contract has been developed primarily to deal with the

[120] See, eg, *New South Wales v Bardolph* (1934) 52 CLR 455, 509 (Dixon J); *Attorney-General (Vic) v Commonwealth* (1935) 52 CLR 533, 567 (Starke J); *Barton* (n 37) 498 (Mason J); *Victoria v Commonwealth and Hayden* (1975) 134 CLR 338, 362 (Barwick CJ), 396–97 (Mason J), 379 (Gibbs J), 405–06 (Jacobs J) ('*AAP case*'); *R v Duncan; Ex parte Australian Iron & Steel Pty Ltd* (1983) 158 CLR 535, 560 (Mason J); *Davis* (n 5) 110 (Brennan J); *R v Hughes* (2000) 202 CLR 535, 554–55 [38] (Gleeson CJ, Gaudron, McHugh, Gummow, Hayne and Callinan JJ); *Western Australia v Ward* (2002) 213 CLR 1, 391 [962]; *Pape* (n 5) 63 [132] (French CJ).

[121] See especially Winterton, *Parliament* (n 12) 30; Zines, *The High Court and the Constitution* (n 12) 347; Twomey, 'Pushing the Boundaries' (n 92) 320–21, 329; Gerangelos, 'The Executive Power of the Commonwealth of Australia' (n 89) 97, 103; C Saunders, 'The Sources and Scope of Commonwealth Power to Spend' (2009) 20 *Public Law Review* 251, 261–62.

[122] *Williams [No 1]* (n 5) 319 [403] (Heydon J).

[123] ibid 236 [151] (Gummow and Bell JJ), 241 [173], 258–59 [216] (Hayne J), 351–52 [516], [519] (Crennan J), 368–69 [577] (Kiefel J).

[124] ibid 192–93 [37] (French CJ), 218 [89] (Gummow and Bell JJ), 248–52 [192]–[199] (Hayne J), 353 [522] (Crennan J), 370 [581], 372 [586]–[590] (Kiefel J).

[125] *Cadia* (n 57) 219 [63] (Gummow, Hayne, Heydon and Crennan JJ); *Williams [No 1]* (n 5) 184 [21] (French CJ), 237 [154] (Gummow and Bell JJ), 253–54 [204] (Hayne J), 342 [484] (Crennan J).

[126] *Williams [No 1]* (n 5) 193 [38] (French CJ), 237–38 [154]–[155] (Gummow and Bell JJ), 253–54 [204] (Hayne J), 352 [518] (Crennan J), 373–74 [595] (Kiefel J).

[127] ibid 236–37 [151]–[152] (Gummow and Bell JJ), 241 [173] (Hayne J), 352 [519] (Crennan J), 368–69 [577] (Kiefel J).

interests of private parties. Accordingly, while the juristic capacities of a natural person are potentially unlimited, 'where public moneys are involved, questions of contractual capacity are to be regarded "through different spectacles"'.[128] As such, the Court did not accept that the executive power to contract and spend was limited only by the general law.[129] The principles of representative and responsible government required that the Parliament approve the expenditure of money by the Commonwealth Executive Government in the appropriations process.[130] In *Williams v Commonwealth [No 1]* the added requirement of statutory authorisation before the Commonwealth Executive Government could spend money was seen by the High Court as being consistent with, and giving effect to, these principles because the passage of ordinary legislation through the parliamentary process affords the Parliament an opportunity for enhanced scrutiny and oversight of executive action.

The federal character of the polity also featured prominently in the majority's reasoning in *Williams v Commonwealth [No 1]*, as evidenced by the emphasis placed on the role of the Senate in providing oversight and control of Commonwealth spending. Even though French CJ noted that, with the rise of Party politics, the Senate's role in protecting the interests of the states was 'vestigial', the requirement of statutory support for executive spending would ensure that its role would not be undermined by 'any constitutional inflation of the scope of executive power'.[131] Chief Justice French and Gummow and Bell JJ considered that if executive contracting and spending could be authorised solely by an appropriation Act, the Senate's constitutional role in providing oversight of executive spending would be diminished.[132] The only parliamentary oversight that would be provided would be the appropriation of funds. The Constitution, however, grants the Senate limited power over appropriation and taxation laws.[133] The requirement of prior statutory authorisation for Commonwealth contracting and expenditure was one way to afford the Senate a greater role in the supervision of Commonwealth activities.

The principle of federalism also limited the exercise of capacities by the Commonwealth in *Williams v Commonwealth [No 1]*. The Court reasoned that the Commonwealth is a government of limited and defined powers, and, as such, can only exercise its capacity to contract and spend for purposes that fall within areas of responsibility allocated to it by the Constitution. The majority in *Williams v Commonwealth [No 1]* placed emphasis on the fact that the governments of the

[128] ibid 236 [151]. Scholars had pointed out that the acts done in the exercise of the common law capacities differed significantly from those performed by individuals: Winterton, *Parliament* (n 12) 44–47, 121; M Cohn, 'Medieval Chains, Invisible Inks: On Non-Statutory Powers of the Executive' (2005) 25 *Oxford Journal of Legal Studies* 97.

[129] Saunders, 'Separation of Legislative and Executive Power' (n 1) 639.

[130] *Williams [No 1]* (n 5) 232–33 [136] (Gummow and Bell JJ), 351–52 [516] (Crennan J). See also Appleby and McDonald (n 6) 270.

[131] *Williams [No 1]* (n 5) 205–06 [61].

[132] ibid 234 [143].

[133] Australian Constitution, s 53.

States had the 'legal and practical capacity to provide for a scheme such as the NSCP' and, indeed, the conduct of the public school system in Queensland was the 'responsibility' of that state.[134]

The majority also considered that s 96 of the Constitution would be made redundant if the Commonwealth was conferred with a broad power to contract and spend public funds without statutory authorisation.[135] Section 96 allows the Commonwealth to grant financial assistance to the states on certain conditions. The majority held that the NSCP could have been made the subject of a s 96 grant and expressed concern that a wide Commonwealth spending power would remove this 'consensual' aspect of Commonwealth funding.[136]

The significance of *Williams v Commonwealth [No 1]* is that the Commonwealth Executive Government is generally required to obtain statutory authorisation prior to entering into contracts and spending public money. There were, however, suggestions made by several justices that s 61 could, in limited circumstances, authorise the Commonwealth Executive Government to make contracts and engage in other types of administrative action without statutory authorisation if they fell within an 'exempt class'.[137] An exempt class includes contracts and expenditure undertaken in the execution of prerogative powers[138] as well as contracts made 'in the ordinary course of administering a recognised part of the Commonwealth government', including for the administration of departments of state established under s 64 of the Constitution.[139] Chief Justice French suggested expenditure supported by the nationhood power could also fall within an exempt class, but this proposition was not adopted by the majority.[140] The NSCP did not fall within any of these categories. As it was not supported by legislation, save for an appropriation Act, it was held to be invalid.

The Commonwealth responded swiftly to the High Court's decision in *Williams v Commonwealth [No 1]* by inserting a new s 32B into the *Financial Framework (Supplementary Powers) Act 1997* (Cth). It needed to save many of its directly funded programmes which did not have legislative support. Section 32B

[134] *Williams [No 1]* (n 5) 234 [143] (Gummow and Bell JJ), 272–73 [257] (Hayne J), 346–47 [497]–[499], 348 [503] (Crennan J), 372–73 [590]–[591] (Kiefel J).

[135] ibid 267 [243], 269 [247] (Hayne J), 373 [593] (Kiefel J).

[136] ibid 235–36 [146]–[149] (Gummow and Bell JJ), 348 [503] (Crennan J), 373 [591]–[593] (Kiefel J). See also 267–68 [243], 267–71 [243]–[253] (Hayne J).

[137] ibid 180 [4], 184–85 [34] (French CJ), 249–50 [194], 250–51 [196] (Hayne J), 319 [402] (Heydon J), 342 [485] (Crennan J), 370 [582]–[583] (Kiefel J). See further A Twomey, 'Post-*Williams* Expenditure – When Can the Commonwealth and States Spend Public Money Without Parliamentary Authorisation?' (2014) 33 *University of Queensland Law Journal* 9, 9–10, 23–25; A Twomey, 'Executive Power Following the *Williams* Cases' in J Griffiths and J Stellios (eds), *Current Issue in Australian Constitutional Law: Tributes to Professor Leslie Zines* (Alexandria, Federation Press, 2020) 33, 33; Stellios (n 70) 398–99.

[138] *Williams [No 1]* (n 5) 180 [4], 184–85 [22], 191 [34] (French CJ), 342 [484] (Crennan J), 370 [582] (Kiefel J).

[139] ibid 180 [4], 184–85 [34] (French CJ), 233 [139]–[143] (Gummow and Bell JJ), [212] (Hayne J), 355 [532] (Crennan J), 370 [582] (Kiefel J).

[140] ibid 180 [4] (French CJ), 233 [139] (Gummow and Bell JJ), 249–51 [194], [196], 255–56 [208]–[209] (Hayne J), 342 [484], 345 [493], 354–55 [530]–[532] (Crennan J), 370–71 [582]–[583] (Kiefel J).

was inserted as an attempt to authorise these programmes, which were listed in the *Financial Framework (Supplementary Powers) Regulations 1997* (Cth). Over 400 arrangements and grants were included in the *Financial Framework Regulations*, including the NSCP.

Ron Williams successfully challenged the legislative authorisation of the NSCP in *Williams v Commonwealth [No 2]*. The Court held in *Williams v Commonwealth [No 2]* that the legislative authorisation of the NSCP was not valid because it lacked a sufficient connection to a head of Commonwealth legislative power. The Court dismissed an attempt by the Commonwealth to reopen the decision in *Williams v Commonwealth [No 1]* and confirmed that s 61 did not authorise the expenditure in that case.[141] The Court in *Williams v Commonwealth [No 2]* also rejected the assumption that the executive power to contract and spend in Australia needed to be the same as the powers of the British Executive, which 'operates under a unitary system or under a flexible Constitution where the Parliament is supreme'.[142] The Court placed emphasis on the fact that, in contrast to the United Kingdom, the character and status of the Commonwealth Executive Government in Australia is that of 'the central polity of a federation in which independent governments exist in the one area and exercise powers in different fields of action carefully defined by law'.[143]

*Williams [No 1]* and *Williams [No 2]* are undoubtedly 'fundamental'[144] decisions. While they have helped to clarify the nature and scope of Commonwealth executive power, there are issues that remain to be resolved and which fall outside the scope of this book. For example, it is not clear whether the Commonwealth Executive Government can continue to exercise other capacities, such as the power to conduct inquiries, without statutory authorisation[145] and whether these developments could have implications for the scope of the executive power of the States.[146]

## E. The Nationhood Power

The High Court has also confirmed that, in addition to the powers derived from the royal prerogative, as are attributable to the Commonwealth and the capacities derived from the legal personality of the Commonwealth as a polity, the Commonwealth Executive Government also enjoys a 'capacity to engage in enterprises and activities peculiarly adapted to the government of a nation'.[147]

[141] *Williams v Commonwealth [No 2]* (2014) 252 CLR 416, 463–70 [57]–[87] (French CJ, Hayne, Kiefel, Bell and Keane JJ).
[142] ibid 469 [83] (French CJ, Hayne, Kiefel, Bell and Keane JJ).
[143] ibid.
[144] Twomey, 'Post-*Williams* Expenditure' (n 137) 9.
[145] See also Appleby and McDonald (n 6) 262; N Aroney, 'A Power "Singular and Eccentrical": Royal Commissions and Executive Power after Williams' (2014) 25 *Public Law Review* 99, 101, 109–10.
[146] See also Saunders, 'The Concept of the Crown' (n 74) 894–95.
[147] *AAP case* (n 120) 397 (Mason J).

As discussed in Chapter 1, the High Court has not always referred expressly to the nationhood power, notwithstanding its widespread use in the academic commentary.[148] The 'nationhood power' is a useful shorthand description of the executive power that has variously been described as having its basis in the 'character and status of the Commonwealth as a national government';[149] 'fact of nationhood and of international personality';[150] 'formation of the Commonwealth as a polity and its emergence as an international state';[151] 'growth of the Commonwealth to nationhood';[152] or 'idea of Australia as a nation'.[153]

The nationhood power is the subject of this book but it is helpful to introduce it here and provide a brief overview of its development in the case law. The modern formulation of the nationhood power has its roots in early decisions of the High Court, beginning with the *Pharmaceutical Benefits case*.[154] In that case, Dixon J reasoned that power of expenditure 'includes whatever is incidental to the existence of the Commonwealth as a state and to the exercise of the functions of a national government'.[155] Justice Dixon went on to explain that these incidental matters, 'whether in reference to the external or internal concerns of government, should be interpreted widely and applied according to no narrow conception of the functions of the central government of a country in the world of to-day'.[156]

In the post-war decisions in *Burns v Ransley*,[157] *R v Sharkey*[158] (together, the 'sedition cases') and *Australian Communist Party v Commonwealth* ('*Communist Party case*'),[159] the High Court confirmed that the Commonwealth enjoyed an implied power to protect itself against sedition and subversion.[160] However, the judgments in the sedition cases and *Communist Party case* revealed two possible views as to the source of this power. The prevailing view adopted by the majority

[148] There are some references made to the implied executive nationhood power in the case law: see, eg, *AAP case* (n 120) 362 (Barwick CJ); *Re Wakim; Ex parte McNally* (1999) 198 CLR 511, 614–16 [221]–[224] (Kirby J); *Pape* (n 5) 48–49 [92] (French CJ), 177–91 [511]–[546] (Heydon J); *Williams [No 1]* (n 5) 267 [240] (Hayne J), 356–57 [539] (Crennan J); *Williams [No 2]* (n 141) 454 [23] (French CJ, Hayne, Kiefel, Bell and Keane JJ); *CPCF* (n 107) 568 [150] (Hayne and Bell JJ), 596 [260] (Kiefel J).

[149] *AAP case* (n 120) 397 (Mason J) endorsed in *Duncan* (n 120) 560 (Mason J); *Davis* (n 5) 93–94 (Mason CJ, Deane and Gaudron JJ); *Hughes* (n 120) 554–55 [38] (Gleeson CJ, Gaudron, McHugh, Gummow, Hayne and Callinan JJ); *Pape* (n 5) 60–61 [128], 63 [133] (French CJ), 87–88 [228], 91–92 [248] (Gummow, Crennan and Bell JJ); *Williams [No 1]* (n 5) 179–80 [4], 184–85 [22], 191 [34], 216–17 [83] (French CJ), 342 [485] (Crennan J), 370 [583] (Kiefel J).

[150] *AAP case* (n 120) 362 (Barwick CJ).

[151] ibid; *Commonwealth v Tasmania* (1983) 158 CLR 1, 252 (Deane J); *Re Wakim* (n 148) 581–82 [126] (Gummow and Hayne JJ); *Davis* (n 5) 119 (Toohey J).

[152] *AAP case* (n 120) 378 (Gibbs J).

[153] ibid 406 (Jacobs J) affirmed in *Davis* (n 5) 110 (Brennan J); *Tampa case* (n 90) 539 [180] (French J).

[154] *Attorney-General (Vic); Ex rel Dale v Commonwealth* (1945) 71 CLR 237, 266 (Starke J), 269 (Dixon J).

[155] ibid 269.

[156] ibid.

[157] *Burns v Ransley* (1949) 79 CLR 101.

[158] *R v Sharkey* (1949) 79 CLR 121.

[159] *Communist Party case* (n 19) 151 (Latham CJ), 188 (Dixon J), 211–12 (McTiernan J), 231 (Williams J), 233 (Webb J), 260 (Fullagar J), 277 (Kitto J).

[160] *Burns* (n 157) 110 (Latham CJ), 111 (Rich J), 116 (Dixon J), 120 (McTiernan J); *Sharkey* (n 158) 135 (Latham CJ), 145 (Rich J), 148–49 (Dixon J), 157 (McTiernan J), 159 (Williams J), 163 (Webb J).

was that the power arose under the executive power in s 61, which extends to 'the execution and maintenance of this Constitution'. The incidental power in s 51(xxxix) provided the authority for legislation with respect to matters incidental to the exercise of that power.[161]

Justice Dixon adopted a different view as to the source of the power. While he accepted that the executive power conferred by s 61 in combination with s 51(xxxix) could support laws aimed at suppressing seditious or subversive activities, he thought that this textual combination had 'an artificial aspect'.[162] Justice Dixon preferred the view that he had initially expressed in *Burns* and *Sharkey* that the source of the power to legislate against sedition and subversion was based 'in principle that is deeper or wider than a series of combinations of the words of s 51(xxxix) with those of other constitutional powers'.[163] Justice Dixon thought that the power was inherent in the establishment and character of the Commonwealth as a polity.[164]

Justice Dixon's view about the source of the Commonwealth's power of self-protection received limited support from Fullagar J in the *Communist Party case*. Justice Fullagar accepted that the decisions in *Burns* and *Sharkey* had confirmed that the Commonwealth Parliament had power to legislate for the prevention and punishment of sedition and subversion. In commenting on the source of the power, Fullagar J made the following observation:

> The source of part of the power which I have been discussing may be found in s. 51(xxxix), read with s. 61 of the Constitution … But I think that, if it ever becomes necessary to examine it closely, it may well be found to depend really on an essential and inescapable implication which must be involved in the legal constitution of any polity.[165]

Justice Dixon's reasoning in the sedition cases and *Communist Party case* that the Commonwealth Parliament enjoyed an implied *legislative* power derived from the establishment and character of the national polity was a minority view. It has, nevertheless, unquestionably influenced the development of an inherent *executive* power that was underpinned by the same nationhood considerations.[166]

[161] *Communist Party case* (n 19) 211–12 (McTiernan J), 230–31, 232 (Williams J), 260 (Fullagar J), 277 (Kitto J). See also *Burns* (n 157) 109–10 (Latham CJ); *Sharkey* (n 158) 135–36 (Latham CJ), 157–58 (McTiernan JJ).

[162] *Communist Party case* (n 19) 187.

[163] ibid 188.

[164] ibid.

[165] ibid 260, 266.

[166] See further P Gerangelos, 'Sir Owen Dixon and the Concept of "Nationhood" as a Source of Commonwealth Power' in J Eldridge and T Pilkington (eds), *Sir Owen Dixon's Legacy* (Alexandria, Federation Press, 2019) 56; M Gordon, 'Communist Party Case: Core Themes and Legacy' (Speech delivered at the Centre for Comparative Constitutional Studies Constitutional Law Conference, Melbourne, 23 July 2021) 41, 39–43.

This was evident in the *AAP case*.[167] After referring with approval to Dixon J's judgment in the *Communist Party case*, Mason J stated that

> the Commonwealth enjoys, apart from its specific and enumerated powers, certain implied powers which stem from its existence and its character as a polity … So far it has not been suggested that the implied powers extend beyond the area of internal security and protection of the State against disaffection and subversion. But in my opinion there is to be deduced from the existence and character of the Commonwealth as a national government and from the presence of ss 51(xxxix) and 61 a capacity to engage in enterprises and activities peculiarly adapted to the government of a nation and which cannot otherwise be carried on for the benefit of the nation.[168]

He was not alone in this respect. Chief Justice Barwick thought that there was 'no doubt' that 'some powers, legislative and executive, may come from the very formation of the Commonwealth as a polity and its emergence as an international state'.[169] In commenting on the scope of these powers, Barwick CJ stated that

> [t]he extent of the powers which are inherent in the fact of nationhood and of international personality has not been fully explored. Some of them may readily be recognised: and in furtherance of such powers money may properly be spent. One such power, for example, is the power to explore, whether it be foreign lands or seas or in areas of scientific knowledge or technology.[170]

In the decades following the *AAP case* the High Court found that the nationhood power supported the organisation and commemoration of the 1988 bicentenary of European settlement in Australia, including the establishment of a corporation for this purpose,[171] and one-off tax bonus payments made to individual taxpayers in 2009 in response to the global financial crisis.[172] However, it has also been suggested that the nationhood power provided the constitutional basis for the domestic deployment of the ADF by the Commonwealth to maintain internal security and respond to emergencies[173] and action taken by the Commonwealth to prevent the entry of non-citizens into Australia.[174]

This book examines the exercise of the nationhood power in these different contexts, with a view to extracting the clearest possible statement of principles about its scope and the limitations that apply to it. As is shown below, the conceptual framework developed by Winterton between the 'breadth' and the 'depth' of the executive power is helpful in determining the scope of the nationhood power and will be adopted in this book.

[167] *AAP case* (n 120).
[168] ibid 397.
[169] ibid 362, 375 (Gibbs J).
[170] ibid 362.
[171] *Davis* (n 5).
[172] *Pape* (n 5).
[173] RM Hope, *Protective Security Review Report (unclassified version)* (Parliamentary Paper No 397, 1979) 30 [3.10].
[174] *Tampa case* (n 90) 542–43 [191]–[193] (French CJ), 514 [95] (Beaumont J).

## III. A Framework of Analysis: The 'Breadth' and 'Depth' of Commonwealth Executive Power

In *Parliament, the Executive and the Governor-General: A Constitutional Analysis*[175] Winterton developed a conceptual framework for determining the scope of Commonwealth executive power. He explained that the exercise of Commonwealth executive power in Australia had two dimensions, which he labelled 'breadth' and 'depth'.[176]

The 'breadth' of Commonwealth executive power described the subject matters with respect to which the Commonwealth Executive Government may act, having regard to the federal distribution of powers between the Commonwealth and the States effected by the Constitution.[177] Winterton observed that the High Court had, in ascertaining the 'breadth' of the executive power, applied the principle that the 'contours' of the executive power of the Commonwealth generally followed those of Commonwealth legislative power, enumerated in ss 51, 52 and 122 of the Constitution.[178] As such, in Winterton's view, Commonwealth executive power extended to the subject matters on which the Commonwealth Parliament could legislate, including matters 'appropriate' to a national government, which were, in Winterton's view, grounded in either s 51(xxxix), in relation to domestic matters, or s 51(xxix) in relation to foreign affairs.[179]

'Depth', on the other hand, described the types of actions or activities which the Commonwealth Executive Government is empowered to undertake in relation to those subject matters.[180] It directed attention to whether the action was an exercise of executive power, or legislative or judicial in nature. The question of 'depth' reflected the separation of powers and required a consideration of the relationship between the Executive Government and the Parliament, as governed by the principle of responsible government.

Winterton argued that the executive action undertaken by the Commonwealth needed to satisfy both of the 'breadth' and the 'depth' dimensions in order to be a valid exercise of non-statutory executive power. As Winterton explained, one must

> ascertain first whether the action falls within the breadth of federal executive power, that is, whether its subject matter falls within federal legislative power. If it does, it is necessary then to consider depth, namely, whether the action is one the executive can undertake without prior legislative authorisation; this will depend on whether the action is authorised by the prerogative, or common law powers of the Crown.[181]

[175] Winterton, *Parliament* (n 12).

[176] ibid 29–34, 40–44 endorsed in *Plaintiff M68* (n 2) 96–97 [130]–[131] (Gageler J). See also L Zines, 'The Inherent Executive Power of the Commonwealth' (2005) 16 *Public Law Review* 279, 281; Gerangelos, 'The Executive Power of the Commonwealth of Australia' (n 89) 103–05, 110–12.

[177] Winterton, *Parliament* (n 12) 29–31, 38–47.

[178] ibid 30.

[179] ibid 44.

[180] ibid 34. See also *Plaintiff M68* (n 2) 96 [130] (Gageler J).

[181] Winterton, *Parliament* (n 12) 29–30, 34. Note Twomey's critique of the order of this analysis in Twomey, 'The French Court' (n 14) 42–43.

Winterton's thesis was that the depth of the executive power was limited to powers conferred expressly by statute, or, in the case of non-statutory executive power, the prerogative.[182] In determining the depth of the executive power, then, the relevant question was whether the executive act or activity fell within the common law powers of the Crown in s 61 of the Constitution. Winterton gave several compelling reasons to support his thesis. First, the limits of prerogative powers are well established in the common law. Winterton also placed considerable emphasis on the fact that the prerogative is subject to control by legislation.[183] It is a constitutional principle that a prerogative power of the Crown may be abrogated, curtailed or displaced by statute which comprehensively regulates the same subject matter as the prerogative.[184] In these circumstances, consistent with the principle of parliamentary sovereignty, the Executive Government derives its authority from the Parliament and must exercise its power in accordance with the provisions of the statute. Winterton thought that it was desirable for executive powers to be regulated by legislation as this promotes executive accountability to the Parliament, which is consistent with the principle of responsible government; encourages parliamentary oversight of the nature and scope of executive power; and promotes the rule of law, by subjecting executive action to judicial review.[185] Indeed, one of Winterton's concerns about the existence of an inherent or implied nationhood power was that its relationship with the Parliament and legislation was unclear, and it could create a field of executive power immune from parliamentary control and oversight.[186]

While Winterton confined the depth of the executive power to the established common law powers of the Crown, he conceded that this approach had not always been adopted by Australian courts.[187] However, in the recent decision of *Plaintiff M68* Gageler J applied the breadth and depth framework to his analysis of the scope of Commonwealth executive power. Justice Gageler explained that

> [w]ithout attempting to define Commonwealth executive power, Professor Winterton usefully drew attention to its dimensions when he distinguished its 'breadth' from its 'depth': 'breadth' referring to the subject matters with respect to which the Executive Government of the Commonwealth is empowered to act having regard to the constraints of the federal system; 'depth' referring to the precise actions which the Executive Government is empowered to undertake in relation to those subject matters.[188]

[182] Winterton, *Parliament* (n 12) 31–34. It is important to note that Winterton favoured Dicey's wider definition of the 'prerogative' as encompassing both the common law capacities and prerogatives of the Crown. Accordingly, he referred only to the 'prerogative' in his writing, but for the sake of consistency in this book, the common law powers of the Crown will be divided into two categories, following Blackstone's classification.

[183] Winterton, *Parliament* (n 12) 115–16, 137–39. See also Winterton, 'The Relationship' (n 29) 35–36.

[184] *De Keyser* (n 48).

[185] Winterton, *Parliament* (n 12) 115–16, 137–39. See also Winterton, 'The Relationship' (n 29) 35–36.

[186] Winterton, *Parliament* (n 12) 33–34.

[187] G Winterton, 'The Limits and Use of Executive Power by Government' (2003) 31 *Federal Law Review* 421, 428; Winterton, 'The Relationship' (n 29) 30.

[188] *Plaintiff M68* (n 2) 96 [130] (Gageler J).

Thus, while Winterton's framework of analysis has not always been consistently applied by Australian courts,[189] the distinction that it draws between the breadth and the depth dimensions of Commonwealth executive power has continuing utility[190] and will be adopted in this book to assist our understanding of the scope and limits of the nationhood aspect of executive power.[191]

## IV. Conclusion

This chapter has provided an overview of the executive power of the Commonwealth conferred by s 61 of the Constitution. It set out the categories of power that have been recognised as informing the content of the executive power of the Commonwealth and their limitations. This chapter has concentrated on the scope of the inherent or non-statutory executive power and introduced the conceptual framework developed by Winterton between the breadth and the depth of executive power that will be adopted to describe the different dimensions of executive power in this book. The chapters that follow examine the scope of the nationhood power, with a view to identifying the limitations that apply to it.

[189] See especially *Tampa case* (n 90) 540 [183], 542 [191] (French J); *Williams [No 1]* (n 5). Compare the approach in *Plaintiff M68* (n 2) 96 [130] (Gageler J).

[190] See its recent application in *Plaintiff M68* (n 2) 96–97 [130]–[132] (Gageler J).

[191] See, eg, Zines, 'The Inherent Executive Power' (n 176) 281; S Evans, 'The Rule of Law, Constitutionalism and the MV Tampa' (2002) 13 *Public Law Review* 94; Gerangelos, 'The Executive Power of the Commonwealth of Australia' (n 89); P Gerangelos, 'Section 61 of the *Commonwealth Constitution* and an "Historical Constitutional Approach": An Excursus on Justice Gageler's Reasoning in the *M68* Case' (2018) 43 *University of Western Australia Law Review* 103, 134–36; P Gerangelos, 'Reflections on the Executive Power of the Commonwealth: Recent Developments, Interpretational Methodology and Constitutional Symmetry' (2018) 37 *University of Queensland Law Journal* 191; C Saunders, *The Constitution of Australia: A Contextual Analysis* (Oxford, Hart Publishing, 2011) 177–81; P Stephenson, 'Nationhood and Section 61 of the Constitution' (2018) 43 *University of Western Australia Law Review* 149.

# PART II

# The Scope of the Nationhood Power

# 3

# The Development of the Nationhood Power in the Australian Case Law

> But in my opinion, there is to be deduced from the existence and character of the Commonwealth as a national government and from the presence of ss 51(xxxix) and 61 a capacity to engage in enterprises and activities peculiarly adapted to the government of a nation and which cannot otherwise be carried on for the benefit of the nation.
>
> Sir Anthony Mason, 1975[1]

The High Court of Australia has recognised that the Commonwealth Executive Government enjoys 'inherent' or 'implied' power derived from its character and status as a national government.[2] This power is often referred to as the 'nationhood power' aspect of s 61. The description of the nationhood power that has received judicial endorsement by the High Court was set out by Mason J in the important and influential decision in the *AAP case*.[3] In his judgment, Mason J explained that

> there is to be deduced from the existence and character of the Commonwealth as a national government and from the presence of ss 51(xxxix) and 61 a capacity to engage in enterprises and activities peculiarly adapted to the government of a nation and which cannot otherwise be carried on for the benefit of the nation.[4]

This chapter traces the development of the nationhood power in the Australian constitutional jurisprudence, beginning with the decision in the *AAP case*,[5] before turning to consider its application in subsequent decisions.

The cases examined in this chapter demonstrate that Australian courts have applied Mason J's formulation of the nationhood power as a test for ascertaining

[1] *Victoria v Commonwealth and Hayden* (1975) 134 CLR 338 (*AAP case*). Reproduced with permission of Thomson Reuters (Professional) Australia Limited, legal.thomsonreuters.com.au.

[2] ibid 362 (Barwick CJ), 375 (Gibbs J), 397 (Mason J), 412 (Jacobs J).

[3] ibid.

[4] ibid 397.

[5] Some of the material in this chapter is drawn from P Stephenson, 'Justice Mason in the Australian Assistance Plan Case (1975): Nationhood, Federalism and Commonwealth Executive Power' in A Lynch (ed), *Great Australian Dissents* (Cambridge, Cambridge University Press, 2016) 169 and has been reproduced with permission.

whether a sufficient connection exists between executive action and that area of responsibility appropriate to the character and status of the Commonwealth as the national government. It is demonstrated that the application of the 'peculiarly adapted' test by the High Court has limited the expansion of the 'breadth' of Commonwealth executive power. The High Court has also recognised that there are limits on the types of executive action that the Commonwealth is empowered to undertake 'for the benefit of the nation' pursuant to the nationhood power. These limits to the 'depth' of the executive power relate to the capacity of the Commonwealth to undertake executive action that interferes with the legal rights and duties of individuals.

## I. The Nationhood Power, Appropriations and Spending in the *Australian Assistance Plan Case*

The *AAP case* concerned a challenge to Commonwealth expenditure for the Australian Assistance Plan. The Australian Assistance Plan was introduced by the Whitlam Labor Government in 1973 and formed a central pillar in its agenda for social welfare reform in Australia. Under the Australian Assistance Plan, the Commonwealth Government would provide direct grants to Regional Councils for Social Development ('Regional Councils') to facilitate the provision of improved social welfare services and programmes in local communities across Australia. Whitlam referred to this widening of the role of local government as 'a new federalism'.[6] Traditionally, the Commonwealth would have provided the States with a conditional grant made under s 96 of the Constitution. However, Whitlam was of the view that the existing federal system was inefficient, dysfunctional and 'wholly inadequate to the needs of a modern federal state'.[7] As such, it was never intended that the Commonwealth Government would administer the Australian Assistance Plan through the State governments.[8]

In order to fund the Australian Assistance Plan, the Commonwealth Government appropriated \$5,970,000 from the Consolidated Revenue Fund (CRF), consisting of \$5,620,000 for the direct grants to the Regional Councils and \$350,000 for 'development and evaluation expenses'. The Australian Assistance Plan was not authorised by legislation, save for a brief description of it in item 4 div 530 of sch 2 of the *Appropriation Act (No 1) 1974–1975* (Cth).

[6] EG Whitlam, 'A New Federalism' (1971) 43 *Australian Quarterly* 6, 6–17.

[7] EG Whitlam, 'The Labor Government and the Constitution' in G Evans (ed), *Labor and the Constitution 1972–1975: Essays and Commentaries on the Constitutional Controversies of the Whitlam years* (Richmond, Heinemann Educational Australia, 1977) 305.

[8] See also C Saunders, 'The Development of the Commonwealth Spending Power' (1978) 11 *Melbourne University Law Review* 369, 402.

The details of the Australian Assistance Plan were contained in two discussion papers and a document entitled 'Guidelines for Pilot Programme – Australian Assistance Plan'. Although it was intended that the Australian Assistance Plan would subsequently be enshrined in legislation, this never eventuated. For the duration of its lifetime, the Australian Assistance Plan was administered by the Commonwealth Government, free of any underpinning legislative foundation.

The State of Victoria and its Attorney-General challenged the constitutional validity of the Australian Assistance Plan in the High Court and sought a declaration that the appropriation for the Australian Assistance Plan was invalid insofar as it exceeded the limited social welfare activities which the Commonwealth was authorised to carry out pursuant to ss 51(xxiii) and 51(xxiiiA) of the Constitution. The plaintiffs also sought an injunction restraining the defendants, the Commonwealth and the Minister for Social Security, Bill Hayden, from expending any funds for the purposes of the Australian Assistance Plan. The defendants asserted the validity of the Australian Assistance Plan and the associated appropriation.

Argument began on 6 May 1975 and concluded two days later. The High Court handed down its decision on 17 October 1975. In a narrow 4:3 decision, the High Court dismissed the plaintiffs' action. Justices McTiernan, Jacobs and Murphy were members of the majority which upheld the appropriation for the Australian Assistance Plan. Chief Justice Barwick and Gibbs and Mason JJ, in dissent, found respectively that the appropriation or the activities which required the expenditure of funds[9] were invalid. Justice Stephen did not decide the issue, having concluded that Victoria and its Attorney-General lacked standing to institute the proceedings. As such, the appropriation for the Australian Assistance Plan and the associated expenditure survived the challenge.

## A. Validity of the Appropriation

The central issue in the *AAP case* concerned whether the appropriation for the Australian Assistance Plan was 'for the purposes of the Commonwealth', as required by s 81 of the Constitution. At the time, there were two competing views about the meaning of this phrase that had emerged from the earlier decision in *Attorney-General (Vic); Ex rel Dale v Commonwealth* ('*Pharmaceutical Benefits case*').[10] In that case Latham CJ and McTiernan J adopted a wide interpretation of the phrase, finding that the Commonwealth Parliament could appropriate funds for any purpose that it chose.[11] This wide view of s 81 was not accepted by Rich, Starke, Williams and Dixon JJ, who saw the words 'purposes of the Commonwealth'

[9] *AAP case* (n 1) 396, 400–01 (Mason J).

[10] *Attorney-General (Vic); Ex rel Dale v Commonwealth* (1945) 71 CLR 237 (*Pharmaceutical Benefits case*).

[11] ibid 254 (Latham CJ), 273–74 (McTiernan J).

in s 81 as limiting the power of appropriations. Justices Starke and Williams considered that the phrase referred to the purposes of the Commonwealth as a body politic.[12] Accordingly, the Commonwealth could only appropriate funds for purposes within Commonwealth power. Those purposes needed to be found 'within the four corners of the Constitution'[13] and included legislative, executive and judicial functions vested in the Commonwealth by the Constitution or any other Act and 'matters arising from the existence of the Commonwealth and its status as a Federal Government'.[14] Justice Dixon (with whom Rich J concurred) confined the phrase 'purposes of the Commonwealth' to matters within the legislative power of the Commonwealth, including matters 'incidental to the existence of the Commonwealth as a state and to the exercise of the functions of a national government'.[15]

In considering the validity of the appropriation in the *AAP case*, McTiernan, Mason and Murphy JJ held that the appropriation was for the 'purposes of the Commonwealth' and was therefore valid. In reaching this conclusion, McTiernan J relied extensively on Latham CJ's judgment in the *Pharmaceutical Benefits case*, finding that s 81 was essentially unlimited in scope.[16] Mason and Murphy JJ also afforded s 81 a wide operation and concluded that it extended to 'such purposes as the Parliament may determine'.[17]

Justice Jacobs adopted what he understood to be the majority view in the *Pharmaceutical Benefits case*, namely that the 'purposes of the Commonwealth' were limited to purposes falling within 'a subject matter of general or particular power prescribed in the *Constitution*', including purposes that could be implied from the status of 'Australia as a nation externally and internally sovereign'.[18] Justice Jacobs took a wide view of these purposes, finding that public funds could be appropriated for activities that required national coordination and reflected 'the complexity and values of a modern national society'.[19] Justice Jacobs held that the expenditure for the Australian Assistance Plan was a valid exercise by the Commonwealth Executive Government of its power to 'formulate and co-ordinate plans and purposes which require national rather than local planning and of its legislative power to appropriate its funds accordingly'.[20]

Chief Justice Barwick and Gibbs J, in dissent, adopted a narrow interpretation of 'purposes of the Commonwealth' in s 81, finding that it was limited to those purposes that fell within the legislative and executive powers of the Commonwealth, including powers inherent in its establishment as a nation.[21]

[12] ibid 266 (Starke J), 282 (Williams J).
[13] ibid 282 (Williams J).
[14] ibid 266 (Starke J).
[15] ibid 269 (Dixon J).
[16] *AAP case* (n 1) 367–69.
[17] ibid 396 (Mason J), 419 (Murphy J).
[18] ibid 412–13.
[19] ibid 412.
[20] ibid 413.
[21] ibid 361–62 (Barwick CJ), 373–74 (Gibbs J).

As the appropriation for the Australian Assistance Plan was not supported by these powers, it was invalid.

In their respective judgments in the *AAP case* Mason and Jacobs JJ considered the nature of an appropriation. Jacobs J remarked that an appropriation Act merely 'earmark[ed]' the money.[22] He thought that the source of the power to spend the funds was the prerogative.[23] Justice Mason also observed that an appropriation had a limited effect. Sections 81 and 83 enabled the Commonwealth to withdraw money from the CRF, but did not authorise the Commonwealth's engagement in the relevant activities which called for the expenditure of the funds.[24] While Mason J accepted the validity of the appropriation for the Australian Assistance Plan, he found that the appropriation Act did not provide the authority for the activities associated with it.[25] That power needed to be found elsewhere in the Constitution. As the Australian Assistance Plan operated as an administrative scheme which was not supported by legislation, the issue arose as to whether it fell within the executive power of the Commonwealth in s 61 of the Constitution.

## B. Judicial Recognition of 'Nationhood' Powers

It is difficult to identify the principle that the *AAP case* stands for because there was no clear majority finding about the source of the appropriation and spending powers.[26] For present purposes, however, the significance of the *AAP case* stems largely from the way in which it reconceptualised our understanding of the nature and scope of the executive power of the Commonwealth. In their respective judgments in the *AAP case* Mason and Jacobs JJ recognised that the Commonwealth Executive Government enjoyed inherent 'nationhood' powers. However, they adopted different approaches as to the source of these powers. While Jacobs J equated nationhood powers with the royal prerogative,[27] Mason J was of the view that the Commonwealth Executive enjoyed power derived from the 'existence and character of the Commonwealth as the national government'.[28] As is shown below, Mason J's judgment in the *AAP case* has proven to have a profound and enduring influence on the High Court's interpretation of the nature and scope of the nationhood power in subsequent decisions.

[22] ibid 411.
[23] ibid 404–05.
[24] ibid 396.
[25] ibid.
[26] See also *Pape v Federal Commissioner of Taxation* (2009) 238 CLR 1, 113 [321] (Hayne and Kiefel JJ); A Twomey, 'The French Court, the Nature of the Executive Power and its Reconciliation with the Expenditure Power' in H Jackson (ed), *Essays in Honour of Chief Justice French* (Alexandria, Federation Press, 2019) 30. Saunders, 'The Development' (n 8) 373, 401–03.
[27] *AAP case* (n 1) 405–06 (Jacobs J).
[28] ibid 397 (Mason J).

### *i. 'Maintenance of this Constitution' in s 61*

In his judgment Jacobs J recognised that the executive power of the Commonwealth extended to 'all matters which are the concern of Australia as a nation'.[29] However, while Mason J recognised the existence of the nationhood power as a separate category of executive power, the 'nationhood' powers recognised by Jacobs J were powers derived from the royal prerogative, which had become exercisable by the Commonwealth Executive as Australia had attained independence. These powers were, therefore, appropriate to the character and status of the Commonwealth as the national government. He was of the view that executive powers in the nature of the prerogative were encompassed by the reference in s 61 to the 'maintenance of this Constitution', rather than the opening declaration in that provision vesting the executive power of the Commonwealth in the Queen. As Jacobs J explained,

> [t]he prerogative is now exercisable by the Queen through the Governor-General acting on the advice of the Executive Council on all matters which are the concern of Australia as a nation. Within the words 'maintenance of this Constitution' appearing in s 61 lies the idea of Australia as a nation within itself and in its relationship with the external world, a nation governed by a system of law in which the powers of government are divided between a government representative of all the people of Australia and a number of governments each representative of the people of the various States.[30]

Previously, the reference to 'maintenance of this Constitution' in s 61 had been understood as being confined to 'the protection and safeguarding of something immediately prescribed or authorized by the Constitution without the intervention of Federal legislation'.[31] The concept of 'maintaining' the Constitution included protecting the nation and the institutions, functions and operations of the Commonwealth Government.[32] In his judgment in the *AAP case*, Jacobs J adopted a wider interpretation of this phrase. He was of the view that the extension of the executive power to the 'maintenance of this Constitution' in s 61 empowered the Commonwealth to undertake activities 'which have an Australian rather than a local flavour'.[33]

Justice Jacobs was satisfied that the Australian Assistance Plan was an example of a type of activity that had a 'national flavour'[34] and was within the scope of the executive power conferred by s 61. He placed emphasis on the fact that the purpose of the Australian Assistance Plan was to coordinate the provision of social welfare services across the nation. According to Jacobs J, executive activities would be supported by the executive power if they required national coordination rather

[29] ibid 405–06.

[30] ibid 406.

[31] *Australian Communist Party v Commonwealth* (1951) 83 CLR 1, 230 (Williams J) (*Communist Party case*).

[32] This was confirmed in *Pape* (n 26) at 171 [498] (Heydon J). See also Hayne and Kiefel JJ at 125 [364].

[33] *AAP case* (n 1) 412–13.

[34] ibid 413.

than local planning. National inquiries, research and exploration were examples given by Jacobs J of activities with a 'national flavour' that were supported by the nationhood aspect of the executive power.[35]

As is discussed below, Jacobs J's reasoning was relied on by Brennan J in *Davis* to support a finding that the extension of the executive power to the 'maintenance of this Constitution' in s 61 assigned functions to the Commonwealth Executive Government relating to 'the protection and *advancement* of the nation' (emphasis added).[36] However, the extension of 'maintenance' to 'advancement' of this Constitution does not appear to have been widely endorsed in subsequent decisions.[37]

### *ii. Power Derived from the Character and Status of the Commonwealth as the National Government*

Justice Mason accepted that funds validly appropriated in accordance with ss 81 and 83 could be spent by the Commonwealth Executive Government, but a further source of power was required to engage in the activities associated with the Australian Assistance Plan. As no legislation had been enacted to support the Australian Assistance Plan, Mason J considered whether it fell within the scope of the executive power of the Commonwealth conferred by s 61 of the Constitution. Justice Mason explained, in this respect, that the breadth of Commonwealth executive power included

> the area of responsibilities allocated to the Commonwealth by the Constitution, responsibilities which are ascertainable from the distribution of powers, more particularly the distribution of legislative powers, effected by the Constitution itself and the character and status of the Commonwealth as a national government.[38]

Justice Mason accepted that Commonwealth executive power included power derived from 'the character and status of the Commonwealth as the national government'. This was evident where he explained, in the critical and influential passage in the *AAP case*, that

> there is to be deduced from the existence and character of the Commonwealth as a national government and from the presence of ss 51(xxxix) and 61 a capacity to engage

[35] ibid.

[36] *Davis v Commonwealth* (1988) 166 CLR 79, 110 (Brennan J).

[37] See also A Sapienza, *Judicial Review of Non-Statutory Executive Action* (Alexandria, Federation Press, 2020) 20.

[38] *AAP case* (n 1) endorsed in *R v Duncan; Ex parte Australian Iron & Steel Pty Ltd* (1983) 158 CLR 535, 560 (Mason J); *Davis* (n 36) 93–94 (Mason CJ, Deane and Gaudron JJ); *R v Hughes* (2000) 202 CLR 535, 554–55 [38] (Gleeson CJ, Gaudron, McHugh, Gummow, Hayne and Callinan JJ); *Pape* (n 26) 114 [323], 115–16 [327], 124 [357] (Hayne and Kiefel JJ); *Williams v Commonwealth [No 1]* (2012) 248 CLR 156, 188 [29] (French CJ), 156 [133] (Gummow and Bell JJ), 251 [197] (Hayne J), 356–57 [539] (Crennan J), 364 [564], 371 [586] (Kiefel J). This cohered with his earlier view in *Barton v Commonwealth* (1974) 131 CLR 477, 498 (Mason J).

> in enterprises and activities peculiarly adapted to the government of a nation and which cannot otherwise be carried on for the benefit of the nation.[39]

Without attempting to exhaustively define the scope of this power, Mason J suggested that it could support national scientific research, including the establishment of the CSIRO[40] and Commonwealth expenditure on 'inquiries, investigation and advocacy in relation to matters affecting public health'.[41] These examples were not exhaustive and Mason J accepted that

> the functions appropriate and adapted to a national government will vary from time to time. As time unfolds, as circumstances and conditions alter, it will transpire that particular enterprises and activities will be undertaken if they are to be undertaken at all, by the national government.[42]

While Mason J contemplated that a potentially wide range of executive activities could enliven the nationhood power, he also accepted that there were limits on its scope. The nationhood power could not be exercised to effect a 'radical transformation' of the federal constitutional structure.[43] Justice Mason explained that the mere fact that an enterprise or activity could be 'conveniently formulated and administered by the national government'[44] was not sufficient to render it peculiarly adapted to the national government and within the scope of the nationhood power. In these ways, Mason J attempted to place limits on the expansion of the breadth of the executive power of the Commonwealth.

Ultimately, Mason J held that the establishment and funding of the Regional Councils to provide social welfare support and functions under the Australian Assistance Plan did not satisfy the 'peculiarly adapted' test and fell 'outside the realm of the executive power of the Commonwealth'.[45] He observed that the purpose of the Australian Assistance Plan was to reconfigure the Australian community into regions for the purpose of coordinating and providing a wide range of social welfare services. The Regional Councils would be established and directly financed to provide these services, which extended to childcare, parent education, family counselling and housekeeping services, and which fell within areas of State responsibility. Justice Mason expressed concern that the Regional Councils would be 'operating not under the aegis of the States, but independently of and perhaps in competition with them and their institutions'.[46]

Justice Mason also explained that the establishment and direct financing of the Regional Councils was not the only way in which the Commonwealth could have

[39] *AAP case* (n 1) 397.
[40] ibid.
[41] ibid.
[42] ibid 397–98.
[43] ibid 398.
[44] ibid.
[45] ibid 401.
[46] ibid 400.

implemented the Australian Assistance Plan. The Commonwealth could have made a conditional grant to the States under s 96 of the Constitution, and Mason J did not accept that this constitutional mechanism could be bypassed simply because it was less convenient for the Commonwealth.[47] Justice Mason was not prepared to allow the Commonwealth to rely on its executive power to circumvent the States in this way. While Mason J recognised that there were implied powers derived from the character and status of the Commonwealth as the national government, he emphasised that the position of the Commonwealth Executive Government under the Constitution was that of a central government in a federal polity. Justice Mason was not prepared to afford the nationhood power a wide interpretation that would effect 'a radical transformation' of the federal constitutional structure.[48]

This interpretation of the nationhood power was adopted in *R v Duncan; Ex parte Australian Iron & Steel Pty Ltd*.[49] In that case Mason J found that the nationhood power could support the Commonwealth's entry into an intergovernmental agreement with the States on matters of joint interest, provided that 'the end to be achieved and the means by which it is to be achieved are consistent with and do not contravene the Constitution'.[50] In finding that the nationhood power supported the agreement, Mason J placed emphasis on its consensual nature.[51] The nationhood power was not being used to override or circumvent the federal distribution of powers, but to facilitate joint cooperative executive (and legislative) action on certain matters of interest to both the Commonwealth and the States.

## II. The Development of the Nationhood Power in *Davis v Commonwealth*

Justice Mason's formulation of the nationhood power in the *AAP case* was endorsed 13 years later by a majority of the High Court in *Davis v Commonwealth*.[52] By the time *Davis* was decided in 1988, Mason J had been appointed Chief Justice of the High Court. During his tenure as Chief Justice, Mason CJ's judgments would be influenced by what McHugh J described as a particular 'attitude of mind', which was characterised by

> the belief that Australia was now an independent nation whose political, legal and economic underpinnings had recently and essentially changed. These developments

[47] ibid 398, approved in *Commonwealth v Tasmania* (1983) 158 CLR 1, 109 (Gibbs CJ) (*Tasmanian Dam case*). Compare *AAP case* (n 1) 412–13 (Jacobs J), where national coordination was held to be sufficient.

[48] *AAP case* (n 1) 398 (Mason J).

[49] *Duncan* (n 38).

[50] ibid 560.

[51] C Saunders, 'Intergovernmental Agreements and the Executive Power' (2005) 16 *Public Law Review* 294, 307.

[52] *Davis* (n 36).

> outside the pages of the *Commonwealth Law Reports* required a different approach to the interpretation of the *Constitution* and a different approach to judging, generally.[53]

The enactment of the *Australia Acts* in 1986 by the Commonwealth and UK Parliaments just two years prior to *Davis* had formally severed Australia's remaining constitutional links with the UK,[54] which had 'been weakening for decades'.[55] Accordingly, when *Davis* was decided, Australia's status as a sovereign, independent nation continued to be a relevant factor in ascertaining the scope of the Commonwealth's executive power in its domestic application.[56] As Chief Justice of the Court, Mason CJ was able to command the support of other members of the bench who shared his 'attitude of mind'.

The central issue in *Davis* concerned whether activities associated with the commemoration of the 1988 bicentenary of European settlement in Australia ('Bicentenary') fell within the scope of the executive power of the Commonwealth.[57] These activities included the establishment by the Commonwealth of the Australian Bicentennial Authority for the purpose of organising the commemoration ('Authority'). The Authority was a private company that was incorporated on 21 January 1980 in the Australian Capital Territory under the *Companies Ordinance Act 1962* (ACT). The Commonwealth Parliament had also enacted the *Australian Bicentennial Authority Act 1980* (Cth) ('*Bicentennial Authority Act*') pursuant to the incidental legislative power in s 51(xxxix) and s 61. The *Bicentennial Authority Act* regulated the administration and procedures of the Authority and conferred certain powers on it.[58]

A majority of four justices of the High Court accepted that the commemoration of the Bicentenary was a matter falling within the scope of the nationhood power. It followed from this conclusion that s 61 authorised the Commonwealth Executive Government to establish the Authority as a means of organising and facilitating the commemoration. The majority also held that the incidental power in s 51(xxxix) supported the *Bicentennial Authority Act* as incidental to the exercise of the executive power. There were, however, certain measures in the legislation that the majority held to be invalid on the basis that they went beyond what was reasonably appropriate and adapted to protecting the Authority and the commemoration of the Bicentenary, which is considered in more detail below.[59]

The plurality, consisting of Mason CJ and Deane and Gaudron JJ, accepted that the Commonwealth Executive Government enjoyed power to engage in activities

[53] M McHugh, 'The Constitutional Jurisprudence of the High Court: 1989–2004' (Inaugural Sir Anthony Mason Lecture, Sydney, 26 November 2004).

[54] *Sue v Hill* (1999) 199 CLR 462, 528 (Gaudron J); *Pape* (n 26) 84 [217] (Gummow, Crennan and Bell JJ).

[55] McHugh (n 53).

[56] *Davis* (n 36) 94 (Mason CJ, Deane and Gaudron JJ).

[57] ibid 93 (Mason CJ, Deane and Gaudron JJ), 111 (Brennan J).

[58] ibid 94–95 (Mason CJ, Deane and Gaudron JJ), 114 (Brennan J).

[59] ibid 100 (Mason CJ, Deane and Gaudron JJ), 115–17 (Brennan J).

falling within the 'peculiar province of the Commonwealth in its capacity as the national and federal government'.[60] Their Honours held that the commemoration of the Bicentenary was 'pre-eminently the business and the concern of the Commonwealth as the national government'[61] and, as such, fell squarely within the scope of the nationhood power.[62] The plurality stressed that the existence of this power would be clearest in areas where there was no competition with the competence of the States. In that regard, Mason CJ and Deane and Gaudron JJ asserted that the executive action undertaken in this case did not involve any interference with the States. The interest of the States in the commemoration of the Bicentenary was 'of a more limited character'.[63]

Justice Brennan reached the same conclusion in his judgment in *Davis*. Justice Brennan approved the statement made by Jacobs J in the *AAP case* that the phrase 'maintenance of this Constitution' in s 61 imported 'the idea of Australia as a nation'. He relied on this statement to find that this phrase in s 61 assigned to the Commonwealth Executive functions relating to 'the protection and advancement of the Australian nation'.[64]

Justice Brennan accepted that s 61 authorised the Commonwealth Executive Government to 'engage in enterprises and activities peculiarly adapted to the government of a nation and which cannot otherwise be carried on for the benefit of the nation'. He thought that Mason J's 'peculiarly adapted' test was the 'appropriate formulation of a criterion to determine whether an enterprise or activity lies within the executive power of the Commonwealth'.[65] This was because 'it invit[ed] consideration of the need for national action (whether unilateral or in co-operation with the States) to secure the contemplated benefit'.[66] Justice Brennan held that the 'peculiarly adapted' test was satisfied in the circumstances of the case. He acknowledged that it was 'arguable' that the commemoration was a 'State affair', as European settlement had first occurred in New South Wales, but concluded that it had 'undoubted significance for the whole of Australia' and could 'properly be seen as a matter for commemoration by the Commonwealth'.[67]

Justices Wilson and Dawson also held that the Commonwealth had the capacity to recognise and celebrate its own origins and history but they did not accept that nationhood should form the basis of a 'new or independent source of power', preferring instead to source the power in ss 61 and 51(xxxix) of the Constitution.[68] Their Honours were, however, willing to use the character and status of the Commonwealth as a national government as an element to be considered in the

[60] ibid 93, citing *Barton* (n 38) 498 (Mason J); *AAP case* (n 1) 396–97 (Mason J).
[61] *Davis* (n 36).
[62] ibid 94.
[63] ibid.
[64] ibid 110.
[65] ibid 111.
[66] ibid.
[67] ibid 114.
[68] ibid 103.

construction of s 61 of the Constitution.[69] Justice Toohey largely agreed with the reasons of Wilson and Dawson JJ.[70] However, he was willing to accept the existence of an implied power of self-protection that was inherent in the establishment of the Commonwealth, although ultimately found that it was not enlivened in this case.[71]

The decision in *Davis* has been criticised for expanding the scope of the nationhood power. At the fore of those who have expressed disquiet about the majority judgment in *Davis* is Professor Anne Twomey, who has argued that the majority in *Davis* uncritically accepted that it was more appropriate for the Commonwealth to commemorate the Bicentenary, rather than the States, and especially the State of New South Wales, to which the event was most relevant.[72] Furthermore, the majority made no attempt to even pay 'lip-service' to the second limb of the 'peculiarly adapted' test.[73] In this regard, Twomey has observed that the actual event being celebrated was the settlement of the colony of New South Wales, rather than federation.[74] The Court did not provide any compelling reason as to why the Bicentenary could not have been celebrated by the Australian States, and New South Wales in particular, rather than the Commonwealth.

While there was recognition in *Davis* that the nationhood power could accommodate matters associated with the 'symbolic aspects of nationhood',[75] such as the regulation of the national flag and emblems, as well as national days and celebrations, it is also significant that the majority considered whether the commemoration of the Bicentenary involved competition with the executive and legislative competence of the State government. In their joint judgment, Mason CJ and Deane and Gaudron JJ cautioned that the nationhood power could not be exercised to 'circumvent limitations or restrictions which would otherwise attach to the federal executive power in so far as it extends to the commemoration of the Bicentenary'.[76] In these ways, the majority prevented any great expansion of the scope of the nationhood power.

## III. The Nationhood Power and Commonwealth Spending

In *Davis* the majority considered not only the national character of the commemoration, but also whether it involved competition with the executive and legislative

[69] ibid.

[70] ibid 119.

[71] ibid.

[72] A Twomey, 'Pushing the Boundaries of Executive Power: *Pape*, the Prerogative and Nationhood Powers' (2010) 34 *Melbourne University Law Review* 313, 328–29.

[73] ibid 329. See also *Pape* (n 26) 177–78 [511] (Heydon J).

[74] Twomey, 'Pushing the Boundaries' (n 72) 328; Twomey, 'The French Court' (n 26) 34.

[75] *Pape* (n 26) 182 [521] (Heydon J).

[76] ibid 94–95.

competence of the State governments. The adoption of Mason J's 'peculiarly adapted' test required the Court to have regard to federal considerations and provide a justification as to why the activity fell within that area of responsibility appropriate to the character and status of the Commonwealth as the national government. As is shown below, this approach to ascertaining the scope of Commonwealth executive power was adopted by the majority of the High Court in the significant decisions in *Pape*, *Williams v Commonwealth [No 1]* and *Williams v Commonwealth [No 2]*.

## A. *Pape v Federal Commissioner of Taxation*

In the decision in *Pape*[77] a majority of four justices of the High Court held that the Commonwealth Executive Government enjoyed, under s 61 of the Constitution, an implied executive nationhood power to respond to a national emergency, to which the global financial crisis had given rise.[78] Their Honours accepted that this power supported short-term fiscal measures that were employed by the Commonwealth to stimulate the national economy, and that s 51(xxxix) of the Constitution supported the enactment of the *Tax Bonus for Working Australians Act (No 2) 2009* (Cth) ('*Tax Bonus Act*') as being incidental to the execution of that power.

Under the *Tax Bonus Act*, individuals who met the eligibility criteria were entitled to the payment of one-off 'tax bonuses', which ranged from $250 to $900.[79] These measures comprised part of the Federal Government's financial stimulus package, which was aimed at mitigating the impact of the global financial crisis (GFC) on the national economy. In *Pape* all parties accepted statements made by international bodies, including the Group of 20 (G20), the International Monetary Fund (IMF) and the Organisation for Economic Co-operation and Development (OECD) that there had been 'rapid adverse changes in macroeconomic circumstances globally and in Australia in 2008 and 2009' that had triggered a global recession.[80] It was also accepted that the implementation of a domestic fiscal stimulus package was an appropriate national response to the GFC.[81]

The High Court held, by a 4:3 majority consisting of French CJ, and in a separate joint judgment, Gummow, Crennan and Bell JJ, that the *Tax Bonus Act* was validly enacted under the incidental legislative power in s 51(xxxix) in support of the execution of executive power in s 61. Justices Hayne and Kiefel considered that the *Tax Bonus Act* could be read down to ensure that the amount of the tax

[77] M Gordon, 'Communist Party Case: Core Themes and Legacy' (Speech delivered at the Centre for Comparative Constitutional Studies Constitutional Law Conference, Melbourne, 23 July 2021) 41.

[78] *Pape* (n 26) 23–24 [8]–[9], 63–64 [133]–[134] (French CJ), 91–92 [241]–[243] (Gummow, Crennan and Bell JJ).

[79] *Tax Bonus for Working Australians Act (No 2) 2009 (Cth)* s 5.

[80] *Pape* (n 26) 26–27 [19].

[81] ibid 27–29 [21]–[28].

bonus did not exceed the individual recipient's tax liability and, as such, could be supported under the taxation power in s 51(ii). Justice Heydon issued a strong dissent, finding that the *Tax Bonus Act* was invalid.

The High Court confirmed in *Pape* what had been foreshadowed in the *AAP case*, that ss 81 and 83 were not the source of the Commonwealth's power to spend public money. The appropriations provisions were held to be the constitutional mechanism by which the Parliament retained control over public funds.[82] While an appropriation was a necessary precondition for the disbursement of funds, it did not provide the source of power for the expenditure of those funds.

The Court's rejection of ss 81 and 83 as the constitutional basis for the spending power in *Pape* has shifted the field of debate away from appropriations to the question of whether the Commonwealth's spending programmes were authorised either by the executive power in s 61 of the Constitution or legislation enacted under a head of Commonwealth legislative power. In *Pape* the Court was required to consider whether the *Tax Bonus Act* could be supported by the incidental legislative power in s 51(xxxix), in connection with the executive power of the Commonwealth in s 61 of the Constitution.

A majority of four justices accepted that the nationhood power supported short-term measures taken to respond to a national financial and economic crisis.[83] Chief Justice French reasoned that the payment of the tax bonuses was an executive activity 'peculiarly within the capacity of the national government' because only the Commonwealth had the resources and the capacity to respond on the scale, and within the time frame, that was necessary to address the adverse effects of a global financial crisis on the Australian economy.[84]

Chief Justice French therefore accepted that the *Tax Bonus Act* was incidental to the execution of the nationhood power and supported by ss 51(xxxix) and 61 of the Constitution.[85] However, he cautioned that it did not equate to 'a general power to manage the national economy'[86] or to address matters of 'national concern' or 'national emergency'.[87] Chief Justice French appeared to ascribe particular significance to the short-term nature of the measures in *Pape*[88] because this meant that the nationhood power would not 'in any way' interfere with the constitutional

[82] C Saunders, 'Separation of Legislative and Executive Power' in C Saunders and A Stone (eds), *The Oxford Handbook of the Australian Constitution* (Oxford, Oxford University Press, 2018) 626. See also G Appleby and S McDonald, 'The Ramifications of *Pape v Federal Commissioner of Taxation* for the Spending Power and Legislative Powers of the Commonwealth' (2011) 37 *Monash University Law Review* 162, 167–68. See *Pape* (n 26) 23 [8], 36 [53]–[54], 63 [113] (French CJ), 73 [178], 75 [184], 80 [202], 81 [204] (Gummow, Crennan and Bell JJ), 113 [320] (Hayne and Kiefel JJ), 210–11 [600]–[602] (Heydon J).

[83] *Pape* (n 26) 23 [8], 63 [133] (French CJ), 87–88 [228], 91 [241] (Gummow, Crennan and Bell JJ).

[84] ibid 23 [8], 63 [133].

[85] ibid 23 [8].

[86] ibid 63 [133].

[87] ibid 24 [10], 63 [133] (French CJ). See also 124–25 [359] and 125 [363]–[364] (Hayne and Kiefel JJ) and 176–77 [509], 192–93 [550]–[552] (Heydon J).

[88] ibid 60 [127].

distribution of powers between the Commonwealth and the States.[89] The States did not have the capacity or the resources to implement, within a short time frame, measures that were 'rationally adjudged' as 'avoiding or mitigating' the adverse effects of the GFC in Australia.[90]

Justices Gummow, Crennan and Bell also thought that the measures in *Pape* were 'peculiarly adapted' to the national government because 'only the Commonwealth has the resources available to respond promptly to the present financial crisis on the scale exemplified by the *Bonus Act*'.[91] Their Honours likened the financial crisis to war or a natural disaster and concluded that the Executive Government was the branch 'capable of and empowered' to respond to the crisis. According to their Honours,

> in considering what enterprises and activities are peculiarly adapted to the government of the country and which cannot otherwise be carried on for its benefit, this case may be resolved without going beyond the notions of national emergency and the fiscal means of promptly responding to that situation.[92]

Justices Gummow, Crennan and Bell considered that Commonwealth executive power could be limited by 'some constraint having its source in the position of the Executive Governments of the States'.[93] They also acknowledged judicial statements made in *Davis* that the executive power is clearest where it involves no competition with areas of State executive competence.[94] There was recognition that when the Commonwealth is exercising the nationhood power in relation to matters that fall outside the areas of responsibility allocated to it by the Constitution, the Court will assess the capacity of the States to undertake the activities in question.[95] In that regard, it was significant that, as a result of the 'aggregation of fiscal power in the hands of the Commonwealth over the last century', *only* the Commonwealth had the capacity and resources to respond promptly and effectively to the financial crisis.[96]

In dissent, Hayne and Kiefel JJ were critical of the majority's reliance on the existence of an 'emergency' or 'crisis' to enliven the nationhood power. While they accepted that the Commonwealth Executive Government had power to engage in executive action appropriate to its character and status as a national government, to be ascertained by the application of Mason J's 'peculiarly adapted' test,[97] they did not accept that this power could support the implementation of any measures that the Commonwealth Government deemed necessary to respond to a national

[89] ibid 60 [127].
[90] ibid 63 [133].
[91] ibid 91 [241].
[92] ibid 91 [241].
[93] ibid 85 [220].
[94] ibid 90–91 [239].
[95] ibid, quoting *Davis* (n 36) 93–94.
[96] *Pape* (n 26) 91 [241].
[97] ibid 116 [328]–[329].

crisis or emergency. According to their Honours, the approach adopted by the majority conflated 'distinct questions about ends and means'.[98]

Justices Hayne and Kiefel thought that words like 'crisis' or 'emergency' were vague and imprecise, and 'do not readily yield criteria of constitutional validity'. They noted that this case did not require the Court to consider whether a national crisis or emergency existed, but pointed out that if there was a general executive power to respond to a national emergency, this might require the Court to examine the constitutional facts on which it was based, otherwise 'the Executive's powers in such matters would be self-defining'.[99] Their Honours thought that claims of an executive power to respond to a national emergency still required the Court to examine whether the measures chosen by the executive to deal with the crisis were appropriate and lawful exercises of executive power. In that regard, Hayne and Kiefel JJ observed that the direct payment of the tax bonuses was not the only means available to the Commonwealth to respond to the financial crisis. The Commonwealth could have stimulated the economy through other means, namely by enacting legislation under the taxation power in s 51(ii) or by increasing welfare payments under s 51(xxiiiA).[100] Alternatively, the Commonwealth could have made conditional grants to the States under s 96 of the Constitution.[101]

In similar vein, Heydon J emphasised in his dissent that the second limb of Mason J's 'peculiarly adapted' test had not been satisfied because there were other constitutional mechanisms that could have been utilised by the Commonwealth Government to implement a fiscal stimulus, either alone or in cooperation with the governments of the States. Justice Heydon was also sceptical of a nationhood power to respond to emergencies. He thought that if courts deferred to the opinion of the executive or the legislature, this would give 'an "unexaminable" power to the Executive'.[102] This was evident where he remarked that

> [e]ven if only a very narrow power to deal with an emergency on the scale of the global financial crisis were recognised, it would not take long before constitutional lawyers and politicians between them managed to convert that power into something capable of almost daily use. The great maxim of governments seeking to widen their constitutional powers would be: 'Never allow a crisis to go to waste'.[103]

Notwithstanding the criticism that has been levelled at it, the reasoning of the majority in *Pape* signalled renewed willingness on the part of the High Court to ascertain the scope and limits of the nationhood power by reference to the federal distribution of powers between the Commonwealth and the States effected by the Constitution. Indeed, these federal considerations would prove to be influential in the High Court's decision to invalidate a contract and associated expenditure made under the Commonwealth's National School Chaplaincy Program (NSCP) just a few years later in *Williams v Commonwealth [No 1]*.

[98] ibid 122 [349].
[99] ibid 123 [353].
[100] ibid 124 [356] (Hayne and Kiefel JJ).
[101] ibid 178–79 [513] (Heydon J); Twomey, 'Pushing the Boundaries' (n 72) 330.
[102] ibid 193 [552].
[103] ibid 193 [551] (Heydon J).

## B. *Williams v Commonwealth [No 1]*

Chapter 2 explained that *Williams v Commonwealth [No 1]* concerned a challenge to Commonwealth funding for the NSCP. The NSCP was supported by a parliamentary appropriation but was not authorised by legislation. Under the NSCP, the Commonwealth entered into a contract with Scripture Union Queensland for the provision of chaplaincy services at the Darling Heights state school in Queensland ('Funding Agreement'). While it did not fall directly for consideration, the Court held that the Funding Agreement and associated expenditure could not be supported by the nationhood power.

According to the majority, the NSCP was not an activity that was 'peculiarly adapted to the government of the nation and which cannot otherwise be carried on for the benefit of the nation' because it fell within an area 'dominated by State legislation, administration, and policy' and several States, including Queensland, already provided chaplaincy services in state schools.[104] Justices Gummow and Bell observed, in this regard, that the States had the 'legal and practical capacity to provide for a scheme such as the NSCP'.[105] Furthermore, their Honours were of the view that the conduct of the public school system in Queensland was the 'responsibility' of that State.[106] Similar observations were made by Hayne J, Crennan J and Kiefel J in their respective judgments.[107] They were of the view that the States were capable of providing the services covered by the NSCP, as underscored by Queensland's own funding scheme for school chaplaincy services. There was, therefore, 'direct competition' with an area of State competence and the capacity of the Executive Government of the States.

Furthermore, the case did not involve a national crisis or emergency, as in *Pape*, that could only be addressed by the Commonwealth.[108] In the absence of any such emergency, the Court concluded that the nationhood power was not enlivened. Indeed, since *Pape*, the nationhood power has been defined as a power to respond to national emergencies.[109] In *CPCF* Hayne and Bell JJ referred to the 'implied executive "nationhood power" to respond to national emergencies',[110] and Kiefel J

[104] Saunders, 'Separation of Legislative and Executive Power' (n 82) 638.
[105] *Williams [No 1]* (n 38) 235 [146].
[106] ibid.
[107] ibid 272–73 [257] (Hayne J), 347–48 [501]–[503] (Crennan J), 373 [591] (Kiefel J).
[108] ibid 235 [146] (Gummow and Bell JJ), 250–51 [196], 267 [240] (Hayne J), 346–47 [499] (Crennan J), 362 [599] (Kiefel J).
[109] See also Twomey, 'The French Court' (n 26); A Twomey, 'Post-*Williams* Expenditure – When Can the Commonwealth and States Spend Public Money Without Parliamentary Authorisation?' (2014) 33 *University of Queensland Law Journal* 9, 24. This raises questions that are beyond the scope of this book about the appropriate role for the Court in determining whether there is an emergency and justiciability more generally: see *Pape* (n 26) 123 [353] (Hayne and Kiefel JJ); A Hanna, 'Nationhood Power and Judicial Review: A Bridge Too Far' (2015) 39 *University of Western Australia Law Review* 327; T Poole, 'The Law of Emergency and Reason of State' in E Criddle (ed), *Human Rights in Emergencies* (New York, Cambridge University Press, 2016) 148.
[110] *CPCF v Minister for Immigration and Border Protection* (2015) 255 CLR 514, 568 [150] (Hayne and Bell JJ).

described the nationhood power as being 'capable of responding to events such as a national emergency'.[111]

As Crennan J explained in *Williams v Commonwealth [No 1]*, the nationhood power did not apply in this case because

> [t]here was nothing in the facts here amounting to a circumstance in which the nation needed protection, or invoking Commonwealth executive powers otherwise peculiarly referable to the government of Australia as a nation, such that the Commonwealth Executive was, for this or any other identifiable reason, the arm of government exclusively, best, or uniquely authorised to act in respect of the NSCP. There was nothing to explain or justify the absence of special legislation or any involvement of Parliament, beyond the appropriation Acts or the bypassing of s 96.[112]

Justice Crennan also took the opportunity in her judgment in *Williams v Commonwealth [No 1]* to clarify the scope and limits of the nationhood power, by drawing on observations made in earlier decisions. Justice Crennan explained that

> the fact that an initiative, enterprise or activity can be 'conveniently formulated and administered by the national government', or that it ostensibly does not interfere with State powers, is not sufficient to render it one of 'truly national endeavour' or 'pre-eminently the business and the concern of the Commonwealth as the national government'.[113]

Thus, in *Williams v Commonwealth [No 1]* the High Court demonstrated that it was not prepared to accept a wide interpretation of the nationhood power. The NSCP and associated expenditure could not be characterised as an enterprise or activity that was 'peculiarly adapted to the government of the nation'. In rejecting the application of the nationhood power in this case, the High Court has indicated that it is not prepared to find that the nationhood power is a general power to act in respect of matters that it deems as being of national interest or concern.

## C. *Williams v Commonwealth [No 2]*

In *Williams v Commonwealth [No 2]* the majority of the High Court, consisting of French CJ, Hayne, Kiefel, Bell and Keane JJ, reiterated the limits on the nationhood power. In that case, the Commonwealth had purported to argue that

> executive power to contract and spend under s 61 of the *Constitution* extends to *all* those matters that are *reasonably capable* of being *seen* as of national benefit or concern; that is, *all* those matters that befit the national government of the federation, *as discerned from the text and structure of the Constitution.*[114]

[111] ibid 596 [260] (Kiefel J).
[112] *Williams [No 1]* (n 38) 348 [503] (Crennan J).
[113] ibid 348 [504] (Crennan J) (citations omitted).
[114] *Williams v Commonwealth [No 2]* (2014) 252 CLR 416, 466 [70].

This argument was rejected, with the Court noting that 'the proposition is one of great width'.[115] The High Court acknowledged that the Commonwealth must 'possess all the powers that it needs in order to function as a polity',[116] however it also described the character and status of the Commonwealth Government as that of 'the central polity of a federation in which independent governments exist in the one area and exercise powers in different fields of action carefully defined by law'.[117] The federal distribution of powers and functions between the Commonwealth and the States was the 'basal consideration'[118] in determining the scope of the executive power of the Commonwealth.

In *Williams v Commonwealth [No 2]* the High Court recognised 'those aspects of executive power which might be referred to loosely as the Executive's power to deal with or respond to a national emergency (considered in *Pape*) or other matters of the kind commonly grouped under the heading "nationhood"'.[119] However, the High Court has also imposed limitations on the nationhood power so that it cannot be invoked by the Commonwealth to support initiatives, enterprises and activities in relation to matters that it deems to be of 'national benefit or concern' or in the 'national interest'. These limitations are examined in the next section of this chapter.

## IV. Limitations on the Nationhood Power

The decisions of the High Court that have recognised the existence of the nationhood power have been the subject of criticism in the academic literature. George Winterton criticised the approach that was adopted by Mason J in the *AAP case* on the basis that it required the Court to grapple with 'political questions unsuited to judicial determination'.[120] Winterton observed that

> [o]pinions may justifiably differ as to whether a particular activity must be conducted by the Commonwealth if the nation is to derive benefit, and opinions will also differ on the question whether activities are to Australia's benefit or detriment.[121]

Leslie Zines was also critical of what he perceived to be an expansion of federal executive power, noting that in these cases 'the predilections of the individual judges will be dominant'.[122] Twomey has criticised the existence of the nationhood

[115] ibid 466 [71].
[116] ibid 467–68 [78].
[117] ibid 469 [83].
[118] ibid 469 [83] (French CJ, Hayne, Kiefel, Bell and Keane JJ).
[119] ibid 454. See also *CPCF* (n 110) 568 [150] (Hayne and Bell JJ), 597–99 [266]–[271], 600 [277] (Kiefel J).
[120] G Winterton, 'The Limits and Use of Executive Power by Government' (2003) 31 *Federal Law Review* 421, 427.
[121] ibid 427.
[122] L Zines, *The High Court and the Constitution*, 5th edn (Annandale, Federation Press, 2008) 417.

power as being based on a conception of 'the types of powers that the national government *should* be able to exercise, regardless of the actual powers distributed to that government by the *Constitution*',[123] although in more recent works has recognised that the Court has taken 'a more limited and grounded view of it' in the *Pape* and *Williams* decisions.[124]

While some justices contemplated in early decisions that the nationhood power could be exercised in respect of matters associated with 'national advancement', the cases examined in this chapter demonstrate that Australian courts have imposed limitations on the scope of the nationhood power. The remainder of this chapter demonstrates that the High Court has assessed the limits of the nationhood power by reference to the federal system of government established by the Constitution. In doing so, the Court has limited any great expansion of the 'breadth' of the executive power. It is also shown that the High Court has recognised that there are limits on the types of executive action that the Commonwealth is empowered to undertake pursuant to the nationhood power. These limits to the 'depth' of the executive power relate to the capacity of the Commonwealth to undertake executive action that interferes with the legal rights and duties of individuals.

## A. Limits to the Breadth of the Nationhood Power

The federal character of the Commonwealth has been an influential factor for the High Court in determining the scope of the nationhood power. The extent to which the principle of federalism operates as a limit on the nationhood power is explored more fully in Chapter 6. For present purposes it suffices to make a few brief observations about the High Court's willingness to rely on 'federal considerations' to limit the scope of the nationhood power in each of the cases that have been considered in this chapter.

Justice Mason acknowledged such limits in his judgment in the *AAP case*. While Mason J contemplated that a potentially wide range of executive activities could enliven the nationhood power, he cautioned that its scope was not unlimited. Justice Mason explained that

> [i]t would be inconsistent with the broad division of responsibilities between the Commonwealth and the States achieved by the distribution of legislative powers to concede to this aspect of the executive power a wide operation effecting a radical transformation in what has hitherto been thought to be the Commonwealth's area of responsibility under the *Constitution*, thereby enabling the Commonwealth to carry out within Australia programmes standing outside the acknowledged heads of legislative

[123] Twomey, 'Pushing the Boundaries' (n 72) 335.

[124] A Twomey, 'Executive Power Following the *Williams* Cases' in J Griffiths and J Stellios (eds), *Current Issues in Australian Constitutional Law: Tributes to Professor Leslie Zines* (Alexandria, Federation Press, 2020) 41–43; Twomey, 'The French Court' (n 26) 33–40.

> power merely because these programmes can be conveniently formulated and administered by the national government.[125]

The other dissenting judges in the *AAP case* were also wary of a wide nationhood power and took steps to define and limit it. Chief Justice Barwick, for example, warned that the nationhood power would not be enlivened simply because a matter was of 'national interest or concern' or because it was more convenient for the matter to be dealt with on a national basis.[126] Chief Justice Barwick remarked, in this regard, that

> [t]hough some power of a special and limited kind may be attracted to the Commonwealth by the very setting up and existence of the Commonwealth as a polity, no power to deal with matters because they may conveniently and best be dealt with on a national basis is similarly derived. However desirable the exercise by the Commonwealth of power in affairs truly national in nature, the federal distribution of power for which the Constitution provides must be maintained.[127]

The 'national nature of the subject matter' was not enough to bring the Australian Assistance Plan within the scope of Commonwealth executive power.[128] Justice Gibbs similarly observed that 'the growth of the Commonwealth to nationhood did not have the effect of destroying the distribution of powers carefully effected by the Constitution'.[129] Each of the justices emphasised the position of the Commonwealth as the central government in a federal polity.[130] Thus, their Honours were not prepared to afford the nationhood power a wide interpretation that would undermine the federal distribution of powers for which the Constitution provides.

In *Davis* Mason CJ and Deane and Gaudron JJ acknowledged the federal limitations that applied to the nationhood power. They were of the view that the existence of the nationhood power would be 'clearest' where it 'involves no real competition with State executive or legislative competence'.[131] They recognised that the nationhood power was subject to limits derived from federalism. This was evident where their Honours considered whether the States could have effectively organised and commemorated the Australian Bicentenary. The plurality noted, in this regard, that while the States had a 'part to play, whether as part of an exercise in co-operative federalism or otherwise',[132] this could not be allowed 'to obscure the plain fact that the commemoration of the Bicentenary is pre-eminently the business and the concern of the Commonwealth as the national government'.[133]

[125] *AAP case* (n 1) 398 endorsed in *Davis* (n 36) 103 (Wilson and Dawson JJ); *Pape* (n 26) 50 [96] (French CJ), 117 [330], 124 [357] (Hayne and Kiefel JJ), 181 [519], 187 [533] (Heydon J); *Williams [No 1]* (n 38) 303–04 [363] (Heydon J), [504] 348 (Crennan J), 371 [584], 372 [587] (Kiefel J).
[126] *AAP case* (n 1) 362, 364. See also 378 (Gibbs J).
[127] ibid 362 (Barwick CJ).
[128] ibid 362.
[129] ibid 378 (Gibbs J).
[130] This point was also noted in *Pape* (n 26) 181 [519] (Heydon J).
[131] *Davis* (n 36) 93–94.
[132] ibid 94.
[133] ibid.

The interest of the States in the commemoration of the Bicentenary was 'of a more limited character'.[134]

Justice Brennan also observed that the second limb of the 'peculiarly adapted' test invited

> consideration of the sufficiency of the powers of the States to engage effectively in the enterprise or activity in question and of the need for national action (whether unilateral or in co-operation with the States) to secure the contemplated benefit.[135]

Justice Brennan similarly acknowledged that it was 'arguable' that the commemoration was a 'State affair', as European settlement had first occurred in New South Wales, but was of the opinion that it had 'undoubted significance for the whole of Australia'.[136]

The majority in *Pape* also relied on 'federal considerations' to limit the scope of the nationhood power. While French CJ accepted that 'short-term fiscal measures to meet adverse economic conditions affecting the nation as a whole' were, in the circumstances of a national financial crisis, 'peculiarly within the capacity of the Commonwealth', he cautioned that this conclusion did not mean that the Commonwealth enjoyed a broad executive power to 'manage the national economy'[137] or deal with matters arising under the 'general rubric such as "national concern" or "national emergency"'.[138] As French CJ explained, 'the exigencies of "national government" cannot be invoked to set aside the distribution of powers between Commonwealth and States'.[139] The Commonwealth's position was 'peculiar' because a short-term response was required and only the Commonwealth had the resources to address the emergency. The short-term nature of the measures in *Pape* was significant for French CJ because this meant that the exercise of executive power would not, 'in any way', interfere with the federal distribution of powers between the Commonwealth and the States. By imposing these limitations on the scope of the nationhood power, French CJ prevented a significant expansion of the 'breadth' of Commonwealth executive power that would undermine the federal system established by the Constitution.

Justices Gummow, Crennan and Bell also accepted that the emergency expenditure in *Pape* was 'peculiarly adapted' to the national government because 'only the Commonwealth has the resources available to respond promptly to the present financial crisis on the scale exemplified by the *Bonus Act*'.[140] In their application of the second limb of the 'peculiarly adapted' test, the majority considered it as being

[134] ibid.

[135] ibid 111.

[136] ibid 114.

[137] *Pape* (n 26) 63 [133].

[138] ibid 24 [10], 63 [133] (French CJ). See also 124–25 [359], 125 [363]–[364] (Hayne and Kiefel JJ) and 176–77 [509], 192–93 [550]–[552] (Heydon J).

[139] ibid 60 [127].

[140] ibid 91 [241].

significant that only the Commonwealth Government had the legal and *practical* capacity and resources to respond, as swiftly and urgently as was required, to avoid or mitigate the adverse effects of a global financial crisis on the national economy. However, Gummow, Crennan and Bell JJ also recognised that the breadth of the executive power could be limited by 'some constraint having its source in the position of the Executive Governments of the States'.[141] This is evident where they remarked that

> the polity which the Constitution established and maintains is an independent nation state with a federal system of government ... [W]hile s 51(xxxix) authorises the Parliament to legislate in aid of the executive power, that does not mean that it may do so in aid of any subject which the Executive Government regards as of national interest and concern.

Consistently with the majority judgments in *Pape*, the limits of the nationhood power are to be ascertained by reference to the federal system established by the Constitution. *Pape* demonstrates that the nationhood power will be enlivened in circumstances giving rise to a national emergency, where *only* the Commonwealth has the resources and capacity to adequately respond, and where the exercise of executive power will not interfere with the federal distribution of powers.

Federal considerations also featured prominently in the reasoning of the Court in *Williams v Commonwealth [No 1]* to limit the scope of the nationhood power.[142] The Court did not accept that the provision of a school chaplaincy programme in state schools was 'peculiarly adapted to the government of a nation' because it involved functions within the 'province of the States, in their provision of support for school services'[143] that were already being carried out by the Queensland Government. It therefore gave rise to 'real competition' between the Commonwealth and State Executives.[144] The judgments in *Williams v Commonwealth [No 1]* reflect 'concern with the federal structure and the position of the States'[145] and recognise that the limits of the executive power of the Commonwealth more generally are to be ascertained by reference to the federal structure of the Constitution.[146]

In *Williams v Commonwealth [No 2]* the majority joint judgment described the federal distribution of powers and functions between the Commonwealth and the

[141] ibid 85 [220].

[142] ibid 252 [199] (Hayne J). For a discussion of federal considerations and *Williams [No 1]* (n 38), see G Appleby and S McDonald, 'Looking at the Executive Power through the High Court's New Spectacles' (2013) 35 *Sydney Law Review* 253; D Hume, A Lynch and G Williams, 'Heresy in the High Court? Federalism as a Constraint on Commonwealth Power' (2013) 41 *Federal Law Review* 71; G Lindell, 'The Changed Landscape of the Executive Power of the Commonwealth after the *Williams* Case' (2013) 39 *Monash University Law Review* 348; S Chordia, A Lynch and G Williams, '*Williams v Commonwealth*: Commonwealth Executive Power and Australian Federalism' (2013) 37 *Melbourne University Law Review* 189.

[143] *Williams [No 1]* (n 38) 373 [594] (Kiefel J).

[144] ibid 372–73 [590]–[591] (Kiefel J).

[145] ibid 234–35 [144].

[146] ibid 218 [89] (Gummow and Bell JJ).

States as being a 'basal consideration'[147] in determining the ambit of the executive power of the Commonwealth. It was acknowledged that the Commonwealth must 'possess all the powers that it needs in order to function as a polity'.[148] The Court rejected the Commonwealth's argument that the nationhood power extends to 'all those matters that are reasonably capable of being seen as of national benefit or concern' or 'those matters that befit the national government of the federation'.[149] Such a wide interpretation of the nationhood power was not consistent with the character of the Commonwealth as the 'central polity of a federation in which independent governments exist in the one area and exercise powers in different fields of action carefully defined by law'.[150]

## B. Limits to the Depth of the Nationhood Power

In addition to these limits on the breadth of the nationhood power, derived from federalism, several members of the High Court recognised that there were limits on the types of executive action that the Commonwealth can undertake 'for the benefit of the nation' pursuant to the nationhood power. As is shown below, the Court has imposed limitations on the nationhood power that relate to the capacity of the Commonwealth to undertake executive action that interferes with the legal rights and duties of individuals. It is argued that the imposition of these limits on the nationhood power has prevented the expansion of the 'depth' of the executive power of the Commonwealth.

In his judgment in the *AAP case* Mason J described the nationhood power as a *capacity* to engage in enterprises and activities 'peculiarly adapted' to a national government and which could not otherwise be carried on for the national benefit.[151] As discussed in Chapter 2, in *Plaintiff M68/2015 v Minister for Immigration and Border Protection*[152] Gageler J observed that the 'essential difference' between an act done in the execution of prerogative power and an act done in execution of a capacity is that the former 'is an act which is capable of interfering with legal rights of others' whereas the latter

> involves nothing more than the utilisation of a bare capacity or permission, which can also be described as an ability to act or as a 'faculty'. Such effects as the act might have on legal rights or juridical relations result not from the act being uniquely that of the Executive Government but from the application to the act of the same substantive law as would be applicable in respect of the act had it been done by any other actor. In this respect, the Executive Government 'is affected by the condition of the general law'.[153]

[147] *Williams [No 2]* (n 114) 469 [83] (French CJ, Hayne, Kiefel, Bell and Keane JJ).
[148] ibid 467–68 [78].
[149] ibid 466 [70].
[150] ibid 469 [83]. See also *AAP case* (n 1) 396–97 (Mason J).
[151] *AAP case* (n 1) 397.
[152] *Plaintiff M68/2015 v Minister for Immigration and Border Protection* (2016) 257 CLR 42.
[153] ibid 98 [135].

As this chapter has demonstrated, and as other academic commentators have observed, the nationhood power has received judicial support to the extent that it is 'facultative' in nature; that is, as facilitating the implementation of certain initiatives, enterprises and activities that are 'peculiar' to the position of the Commonwealth as the national government, and which are of national benefit.[154] In the *AAP case* several judges remarked that the nationhood power extended to exploration of foreign lands or seas, and in areas of scientific knowledge or technology.[155] Justice Mason agreed and referred specifically to the establishment of the CSIRO.[156] Similar reasoning would support Commonwealth spending on national cultural and literature programmes and the establishment of national institutions to undertake these activities.[157] These activities do not require the exercise of coercive power.[158] They are not capable of producing legal effects and do not involve action aimed at preventing, prohibiting, controlling or regulating the actions taken by others.[159]

To the extent that these activities have involved coercive aspects, they have been contained in legislation enacted under the incidental power in s 51(xxxix) of the Constitution. The High Court has, however, demonstrated considerable reluctance in finding that s 51(xxxix) could support coercive laws as incidental to the exercise of the nationhood power. As French CJ observed in *Pape*:

> Future questions about the application of the executive power to the control or regulation of conduct or activities under coercive laws, absent authority supplied by a statute made under some head of power other than s 51(xxxix) alone, are likely to be answered conservatively.[160]

Section 51(xxxix) of the Constitution confers power on the Federal Parliament to legislate on 'matters incidental to the execution of any power vested by this Constitution … in the government of the Commonwealth.' Therefore, once executive action finds its support in the nationhood power, it can be given legislative expression by the operation of s 51(xxxix), which provides authority for legislation

[154] See also Twomey, 'Pushing the Boundaries' (n 72) 339–42; A Twomey, 'The Prerogative and the Courts in Australia' (2021) 3 *Journal of Commonwealth Law* 55, 65–67, 85; L Zines, 'The Inherent Executive Power of the Commonwealth' (2005) 16 *Public Law Review* 279, 280; C Moore, *Crown and Sword – Executive Power and the Use of Force by the Australian Defence Force* (Canberra, ANU Press, 2017) 72–73; P Stephenson, 'Nationhood and Section 61 of the Constitution' (2018) 43 *University of Western Australia Law Review* 149, 164.

[155] *AAP case* (n 1) 362 (Barwick CJ), 412–13 (Jacobs J).

[156] ibid 397 (Mason J).

[157] It is unclear, following *Williams [No 1]* (n 38), whether the nationhood power would continue to support expenditure for these purposes: Twomey, 'Post-*Williams*' (n 109) 24–25. Note Twomey's argument that the establishment of national institutions in the Australian Capital Territory would fall under the Commonwealth Parliament's power to legislate with respect to the Territories in s 122 of the Constitution. See further: Twomey, 'Pushing the Boundaries' (n 72) 335–38; Twomey, 'The French Court' (n 26) 53–54.

[158] Compare Zines, 'The Inherent Executive Power' (n 154) 281.

[159] ibid 280; Twomey, 'Pushing the Boundaries' (n 72) 339.

[160] *Pape* (n 26) 24 [10] (French CJ).

with respect to matters incidental to the exercise of the executive power in s 61.[161] The High Court has, however, confirmed that there are limits on the scope of the incidental power when it is used in support of the nationhood power.

While the nature of the executive action undertaken in *Davis* was non-coercive, the associated legislation had coercive aspects to it. Section 22(1) of the *Bicentennial Authority Act* made it an offence to use certain expressions and symbols relating to the Authority and the Bicentenary. In particular, s 22(6)(d)(i) prohibited the use of broad expressions such as 'Bicentenary', 'Bicentennial', '200 years', 'Australia', 'Sydney', 'Melbourne', 'Founding', 'First Settlement', 'Exposition', 'Expo', or 'World Fair' when used in conjunction with '1988', '1788' or '88'.[162] Section 23 made provision for the forfeiture of all articles and goods to the Commonwealth where an offence under s 22(1) had been committed. The Commonwealth submitted that the object of the provisions was to 'protect and enhance' the Authority and the commemoration of the Bicentenary.[163]

Chief Justice Mason and Deane and Gaudron JJ recognised that s 51(xxxix) of the Constitution empowers the Commonwealth Parliament to legislate in relation to matters that are incidental to particular exercises of executive power.[164] Their Honours also accepted that the incidental power in s 51(xxxix) was capable of supporting measures that were coercive in nature, if they were necessary for the protection of the Authority.[165] However, Mason CJ and Deane and Gaudron JJ held that the incidental power could not support s 22(6)(d)(i) of the *Bicentennial Authority Act* because it constituted an unreasonable interference with the liberties of individuals and, in particular, freedom of expression and political communication. They warned that the nationhood power could not be exercised to 'circumvent limitations or restrictions which would otherwise attach to the federal executive power in so far as it extends to the commemoration of the Bicentenary'.[166]

Chief Justice Mason and Deane and Gaudron JJ applied a proportionality test to limit the scope of the incidental power in s 51(xxxix) when used in support of the nationhood aspect of the executive power in s 61. Having identified that the Bicentenary was a valid exercise of the nationhood power, their Honours considered whether the offence provisions were 'reasonably appropriate and adapted' to the purpose of protecting the commemoration of the Bicentenary and the authority. They concluded that the measures in the *Bicentennial Authority Act* constituted 'an extraordinary intrusion into freedom of expression' and were regarded as being 'grossly disproportionate' to achieving the legitimate purpose of ensuring the

[161] *Plaintiff M68* (n 152) 93 [121]–[122] (Gageler J). See also C Saunders, 'The Sources and Scope of Commonwealth Power to Spend' (2009) 20 *Public Law Review* 251, 262; Twomey, 'The Prerogative and the Courts' (n 154) 66–67.

[162] *Australian Bicentennial Authority Act 1980 (Cth)* s 22(6)(d)(i).

[163] *Davis* (n 36) 92.

[164] ibid 98–99.

[165] ibid (Mason CJ, Deane and Gaudron JJ).

[166] ibid 94–95.

protection of the commemoration and the Authority.[167] The effect of the provision was to confer power on the Authority to proscribe the use of common expressions. Section 51(xxxix) could not support the wide-ranging prohibitions on the use of certain expressions relating to the Bicentenary and the authority and the creation of criminal offences because such a law went beyond what was necessary to protect the exercise of the nationhood aspect of executive power in this case.

In *Davis*, Brennan J held that s 51(xxxix) could not be used to support a law that created criminal offences, 'except in so far as is necessary to protect the efficacy of the execution by the Executive Government of its powers and capacities'.[168] This limitation on the scope of the incidental power in s 51(xxxix) reflects the inability of the Commonwealth Executive to create an offence, derived from the common law. Indeed, in his judgment, Brennan J recognised that '[a]t least since the *Case of Proclamations*, the exercise of prerogative power has not been capable of creating a new offence. Nor can the exercise by the Executive Government of a non-statutory capacity create an offence'.[169] In his judgment in *Davis*, Brennan J adapted this common law limitation on executive power to the Australian constitutional context by finding that legislation exceeded the limits of s 51(xxxix) because it purported to use the incidental power to create an offence to 'supplement what the Executive Government … proposes to do'.

Justice Brennan reasoned that provisions designed to 'suppress fraud, deceit or the misapplication of Commonwealth funds' were examples of matters incidental to the execution of the executive power and the commemoration of the Bicentenary that would be supported by the incidental power.[170] However, Brennan J also observed that 'where the Executive Government engages in [an] activity in order to advance the nation – *an essentially facultative function* – the execution of executive power is not the occasion for a wide impairment of individual freedom'.[171] While Brennan J was willing to concede that freedom of speech may sometimes be a 'casualty' of legislation enacted for the purpose of protecting the nation, he was not prepared to allow freedom of speech to be a casualty of an activity undertaken by the Executive Government for the purpose of advancing a nation 'which boasts of its freedom'.[172] The 'excessive and unjustified restriction of free expression'[173] through the prohibition and imposition of criminal penalties could not be characterised as being incidental to the execution of the nationhood power in this case.[174]

[167] ibid 99–100 (Mason CJ, Deane and Gaudron JJ).

[168] ibid 112–13 (Brennan J).

[169] ibid 112.

[170] ibid 116 (Brennan J). See also Twomey, 'Pushing the Boundaries' (n 72) 327. Compare *ICM Agriculture Pty Ltd v Commonwealth* (2009) 240 CLR 140, 166 [32] (French CJ, Gummow and Crennan JJ).

[171] *Davis* (n 36) 112–13 (Brennan J). See also Twomey, 'Pushing the Boundaries' (n 72) 327.

[172] *Davis* (n 36) 116 (Brennan J).

[173] J Kirk, 'Constitutional Guarantees, Characterisation and the Concept of Proportionality' (1997) 21 *Melbourne University Law Review* 25, 32.

[174] *Davis* (n 36) 116–17.

Justice Brennan held that s 51(xxxix) could not support a law that created new offences to 'supplement what the Executive Government has done or proposes to do'.[175] Justice Brennan went on to find that

> the legislative power with respect to matters incidental to the execution of the executive power does not extend to the creation of offences except in so far as is necessary to protect the efficacy of the execution by the Executive Government of its powers and capacities.[176]

The limitation on the use of the incidental power to create an offence imposed by Brennan J in *Davis* was subsequently endorsed by the majority of the High Court in *Hughes*.[177] In that case, Kirby J thought that it was 'highly doubtful' that the incidental power could support the 'serious and burdensome consequences of criminal proceedings' provided in a Commonwealth law as incidental to the execution of the nationhood power.[178]

The majority judgment in *Davis* cohered with the earlier decision of the Court in the *Commonwealth v Tasmania* ('*Tasmanian Dam case*').[179] The judges were unanimous that the legislative nationhood power could not support s 6(2)(e) of the *World Heritage Properties Conservation Act 1983* (Cth) ('*Conservation Act*'), which drastically curtailed the legislative and executive powers of the State of Tasmania to authorise or regulate conduct on its own land.[180] In the opinion of Gibbs CJ, the nationhood power could not authorise the Commonwealth Parliament 'to prevent a State from making or permitting such lawful use of its land as it chooses'.[181] Justice Wilson was not aware of any occasion 'when a coercive law declaring certain conduct to be unlawful and imposing penalties has been enacted by the Parliament otherwise than pursuant to a given head of power'.[182] In similar vein, Deane J declared that the Commonwealth could not rely on the nationhood power to

> arrogate to itself control of such property, achievement or endeavour or to oust or override the legislative and executive powers of the State in which such property is situate or such achievement to endeavour has been effected or is being pursued.[183]

In *Pape* there was recognition that the Federal Executive Government could not rely on its executive power to create new legal rights and liabilities that the tax

[175] ibid 112 (Brennan J). See also Twomey, 'Pushing the Boundaries' (n 72) 327.
[176] *Davis* (n 36) 113 (Brennan J). See also Saunders, 'Separation of Legislative and Executive Power' (n 82) 634.
[177] *Hughes* (n 38) 555 [39] (Gleeson CJ, Gaudron, McHugh, Gummow, Hayne and Callinan JJ), 583 [119] (Kirby J). See also *Tasmanian Dam case* (n 47) 109 (Gibbs CJ), 203–04 (Wilson J), 252–53 (Deane J).
[178] *Hughes* (n 38) 583 [119] (Kirby J).
[179] *Tasmanian Dam case* (n 47).
[180] ibid 109 (Gibbs CJ), 203–04 (Wilson J), 252–53 (Deane J).
[181] ibid 109.
[182] ibid 203.
[183] ibid 253.

bonus scheme required.[184] As such, the Commonwealth Parliament relied on s 51(xxxix) to enact the *Tax Bonus Act* to facilitate the exercise of the nationhood aspect of the executive power in s 61. The *Tax Bonus Act* created a statutory right for individual taxpayers to receive the tax bonus payments, and conferred a duty on the Federal Commissioner of Taxation to spend the money and distribute the payments.[185]

Justices Gummow, Crennan and Bell observed that it has long been established that the executive cannot create criminal offences, and that this common law limitation on Commonwealth executive power applies in Australia. In *Pape*, then, there is also evidence in the majority judgments of common law limitations on the prerogative being adapted to the Australian context. Justices Gummow, Crennan and Bell were not prepared to accept that s 51(xxxix) could be relied on to create offences to support the exercise of Commonwealth executive power, unless they were incidental to the execution of another substantive head of legislative power. Their Honours referred with approval to the observation made by the majority in *Hughes* that the incidental power does not authorise the enactment of legislation 'in aid of any subject which the Executive Government regards as of national interest and concern'.[186] However, their Honours concluded that the *Tax Bonus Act* 'is not a use of s 51(xxxix) of such a character'.[187] The *Tax Bonus Act* did not purport to regulate or control the conduct of individuals or create offences. Justices Gummow, Crennan and Bell therefore concluded that the creation of the entitlements in the *Tax Bonus Act* was valid under s 51(xxxix) because the law was 'incidental to the effectuation of the fiscal stimulus policy'.[188]

It has been suggested that a proportionality test may be one way of constraining the scope of the Commonwealth's power to enact coercive laws pursuant to the incidental power in s 51(xxxix) and the nationhood power. However, Twomey has pointed out that while the plurality in *Davis* considered whether the law was proportionate, or 'reasonably appropriate and adapted' to the purpose of facilitating the exercise of the nationhood power, the Court did not apply a proportionality test to assess whether the *Tax Bonus Act* was incidental to the exercise of the nationhood power in *Pape*. Twomey has argued, persuasively in this regard, that this omission could be attributed to the fact that the legislation was regulatory, rather than coercive, in nature.[189] While the *Tax Bonus Act* created rights for individual taxpayers to receive the payments and imposed a duty on the Commissioner to distribute the payments, the provisions did not proscribe certain conduct in the same way as

[184] *Pape* (n 26) 92 [243] (Gummow, Crennan and Bell JJ). See also Saunders, 'Separation of Legislative and Executive Power' (n 82) 634; HP Lee, MWR Adams, C Campbell and P Emerton, *Emergency Powers in Australia*, 2nd edn (Cambridge, Cambridge University Press, 2019) 76.

[185] Twomey, 'Pushing the Boundaries' (n 72) 341; Lee et al (n 184) 76.

[186] *Pape* (n 26) 87–88 [228], citing *Hughes* (n 38) 555 [39] (Gleeson CJ, Gaudron, McHugh, Gummow, Hayne and Callinan JJ).

[187] *Pape* (n 26) 92 [245].

[188] ibid [245] (Gummow, Crennan and Bell JJ). See also Saunders, 'Separation of Legislative and Executive Power' (n 82) 634.

[189] Twomey, 'Pushing the Boundaries' (n 72) 342.

the impugned provisions in the *Conservation Act* and *Bicentennial Authority Act* in the *Tasmanian Dam case* and *Davis*.[190] The legislation was accordingly upheld as a valid exercise of the nationhood power and the incidental legislative power in s 51(xxxix) of the Constitution.

Therefore, the decision in *Pape* did not resolve the question of whether a proportionality test will be applied by the High Court to ascertain whether a law is incidental to the exercise of federal executive power.[191] There is also considerable uncertainty about which proportionality test will apply. In its more recent constitutional jurisprudence, the majority of the High Court has applied a structured proportionality test of a European kind to ascertain the validity of a law burdening the implied freedom of political communication[192] and the freedom of interstate trade, commerce and intercourse in s 92 of the Constitution.[193] The suitability of the structured proportionality test in this context warrants further consideration, but it is beyond the scope of this book to engage in this analysis.[194]

The decisions in *Davis* and *Pape* demonstrate that the High Court has recognised that there are limits on the nationhood power that relate to the capacity of the Commonwealth to undertake executive action that interferes with the legal rights and duties of individuals. While French CJ foreshadowed the adoption of a 'conservative' approach in determining the extent to which s 51(xxxix) will support coercive laws as incidental to the exercise of the nationhood power, this question was not fully explored or settled in *Pape*. The decisions discussed in this chapter certainly suggest that 'the incidental power could not be used to convert a non-coercive executive power into a coercive one',[195] but this remains a live issue for future cases.[196]

## V. Conclusion

This chapter has traced the emergence and development of the nationhood power in the Australian constitutional jurisprudence. It demonstrated that Australian

[190] ibid 341.

[191] There are judicial statements that suggest that the proportionality test applies in relation to incidental law-making powers. See, eg, *Murphy v Electoral Commissioner* (2016) 261 CLR 28, 49–50 [32] (French CJ and Bell J); *McCloy v New South Wales* (2015) 257 CLR 178, 194–95 [2]–[3] (French CJ, Kiefel, Bell and Keane JJ); *Tajjour v New South Wales* (2014) 254 CLR 508, 546 [29], 549–50 [35] (French CJ).

[192] See, eg, *McCloy* (n 188); *Brown v Tasmania* (2017) 261 CLR 328; *Clubb v Edwards* (2019) 267 CLR 171; *Comcare v Banerji* (2019) 267 CLR 373.

[193] *Palmer v Western Australia* (2021) 95 ALJR 229 244–25 [62] (Kiefel CJ and Keane J), 273 [217] (Edelman J).

[194] See further Twomey, 'The French Court' (n 26) 11–12. S Smith, 'The Scope of a Nationhood Power to Respond to COVID-19: Unanswered Questions' (*AUSPUBLAW*, 13 May 2020).

[195] Twomey, 'Pushing the Boundaries' (n 72) 327; Stephenson, 'Nationhood and Section 61' (n 154) 164.

[196] See also Saunders, 'Separation of Legislative and Executive Power' (n 82) 634; Twomey, 'Pushing the Boundaries' (n 72) 340; Twomey, 'The Prerogative and the Courts' (n 154) 66–67.

courts have applied Mason J's formulation of the nationhood power as a test for ascertaining whether the executive action is appropriate to the 'character and status of the Commonwealth as the national government' and therefore within the 'breadth' of Commonwealth executive power.

This chapter has shown that the High Court has imposed limitations on the scope of the nationhood power derived from federalism. In doing so, the Court has limited the expansion of the 'breadth' of the executive power. There was also recognition that there are limits on the types of executive action that the Commonwealth is empowered to undertake 'for the benefit of the nation' pursuant to the nationhood power. These limits to the 'depth' of the executive power relate to the capacity of the Commonwealth to undertake executive action that interferes with the legal rights and duties of individuals.

While the High Court has placed limitations on the nationhood power, the Commonwealth Government continues to rely on it to support expenditure on a wide range of government programmes. There are a significant number of spending programmes listed in the *Financial Framework (Supplementary Powers) Regulations 1997* (Cth) as measures that are 'peculiarly adapted to the government of a nation and which cannot otherwise be carried on for the benefit of the nation'.[197]

While some of these programmes may be supported by the nationhood power on the basis of the reasoning in *Davis*[198] or *Pape*,[199] there are a number of other programmes and initiatives that are premised on an expansive reading of the nationhood power that was rejected by the High Court in the *Williams* decisions.[200] Nevertheless, these programmes will likely remain in effect unless and until they are challenged.

Twomey has expressed concern that the Commonwealth 'appears to be acting on the basis that no one is likely to scrutinise its activities'.[201] Indeed, despite the *Williams* decisions, the Commonwealth Executive Government continues to spend money on programmes where 'the only connection to the national level of government is often that it is "convenient" for it to be done nationally or the Commonwealth has the money to provide the funding'.[202] Furthermore, there

[197] See generally *Financial Framework (Supplementary Powers) Regulations 1997* (Cth) sch 1AB, Part 4. A similar observation has been made in Gordon (n 77) 42–43. See also the discussion in Twomey, 'Executive Power' (n 124) 44–51.

[198] See, eg, funding to support Australia Day Celebrations in the *Financial Framework (Supplementary Powers) Amendment (Prime Minister and Cabinet Measures No. 10) Regulations 2021* (Cth).

[199] See, eg, the Coronavirus economic response – pandemic leave and disaster payments in the *Financial Framework (Supplementary Powers) Amendment (Prime Minister and Cabinet Measures No. 1) 2022* (Cth).

[200] See, eg, *Financial Framework (Supplementary Powers) Regulations 1997* (Cth) Sch 1AB, Part 4, item [58] (Good Sports Programme), item [92] (Stronger Communities Programme), item [191] (Building Better Regions Fund), item [197] (Leadership in Agricultural Industries Fund), item [258] (Water and Snow Safety). For an in-depth discussion and analysis of some of these programmes see Twomey, 'Executive Power' (n 124) 44–51.

[201] Twomey, 'Executive Power' (n 124) 51.

[202] ibid 54.

are a number of programmes listed in the *Regulations* that are capable of being administered by State and Territory governments.[203]

The Commonwealth Government's response to the *Williams* decisions should not, however, detract from the decisions of the High Court considered in this chapter that have identified important limitations on the 'breadth' and 'depth' of the nationhood power. The next chapter considers whether these limitations on the nationhood power also apply to it when it is invoked to support executive action necessary for the protection of the nation. It examines the operation of the nationhood power in the context of internal security and civil emergencies, concentrating on the use of the ADF to respond to the 2019–20 bushfires and the COVID-19 pandemic.

[203] See especially *Financial Framework (Supplementary Powers) Regulations 1997* (Cth) Sch 1AB, Part 4, item [58] (Good Sports Programme), item [258] (Water and Snow Safety).

# 4

# The Nationhood Power and the Use of the Armed Forces During Emergencies

> I prefer the view adopted in the United States … 'it is within the necessary power of the federal government to protect its own existence and the unhindered play of its legitimate activities'.
>
> Sir Owen Dixon, 1951[1]

The Australian Constitution does not contain a framework of emergency powers.[2] In Australia's federal system, the primary responsibility for the maintenance of public order and emergency management lies with the State and Territory governments, which have enacted legislation for this purpose. The Commonwealth has, nevertheless, asserted a prominent role in responding to recent emergencies. A central feature of the Commonwealth Government's response to the devastating 2019–20 'Black Summer' bushfires and the COVID-19 pandemic was the deployment of members of the Australian Defence Force (ADF) to provide assistance to State and Territory authorities.

The Australian Constitution contemplates a limited role for the Commonwealth Government in internal security operations. Section 119 of the Constitution states that 'the Commonwealth shall protect every State against invasion, and on the application of the Executive Government of the State, against domestic violence'. However, the Australian Constitution does not make express provision for action taken by the Commonwealth on its own initiative, to ensure the well-being of the nation, or to protect itself and its interests. These recent crises have, therefore, raised questions about the use and limits of the executive power of the Commonwealth to respond to national emergencies.

This chapter examines the constitutional basis for the use of the ADF during civil emergencies. It proceeds as follows. It begins by setting out the constitutional framework that governs the relationship between the Commonwealth

[1] *Australian Communist Party v Commonwealth* (1951) 83 CLR 1, 188 (Dixon J) (*Communist Party case*). Reproduced with permission of Thomson Reuters (Professional) Australia Limited, legal.thomsonreuters.com.au.

[2] HP Lee, MWR Adams, C Campbell and P Emerton, *Emergency Powers in Australia*, 2nd edn (Cambridge, Cambridge University Press, 2019) 1, 7.

Executive Government and the ADF in Australia. It also considers the effect that Part IIIAAA of the *Defence Act 1903* (Cth) has had on the executive power to use the ADF within Australia. The chapter then examines two defence operations where members of the ADF were deployed to provide disaster relief and emergency assistance during the Black Summer bushfires and COVID-19 pandemic. The chapter concludes by considering the scope of the nationhood power to support the use of the ADF during civil emergencies.

As the utilisation of the ADF for purposes other than external defence raises a number of complex legal issues, it is important to set out what this chapter covers, and what it does not. The focus of this chapter is on the constitutional basis for non-statutory executive action taken to respond to civil emergencies within Australia, with a particular focus on the use of the ADF for these purposes. This chapter does not consider what legal protections and immunities are available to individual members of the ADF when they are called out for this purpose. As the focus of this chapter is on the scope of Commonwealth executive power, it does not examine powers to deal with specific emergencies that are set out in Commonwealth, State and Territory legislation.[3] Issues concerning the justiciability of prerogative powers,[4] the appropriate role of the ADF in civilian security operations,[5] martial law,[6] and the conferral and exercise of law enforcement powers by ADF officers under Commonwealth laws[7] also lie beyond the scope of this chapter.

## I. The Constitutional Framework

Section 51(vi) of the Australian Constitution confers power on the Commonwealth Parliament to make laws with respect to the naval and military defence of the

[3] ibid ch 6. For public health emergencies see P Stephenson, B Bennett and I Freckelton, 'Public Health Emergencies in Australia' in B Bennett and I Freckelton (eds), *Pandemics, Public Health Emergencies and Government Powers: Perspectives on Australian Law* (Annandale, Federation Press, 2021) ch 5.

[4] See A Twomey, 'The Prerogative and the Courts in Australia' (2021) 3 *Journal of Commonwealth Law* 55, 89–99; Lee et al (n 2) 232–60; A Sapienza, *Judicial Review of Non-Statutory Executive Action* (Alexandria, Federation Press, 2020) ch 4.

[5] Michael Head is highly critical of the use of the ADF for internal security in Australia in M Head, 'The Military Call-Out Legislation – Some Legal and Constitutional Questions' (2001) 29 *Federal Law Review* 273; M Head 'Calling out the Troops – Disturbing Trends and Unanswered Questions' (2005) 28 *University of New South Wales Law Journal* 479; M Head, *Calling Out the Troops: The Australian Military and Civil Unrest* (Annandale, Federation Press, 2009); M Head, 'Another Expansion of Military Call Out Powers in Australia: Some Critical Legal, Constitutional and Political Questions' (2019) 5 *University of New South Wales Law Journal Forum* 1.

[6] See C Moore, *Crown and Sword – Executive Power and the Use of Force by the Australian Defence Force* (Canberra, ANU Press, 2017) 129–64.

[7] See, eg, *Biosecurity Act 2015* (Cth) ss 544A, 563(1), which confer powers on ADF officers to make human biosecurity control orders. Provisions of the *Fisheries Act 1952* (Cth) which conferred law enforcement powers on ADF officers were held to be valid in *Li Chia Hsing v Rankin* (1978) 141 CLR 182. See further M White, 'The Executive and the Military' (2005) 28 *University of New South Wales Law Journal* 438, 445–46.

Commonwealth and of the several States, and the control of forces to execute and maintain the laws of the Commonwealth. The *Defence Act 1903* (Cth) was enacted under this provision and provides for the establishment and control of the ADF. The defence power is a purposive power and, as such, laws enacted under it must be reasonably appropriate and adapted to the purpose of the defence of the Commonwealth.[8]

The reference in s 51(vi) to 'the control of forces to execute and maintain the laws of the Commonwealth' has provided a source of power for the employment of members of the ADF to assist in the enforcement of Commonwealth laws within areas of Commonwealth competence, such as fisheries, customs, immigration and quarantine.[9] In the decision in *Re Tracey*, Mason CJ and Wilson and Dawson JJ observed that 'it is not the ordinary function of the armed services to "execute and maintain the laws of the Commonwealth"'.[10] There is, nevertheless, judicial acceptance that the Commonwealth may utilise the ADF to protect itself and its interests, including interests that are protected by Commonwealth legislation. Concerns have been raised about how this use of the ADF sits with the principle of military subordination to the civil authority. However, courts have not been willing to find that there is an implied constitutional prohibition on the use of the ADF for this purpose.[11]

The ADF is part of the Commonwealth Executive. Section 68 vests the command in chief of the armed forces of the Commonwealth in the Governor-General. The 'command' vested in the Governor-General is titular.[12] Sir Ninian Stephen has observed that 'no question of any reserve power lurks within the terms of s 68'.[13] In accordance with the principles of responsible government, the Governor-General must act on ministerial advice when exercising command of the ADF, thereby ensuring the subordination of the armed forces to the civil power.[14]

Several provisions of the Australian Constitution operate to confer exclusive authority on the Commonwealth to maintain a national defence force. Sections 69 and 70 required the departments of naval and military defence in each State, and

[8] *Stenhouse v Coleman* (1944) 69 CLR 457, 471 (Dixon J).

[9] *Li Chia* (n 7).

[10] *Re Tracey; ex parte Ryan* (1989) 166 CLR 518, 540.

[11] See PW Johnston, '*Re Tracey:* Some Implications for the Military-Civil Authority Relationship' (1990) 20(1) *University of Western Australia Law Review* 73, 78; White (n 7) 445–46.

[12] N Stephen, 'The Governor-General as Commander-in-Chief' (1984) 14 *Melbourne University Law Review* 563, 569, 571. See also Johnston (n 11) 80; D Letts and R McLaughlin, 'Call-Out Powers for the Australian Defence Force in an Age of Terrorism: Some Legal Implications' (2016) 85 *Australian Institute of Administrative Law Forum* 63, 67; White (n 7) 443.

[13] Stephen (n 12) 570. It has also been argued that s 68 is constitutional recognition of the important principle of the subjugation of the military to the civil authority. However, it remains unresolved whether that principle operates as an implied constitutional limitation on the power of the Commonwealth to use the ADF to execute Commonwealth laws or to aid civilian law enforcement. Stephen (n 12) 571; Johnston (n 11) 80. HP Lee, *Emergency Powers* (Sydney, Law Book Co, 1984) 218.

[14] Stephen (n 12) 570–71; G Winterton, *Parliament, the Executive and the Governor-General: A Constitutional Analysis* (Melbourne, Melbourne University Press, 1983) 16–17, 23, 127; White (n 7) 442–44.

their associated powers and functions, to be transferred to the Commonwealth at federation. Section 52(ii) confers exclusive power on the Commonwealth Parliament to make laws with respect to any department that was transferred to the Commonwealth. Furthermore, s 114 prohibits the States from raising or maintaining any naval or military forces without the consent of the Commonwealth Parliament.

In return for surrendering their armed forces to the Commonwealth at federation, the States were provided with a guarantee for their protection in s 119 of the Constitution. Section 119 is entitled 'Protection of States from invasion and violence' and appears in Chapter V of the Constitution dealing with 'The States'. Section 119 provides that 'The Commonwealth shall protect every State against invasion, and on the application of the Executive Government of the State, against domestic violence'.

Section 119 has two limbs. The first limb confers a duty on the Commonwealth to protect every State against invasion. The second limb confers an obligation on the Commonwealth to protect every State against domestic violence, when an application is made by the Executive Government of the State. In this context, the phrase 'domestic violence' means internal violence within a State. The term 'domestic violence' as it is used in s 119 has not been defined in legislation[15] or considered by the High Court. However, the words of s 119 derive largely from Article IV Section 4 of the US Constitution (the 'guaranty' clause) where 'domestic violence' is understood to refer broadly to uprisings or insurrections in any State against the government of a State.[16] In Australia, the term is wide enough to encompass insurrection or civil unrest. Importantly, however, the ADF cannot be used to 'stop or restrict any protest, dissent, assembly or industrial action' unless there is a 'reasonable likelihood' of death or serious injury to persons or serious damage to property.[17]

The States have requested Commonwealth assistance on few occasions[18] and have formally applied for assistance under s 119 only once, which was denied by the Commonwealth.[19] While s 119 uses mandatory language by the use of the word

[15] The government elected not to define 'domestic violence' in the 2018 amendments to Part IIIAAA. See Addendum to the Explanatory Memorandum to the Defence Amendment (Call Out of the Australian Defence Force) Bill 2018 (Cth), 3 para 205A. See also Head, 'Another Expansion' (n 5) 4.

[16] *Insurrection Act 1807* (US). See also Lee et al (n 2) 225; P Stephenson, 'Fertile Ground for Federalism? Internal Security, the States and Section 119 of the *Constitution*' (2015) 43 *Federal Law Review* 289, 293–95.

[17] *Defence Act 1903* (Cth) s 39(3).

[18] See, eg, requests for Commonwealth assistance from the Tasmanian Government in 1916 to protect against expected disturbances from the referendum on conscription; the Queensland Government in 1912 to respond to protests associated with the Brisbane general strike; the Western Australian Government in 1919 and 1921 to control the Fremantle Wharf strike and the WA Railway strike; the Victorian Government in 1923 to respond to riots resulting from the police strike; and from the South Australian Government in 1928 to respond to violence associated with the National Waterfront strike in Lee (n 13) 201–02.

[19] HP Lee discovered that the Queensland Government applied to the Commonwealth under s 119 to address protests associated with the Brisbane general strike of 1912 in Lee (n 13) 202.

'shall', the Commonwealth has discretion in deciding whether to provide military assistance when an application is made by a State.[20] The Commonwealth has denied an application for military assistance from a State government, especially in relation to strikes and industrial disputes, on the basis that the relevant States had adequate resources to respond to the disturbance.[21] The Commonwealth will generally only provide military aid in circumstances where the State police forces do not have the capacity to contain and control the domestic violence or prevent it from occurring.[22]

There is an important interaction between ss 61 and 119 of the Constitution. As discussed in Chapter 2, the express extension of executive power to the 'execution … of the Constitution' in s 61 encompasses powers that are necessary for the Commonwealth Executive Government to discharge the duties and obligations conferred on it by provisions of the Constitution.[23] In the *Wool Tops case*, Knox CJ and Gavan Duffy J considered that the phrase 'execution … of this Constitution' in s 61 meant 'the doing of something immediately prescribed or authorized by the Constitution without the intervention of Federal legislation'.[24] In that regard, s 119 confers a duty on the Commonwealth to 'protect every State against invasion and, on the application of the Executive Government of the State, against domestic violence'. Therefore, where the Governor-General makes an order calling out the armed forces pursuant to an application received from a State or Territory government, the Governor-General is exercising executive power to 'execute' the duty under s 119 of the Constitution.[25]

The Commonwealth Parliament has power to make laws with respect to 'matters incidental to the execution of any power vested by this Constitution … in the Government'. Therefore, Commonwealth legislation that made provision for the protection of the States against invasion or domestic violence would be incidental to the execution of the Commonwealth's duty under 119 of the Constitution.[26] Subject to other constitutional limitations, such a law would be supported by ss 61 and 51(xxxix) of the Constitution. As is shown below, the Commonwealth

[20] Lee et al (n 2) 223–24.

[21] See White (n 7) 444; Lee et al (n 2) 225–26.

[22] White (n 7) 444; Lee et al (n 2) 225–26.

[23] For example, s 119 of the Constitution confers a duty on the Commonwealth to protect the States against invasion and, on application, against domestic violence: G Winterton, 'The Relationship between Commonwealth Legislative and Executive Power' (2004) 25 *Adelaide Law Review* 21, 25; P Gerangelos, 'Parliament, the Executive, the Governor-General and the Republic: The George Winterton Thesis' in HP Lee and P Gerangelos (eds), *Constitutional Advancement in a Frozen Continent: Essays in Honour of George Winterton* (Annandale, Federation Press, 2009) 189, 193–91; Stephenson, 'Fertile Ground' (n 16); A Twomey, 'The French Court, the Nature of the Executive Power and its Reconciliation with the Expenditure Power' in H Jackson (ed), *Essays in Honour of Chief Justice French* (Alexandria, Federation Press, 2019) 44–45.

[24] *Commonwealth v Colonial Combing, Spinning and Weaving Co Ltd* (1922) 31 CLR 421, 432 (Knox CJ and Gavan Duffy J) (*Wool Tops Case*) affirmed in *Communist Party case* (n 1) 230 (Williams J).

[25] See Australian Constitution, ss 61 and 68. See also Winterton, 'The Relationship' (n 23) 25–26; Twomey, 'The French Court' (n 23) 45.

[26] See *Defence Act 1903* (Cth), Part IIIAAA. See also Twomey, 'The Prerogative and the Courts' (n 4) 68; Twomey, 'The French Court' (n 23) 45.

Parliament has enacted Part IIIAAA of the *Defence Act*, which governs the procedure for calling out the ADF to protect the States and Territories against domestic violence.

## A. Protection of Commonwealth Interests

Courts have recognised that domestic violence occurring within a State may pose a threat to the security of the Commonwealth or its interests. It is accepted that, in these circumstances, the Commonwealth does not need to wait for a request from a State government in order to intervene. This was evident in *R v Sharkey*[27] where Dixon J quoted with approval the following passage from Quick and Garran's *The Annotated Constitution of the Australian Commonwealth:*

> The maintenance of order in a State is primarily the concern of the State, for which the police powers of the State are ordinarily adequate. But even if the State is unable to cope with domestic violence, the Federal Government has no right to intervene, for the protection of the State or its citizens, unless called upon by the State Executive. If, however, domestic violence within a State is of such a character as to interfere with the operations of the Federal Government, or with the rights and privileges of federal citizenship, the Federal Government may clearly, without a summons from the State, interfere to restore order. Thus if a riot in a State interfered with the carriage of the federal mails, or with inter-state commerce, or with the right of an elector to record his vote at federal elections, the Federal Government could use all the force at its disposal, not to protect the State, but to protect itself. Were it otherwise, the Federal Government would be dependent on the Governments of the States for the effective exercise of its powers.[28]

In this passage Dixon J recognised that the Constitution does not confer on the Commonwealth a general power to maintain the peace and public order.[29] Justice Dixon confirmed that the States have presumptive responsibility for these subject matters. However, the Commonwealth can act where there is a connection with 'the subjects of Federal power, with the administration of the Federal Government or with the security of any of its institutions'.[30] Where the Commonwealth takes action to protect itself and its interests, it is exercising executive power under s 61 and is not required to wait for a request for assistance from a State, as required by s 119 of the Constitution.[31]

[27] *R v Sharkey* (1949) 79 CLR 121.

[28] J Quick and RR Garran, *The Annotated Constitution of the Australian Commonwealth* (Sydney, Angus & Robertson, 1901) 964–65 endorsed in *Sharkey* (n 27) 151 (Dixon J); *Thomas v Mowbray* (2007) 233 CLR 307, 394 [248] (Kirby J).

[29] *Sharkey* (n 27) 152 (Dixon J), quoting with approval *Attorney General v Colonial Sugar Refining Co Ltd* (1913) 17 CLR 644, 654 (Lord Haldane).

[30] *Sharkey* (n 27) 150, 153.

[31] White (n 7) 441.

An example of when the Commonwealth exercised its executive power to protect Commonwealth interests occurred in 1978, in the wake of the bombing of the Hilton Hotel in Sydney. In the very early hours of the morning of 13 February 1978 a bomb exploded in a garbage bin outside the Hilton Hotel in Sydney where 12 Heads of Government from the Asia Pacific region were attending the Commonwealth Heads of Government Regional Meeting (CHOGRM).[32] Three people died as a consequence of the explosion and six others were injured.[33] The CHOGRM meeting primarily took place in Sydney, however it also included a visit to the regional town of Bowral from 14 to 16 February 1978 and there was concern about the adequacy of the security measures for the remainder of the conference.

An emergency Cabinet meeting was held later that afternoon, where it was agreed that the ADF should be formally called out to provide aid to the civilian authorities in securing the route to Bowral. Acting on the advice of the Federal Executive Council, the Governor-General signed an order authorising the deployment of the ADF for the purposes of 'safeguarding the national and international interests of the Commonwealth of Australia; giving effect to the obligations of the Commonwealth of Australia in relation to the protection of internationally protected persons; and for other purposes related to those matters' ('Order').[34] The Order continued 'in force until revoked'.[35] Pursuant to the Order, on the morning of 14 February 1978, heavily armed troops were deployed in and around the towns of Bowral and Mittagong. A total of 1,085 army personnel were deployed in the field and a further 58 air force personnel provided helicopter support to secure the 100-kilometre route to Bowral and the guest house.[36] The Governor-General revoked the Order on 20 February 1978.[37]

The Bowral call out was unprecedented and controversial. It was the first time that the ADF had been called out within Australia during peacetime to provide aid to the civilian authorities. There was also considerable uncertainty surrounding the legal and constitutional basis for the call out. It was not action taken under s 119 of the Constitution because the Commonwealth had not received a request for assistance from the Premier of New South Wales. The call out was not authorised by s 51 of the *Defence Act 1903–1975* (Cth), because the object of the call out was to protect 'Commonwealth interests' rather than the State of New South Wales.[38]

[32] The meeting was attended by Heads of Government from Bangladesh, Fiji, India, Malaysia, Nauru, New Zealand, Papua New Guinea, Singapore, Sri Lanka, Western Samoa and Tonga, and by the Commonwealth Secretary General. See RM Hope, *Protective Security Review (unclassified version)* (Parliamentary Paper No 397, 1979) 257.

[33] ibid 258.

[34] ibid.

[35] ibid.

[36] ibid 261.

[37] ibid 324, Appendix 15, Annex 4: reprint of Revocation of Order by the Governor-General of the Commonwealth of Australia, 20 February 1978.

[38] *Defence Act 1903–1975* (Cth) s 51: 'Where the Governor of a State has proclaimed that domestic violence exists therein, the Governor-General, upon the application of the Executive Government of

Nor was it authorised by the provisions of the *Crimes (Internationally Protected Persons) Act 1976* (Cth)[39] or the *Public Order (Protection of Persons and Property) Act 1971* (Cth), which made it an offence to 'assault, harass, behave offensively towards, or unreasonably obstruct' internationally protected persons, including visiting Ministers.[40]

A comprehensive review of Australia's domestic security arrangements was subsequently undertaken by Justice Robert Hope of the New South Wales Court of Appeal to examine the legal issues raised by the Bowral call out.[41] Sir Victor Windeyer, a former justice of the High Court of Australia, was also engaged to provide an extra-curial legal opinion on the powers and obligations of members of the ADF when called out in aid of the civil authority.

Justice Hope concluded the deployment of armed members of the ADF in aid of civilian security was a valid exercise of the Commonwealth's inherent executive power to protect itself and its interests.[42] This conclusion was supported by Sir Victor Windeyer's legal opinion and a joint opinion provided by the Commonwealth Attorney-General and Solicitor-General.[43] Justice Hope explained that

> [t]he execution and maintenance of the Constitution, to which s. 61 of the Constitution extends the executive power, must include action to ensure that the exercise of its powers by the Commonwealth is not interfered with, even though that interference might not involve an offence under Commonwealth law; and the Governor-General, with the necessary advice, would be entitled to take what steps are necessary to ensure that there is no such interference, or if there has been such an interference, that it is removed or stopped.[44]

In his consideration of what would amount to an interference with 'Commonwealth interests', Hope J noted that 'generally' this would include breaches of the laws of the Commonwealth.[45] However, Hope J was of the view that Commonwealth

the State, may, by proclamation, declare that domestic violence exists in that State, and may call out the Permanent Forces (other than Reserve Forces) and in the event of their numbers being insufficient may also call out such of the Reserve Forces and the Citizen Forces as may be necessary for the protection of that State, and the services of the Forces so called out may be utilized accordingly for the protection of that State against domestic violence'.

[39] This statute implemented obligations under the UN Convention on the Prevention and Punishment of Crimes against Internationally Protected Persons, including Diplomatic Agents: *Convention on the Prevention and Punishment of Crimes against Internationally Protected Persons, including Diplomatic Agents*, opened for signature 14 December 1973, Australian Treaty Series 1977 No 18 (entered into force 20 February 1977).

[40] See Hope (n 32) 129 [9.10], 130 [9.12].

[41] ibid. Notwithstanding its vintage, this review remains, according to a former justice of the Supreme Court of Queensland, 'a comprehensive analysis of the use of the Defence Force for internal civilian security' in White (n 7) 438.

[42] Hope (n 32) 152 [10.33]. Hope also noted that the use of the ADF was authorised under the Constitution to execute and maintain the laws of the Commonwealth and to protect the States.

[43] ibid 273–76.

[44] ibid 152 [10.33].

[45] For example, an interference with Commonwealth voting rights would be an offence under the *Crimes Act 1914* (Cth).

interests included any interference with Commonwealth institutions, functions and property, including interests that may not be protected by Commonwealth statutes.[46] The connection with Commonwealth interests was significant because the Commonwealth was not required to wait for a request for assistance from the States where it was acting to protect itself or its interests. The ADF was called out to ensure the safety of Heads of State travelling between Sydney and Bowral. There was, therefore, a sufficient connection to an area of Commonwealth responsibility, namely the areas of external affairs and defence, to enliven the exercise of Commonwealth executive power.

The executive power to call out the ADF to protect Commonwealth interests and the States and Territories against domestic violence has since been placed on a statutory footing by Part IIIAAA of the *Defence Act*. The next section of this chapter considers the source of the Commonwealth's power to make laws to protect itself from internal threats.

## B. Source of Legislative Power to Protect the Commonwealth against Internal Threats

Since its earliest decisions, the High Court had held that the Commonwealth had power to protect itself and the Constitution.[47] In the 1915 decision in *R v Kidman*[48] both Griffith CJ and Isaacs J found that the Commonwealth possessed a 'right of protection'.[49] In his judgment, Isaacs J accepted that '[t]he Commonwealth carries with it – except where expressly prohibited – all necessary powers to protect itself and punish those who endeavour to obstruct it'.[50] In reaching this conclusion, Isaacs J referred with approval to the judgment of Lord Selborne in the Privy Council decision in *Barton v Taylor*, which concerned the power of the colonial legislatures to punish for contempt. Lord Selborne found that the New South Wales Legislative Assembly had powers that were 'impliedly granted' when it was established and which were 'necessary to the existence of such a body and the proper exercise of the functions which it is intended to execute'.[51] Lord Selborne added that 'for these purposes, protective and self-defensive powers only, and not punitive, are necessary'.[52]

[46] Hope J gave the example of a refuelling station: Hope (n 32) 152. The *Defence Act* includes protection of Commonwealth infrastructure: *Defence Act 1903* (Cth), Part IIIAAA, div 5.

[47] *R v Kidman* (1915) 20 CLR 425, 436 (Griffith CJ), 440–41, 444–45 (Isaacs J); *Ex parte Walsh and Johnson; In re Yates* (1925) 37 CLR 36, 94–95 (Isaacs J); *R v Hush; Ex parte Devanny* (1932) 48 CLR 487, 506 (Rich J) compare 510 (Starke J).

[48] *Kidman* (n 47) 436 (Griffith CJ), 440–41 (Isaacs J).

[49] ibid 436 (Griffith CJ), 440–41 (Isaacs J).

[50] ibid 444–45 (Isaacs J).

[51] *Barton v Taylor* [1886] 11 AC 197, 203 (Lord Selborne) endorsed in *Willis v Perry* (1912) 13 CLR 592, 597 (Griffith CJ). See also *Kidman* (n 47) 440 (Isaacs J).

[52] *Barton* (n 51) 203 (Lord Selborne).

In the post-war decisions of *Burns v Ransley*,[53] *Sharkey*[54] (together, the 'sedition cases') and the *Communist Party case*,[55] the High Court confirmed that the Commonwealth Parliament had power to enact laws to protect itself against sedition and subversion.[56] However, the judgments in the sedition cases and *Communist Party case* revealed two possible views as to the source of this power. The prevailing view adopted by the majority was that the power arose under the executive power in s 61, which extends to 'the execution and maintenance of this Constitution' and was given legislative effect by the incidental power in s 51(xxxix) of the Constitution.[57]

Justice Dixon adopted a different view as to the source of the power. While he accepted that the executive power conferred by s 61 in combination with s 51(xxxix) could support laws aimed at suppressing seditious or subversive activities, he thought that this textual combination had 'an artificial aspect'.[58] Justice Dixon preferred the view that he had expressed in *Burns* and *Sharkey* that the source of the power to legislate against sedition and subversion was based 'in principle that is deeper or wider than a series of combinations of the words of s 51(xxxix) with those of other constitutional powers'.[59] Justice Dixon thought that the power was inherent in the establishment and character of the Commonwealth as a polity.[60]

In the *Communist Party case* Dixon J referred approvingly to the following extract from Henry Campbell Black's *Handbook of American Constitutional Law*:[61]

> [I]t is within the necessary power of the federal government to protect its own existence and the unhindered play of its legitimate activities. And to this end, it may provide for the punishment of treason, the suppression of insurrection or rebellion, and for the putting down of all individual or concerted attempts to obstruct or interfere with the discharge of the proper business of government.[62]

Justice Dixon went on to explain that

> [i]n the United States the power is deduced not only from what is inherent in the establishment of a polity but from the character of the polity set up and more particularly from the power of Congress to make laws which shall be necessary and proper for

[53] *Burns v Ransley* (1949) 79 CLR 101.

[54] *Sharkey* (n 27).

[55] *Communist Party case* (n 1) 151 (Latham CJ), 188 (Dixon J), 211–12 (McTiernan J), 231 (Williams J), 233 (Webb J), 260 (Fullagar J), 277 (Kitto J).

[56] *Burns* (n 53) 110 (Latham CJ), 111 (Rich J), 116 (Dixon J), 120 (McTiernan J); *Sharkey* (n 27) 135 (Latham CJ), 145 (Rich J), 148–49 (Dixon J), 157 (McTiernan J), 159 (Williams J), 163 (Webb J).

[57] *Communist Party case* (n 1) 211–12 (McTiernan J), 230–31, 232 (Williams J), 260 (Fullagar J), 277 (Kitto J). See also *Burns* (n 53) 109–10 (Latham CJ); *Sharkey* (n 27) 135–36 (Latham CJ), 157–58 (McTiernan J).

[58] *Communist Party case* (n 1) 187.

[59] ibid 188.

[60] ibid.

[61] HC Black, *Handbook of American Constitutional Law*, 3rd edn (Saint Paul, West Publishing Co, 1910) 392.

[62] *Communist Party case* (n 1) 188.

> carrying into execution the powers vested in Congress by the Constitution and in the Government or in any Department or officer thereof ... the conditions giving rise to the implied power exist in the Commonwealth Constitution.[63]

Justice Dixon's view about the source of the Commonwealth's power of self-protection received limited support from Fullagar J in the *Communist Party case.* Justice Fullagar accepted that the decisions in *Burns* and *Sharkey* had confirmed that the Commonwealth Parliament had power to legislate for the prevention and punishment of sedition and subversion. In commenting on the source of the power, Fullagar J made the following observation:

> The source of part of the power which I have been discussing may be found in s. 51(xxxix), read with s. 61 of the Constitution ... But I think that, if it ever becomes necessary to examine it closely, it may well be found to depend really on an essential and inescapable implication which must be involved in the legal constitution of any polity.[64]

Since the decision in *Thomas v Mowbray* in 2007, it has been suggested that laws protecting the Commonwealth from sedition, subversion or domestic attack would now fall within the expanded scope of the defence power in s 51(vi), without the need to rely on the operation of ss 61 and 51(xxxix) or Dixon J's implied legislative nationhood power.[65] The majority accepted in *Thomas* that the defence power in s 51(vi) was not limited to the defence of Australia against external threats, but extended to internal threats to the Commonwealth Government, including from terrorism.[66] Such laws would also find support in the incidental power in s 51(xxxix), executing the executive power to 'maintain' this Constitution. In *Pape* Heydon J observed in this regard that such laws could 'be seen as an aspect of the "execution and maintenance of [the] Constitution" within the meaning of those words in s 61'.[67]

## II. The Statutory Framework: Part IIIAAA of the *Defence Act 1903* (Cth)

In reliance on these provisions of the Constitution, the Commonwealth Parliament has enacted Part IIIAAA of the *Defence Act*, which governs the use of the ADF in

[63] ibid.
[64] ibid 260, 266.
[65] *Thomas* (n 28) 363 [145] (Gummow and Crennan JJ), 448 [407] (Hayne J). See also *Pape v Federal Commissioner of Taxation* (2009) 238 CLR 1, 171–72 [498] (Heydon J).
[66] *Thomas* (n 28) 324–25 [7] (Gleeson CJ), 363 [145] (Gummow and Crennan JJ), 448 [407] (Hayne J). See also 395 [250]–[251] (Kirby J). For a critical discussion of the significance of *Thomas* (n 28) see, eg, HP Lee, 'Constitutional Fidelity in Troubled Times' in HP Lee and P Gerangelos (eds), *Constitutional Advancement in a Frozen Continent: Essays in Honour of George Winterton* (Annandale, Federation Press, 2009); H Pintos-Lopez and G Williams, '"Enemies Foreign and Domestic": *Thomas v Mowbray* and the New Scope of the Defence Power' (2008) 27 *University of Tasmania Law Review* 83.
[67] *Pape* (n 65) 171–72 [498].

aid of the civilian authorities to protect Commonwealth interests and the States and Territories against domestic violence. Part IIIAAA confers power on the Governor-General to call out the ADF under a 'Commonwealth interests order' or a 'State protection order'. It also confers coercive powers on the ADF that may be exercised under a call out order. However, Part IIIAAA also places conditions and limits on the exercise of those powers. Part IIIAAA appears to have constitutional support to the extent that its provisions do not contravene s 119 of the Constitution or other implied constitutional limitations.[68]

The next section of this chapter examines Part IIIAAA of the *Defence Act*. It briefly examines the legislative history of Part IIIAAA of the *Defence Act* before setting out its operative provisions. It is demonstrated that the provisions of Part IIIAAA regulate the use of the ADF for domestic violence and internal security operations. However, it is shown that Part IIIAAA does not apply to the use of the ADF by the Commonwealth Executive Government to provide assistance to the civil community in non-violent emergencies, such as natural disasters or a pandemic.[69] As is shown below, the Commonwealth Executive Government has relied on its non-statutory executive power to support the deployment of the ADF to respond to the Black Summer bushfires and COVID-19 pandemic.

## A. Legislative History of Part IIIAAA of the *Defence Act*

The *Defence Act* was amended in 2000, just prior to the Sydney Olympic Games.[70] A new Part IIIAAA was inserted that set out the procedures to be followed when the ADF was called out to protect Commonwealth interests, or to protect the States and Territories against domestic violence. Under this Part, the Governor-General could, by written order and on the advice of an authorising Minister,[71] call out the ADF to protect Commonwealth interests,[72] the States[73] and the Territories[74] against domestic violence. The threshold for making a call out order was that 'a state or territory is not, or is unlikely to be, able to protect the Commonwealth or itself against the domestic violence'.[75] The amendments included some safeguards in respect of the use of the ADF. The ADF could not be utilised in connection with

[68] *Thomas* (n 28) 394–95 [247]–[249] (Kirby J). It is beyond the scope of this chapter to consider this in detail. See, eg, A Gray, 'The Australian Government's Use of the Military in an Emergency and the Constitution' (2021) 44(1) *University of New South Wales Law Journal* 355, 370–72. Note Michael Head's concerns in Head, 'Another Expansion' (n 5).

[69] Twomey, 'The Prerogative and the Courts' (n 4) 71.

[70] See *Defence Legislation Amendment (Aid to Civilian Authorities) Act 2000* (Cth) (No 119, 2000).

[71] ibid s 51(1), defining 'Authorising Minister' as the Prime Minister, Defence Minister or Attorney-General.

[72] ibid s 51A.

[73] ibid s 51B.

[74] ibid s 51C.

[75] ibid ss 51A(1)(b), 51B(1)(a), 51C(1)(c).

protests or industrial action, except where there was 'a reasonable likelihood of the death of, or serious injury to, persons or serious damage to property'.[76]

Part IIIAAA was subsequently amended in 2006 for the Commonwealth Games in Melbourne.[77] The 2006 amendments expanded the scope of Part IIIAAA by making provision for, among other things, the deployment of the ADF to protect Commonwealth interests in the 'offshore area',[78] and to protect against aircraft threats[79] and threats to 'designated critical infrastructure' within a State.[80] In addition, the amendments conferred special powers and protections on members of the ADF called out under Part IIIAAA.

The 2006 amendments established an 'expedited call out' process, where the ADF could be called out in 'sudden and extraordinary emergency' situations.[81] A 'contingent call out' mechanism was also introduced in Part IIIAAA under the 2006 amendments, whereby the ADF was pre-authorised to respond to domestic violence that threatened Commonwealth interests, in the event that specified circumstances or 'trigger events'[82] occurred. The contingent call out mechanism could only be used to protect Commonwealth interests against aviation threats, where an aircraft was used as a weapon, like that of 11 September 2001. In these circumstances, the nature of the anticipated threat or incident of domestic violence would require an immediate ADF response, without waiting for ministerial authorisation.[83]

Substantial amendments were made to Part IIIAAA of the *Defence Act* in the wake of the 2014 Lindt Café siege in Sydney.[84] In 2016 the Commonwealth undertook a comprehensive review of the ADF's role in domestic counter-terrorism operations.[85] In response to the review, in December 2018 there was an 'overhaul'[86] of the call out procedures in Part IIIAAA of the *Defence Act*.[87] The amendments were designed to 'streamline the legal procedures for call out of the ADF and to enhance the ability of the ADF to protect states, self-governing territories, and

[76] ibid s 51G. See also limits on use of Reserve Forces for this purpose in ss 51A(2), 51C(2).
[77] *Defence Legislation Amendment (Aid to Civilian Authorities) Act 2006* (Cth) (No 3, 2006).
[78] ibid Div 3A.
[79] ibid Div 3B.
[80] ibid ss 51CA, CB.
[81] ibid s 51CA.
[82] Letts and McLaughlin, 'Call-Out Powers' (n 12) 73–74.
[83] ibid.
[84] See further State Coroner of New South Wales, *Inquest into the deaths arising from the Lindt Café Siege: Findings and recommendations* (May 2017).
[85] See Australian Department of Defence, 'The Hon Malcolm Turnbull Prime Minister & Senator the Hon Marise Payne Minister for Defence joint media release – Defence Support to domestic Counter-Terrorism arrangements' (Joint Media Release of Prime Minister of Australia Hon Malcolm Turnbull MP and Senator Hon Marise Payne, 17 July 2017) www.minister.defence.gov.au/minister/marise-payne/media-releases/hon-malcolm-turnbull-prime-minister-senator-hon-marise-payne, where the Review of Defence Support to domestic Counter-Terrorism Arrangements was announced.
[86] ibid.
[87] *Defence Amendment (Call Out of the Australian Defence Force) Act 2018* (Cth) (No 158, 2018).

Commonwealth interests, onshore and offshore, against domestic violence, including terrorism'.[88]

## B. Call Out Orders under Part IIIAAA of the *Defence Act*

There are two general types of call out orders under the amended Part IIIAAA of the *Defence Act*, namely a 'Commonwealth interests order'[89] or a 'State protection order'.[90] For both categories of call out order, there is provision for the ADF to be called out immediately or, if specified circumstances arise, under a contingent call out mechanism.[91]

Under s 33, the Governor-General can make an order calling out the ADF to protect Commonwealth interests against domestic violence in Australia[92] or threats in the Australian offshore area[93] ('Commonwealth interests order'). 'Domestic violence' is not defined in the *Defence Act* but is given the same meaning as in s 119 of the Constitution, as discussed above. The Explanatory Memorandum to the *Defence Amendment (Call Out of the Australian Defence Force) Bill 2018* (Cth) defines domestic violence as 'conduct that is marked by great physical force, and would include a terrorist attack, hostage situation, and widespread or significant violence'.[94] Peaceful protests, industrial action or civil disobedience are expressly excluded from the definition of domestic violence.[95]

A Commonwealth interests order can be made in the absence of a request by a State government, however there is a general requirement for consultation in each State or Territory in which domestic violence is occurring, or is likely to occur, before the Governor-General makes a Commonwealth interests order.[96] Consultation will not be required where the authorising Ministers are satisfied that, for reasons of urgency, it is impracticable.[97]

Under s 35, the Governor-General can make an order calling out the ADF to protect the States and Territories against domestic violence that is occurring, or is likely to occur, in the State or Territory upon receiving an application for assistance from the government of the State or Territory ('State protection order'). Section 35, therefore, reflects the constitutional position in s 119.

[88] Explanatory Memorandum to the Defence Amendment (Call Out of the Australian Defence Force) Bill 2018 (Cth), 2 para 3.
[89] *Defence Act 1903* (Cth) s 33.
[90] ibid s 35.
[91] ibid ss 34, 36.
[92] ibid s 33(1)(a)(i).
[93] ibid s 33(1)(a)(ii), (iii).
[94] Addendum to the Explanatory Memorandum to the Defence Amendment (Call Out of the Australian Defence Force) Bill 2018 (Cth), 2 para 165A.
[95] ibid.
[96] *Defence Act 1903* (Cth) s 38(1), (2).
[97] ibid s 38(3).

The amended Part IIIAAA expands the circumstances in which a contingent call out order can be made. A contingent call out order can be made to protect Commonwealth interests against land and maritime threats, in addition to aviation threats.[98] A contingent call out order can also be made to protect the States and Territories against domestic violence.[99] The effect of these provisions is that the ADF is effectively pre-authorised to respond to threats to Commonwealth interests or the States and Territories where specified circumstances arise.[100]

Part IIIAAA imposes conditions on the Governor-General's power to make Commonwealth interests orders and State protection orders.[101] The Governor-General may make a call out order if the 'authorising Ministers'[102] are satisfied of various matters, including that domestic violence is occurring, or is likely to occur, in Australia[103] or there is a threat in the Australian offshore area.[104] In considering whether the ADF should be called out, authorising Ministers are also required to take into account the nature of the domestic violence and whether the utilisation of the ADF would be likely to enhance the ability of the State or Territory to protect itself against domestic violence, as well as any other matter that the authorising Ministers consider relevant.[105]

This is a significant change because it lowers the threshold requirement for a call out.[106] Under the previous provisions, the ADF could only be called out if the States and Territories were not, or were unlikely to be, able to protect themselves or Commonwealth interests against domestic violence. This threshold reflected the language of s 119 of the Constitution. The relevant threshold is no longer that the States and Territories do not have the capability or capacity to deal with the domestic violence, but whether the Prime Minister or two 'authorising ministers' decide that ADF assistance would 'enhance' the law enforcement response.[107] While these amended provisions are intended to make it easier for the States and Territories to request assistance from the ADF, some doubts remain about whether they are consistent with s 119.[108]

There are formal and procedural requirements that the Governor-General must comply with in making a call out order. The order must be in writing[109] and it must define the violence or threats in question, and the Commonwealth interest or the State or Territory that is affected.[110] The requirement for a written

[98] ibid s 34(1)(d).
[99] ibid s 36(1).
[100] ibid ss 34, 36.
[101] ibid ss 33–36.
[102] ibid s 31, defining 'Authorising Ministers' as the Prime Minister, the Defence Minister and the Attorney-General.
[103] ibid ss 35(1), 36(1).
[104] ibid ss 33(1), 34(1).
[105] ibid ss 33(2), 35(2).
[106] See also Lee et al (n 2) 227.
[107] ibid 227.
[108] See Head, 'Another Expansion' (n 5) 5.
[109] *Defence Act 1903* (Cth), ss 33(3), 34(3), 35(3), 36(3).
[110] ibid ss 33(5), 34(5), 35(5), 36(5).

order is that it provides an important record of why the ADF was called out and what it was authorised to do.[111] There are limitations on the duration of the order, which is not longer than 20 days for a Commonwealth interests order or a State protection order.[112] The duration of an order can be extended for a period of up to 20 days for Commonwealth interests and state protection orders.[113] The Governor-General must act with the advice of the Federal Executive Council or, for reasons of urgency, the authorising Minister when making, varying and revoking call out orders.[114]

The Act contains some important restrictions on the powers that can be exercised by the ADF when it is called out to provide aid to the civil authority. Section 39 states that the Chief of the Defence Force must utilise the ADF 'in such manner as is reasonable and necessary, for the purpose specified in the order'.[115] Furthermore, s 39 states that the ADF cannot be used to 'stop or restrict any protest, dissent, assembly or industrial action', except where 'there is a reasonable likelihood of either the death of, or serious injury to, persons or property'.[116] The Reserve Forces cannot be called out or utilised in connection with an industrial dispute.

Section 40 of the *Defence Act* recognises the subordination of the ADF to the civil authority. It requires the Chief of the Defence Force, 'as far as is reasonably practicable', to ensure that the ADF is utilised to cooperate with the police forces of the States and Territories specified in the order, and 'is not utilised for any particular task in any of those States and Territories (except in relation to airborne aircraft)' unless requested to do so by a member of the State or Territory police force.

Divisions 3, 4 and 5 confer extensive, coercive powers on the ADF that can be exercised under a call out order, including power to use lethal force.[117] These powers are similar to those exercised by the police forces, including powers of search and seizure;[118] powers to compel a person to answer questions put to them by ADF members and produce documents;[119] and powers to detain a person in certain circumstances.[120] The Act contains limitations and safeguards on the exercise of these powers. Authorisation from the Chief of the Defence Force is required for ADF members to exercise certain coercive powers, such as the power to enter

[111] Explanatory Memorandum to the Defence Amendment (Call Out of the Australian Defence Force) Bill 2018 (Cth), 37 para 185, 40–41 para 208, 43 para 224, 45 para 241.
[112] *Defence Act 1903* (Cth), ss 33(5)(d), 35(5)(d).
[113] ibid s 37(2).
[114] ibid s 37(5).
[115] ibid s 39(2).
[116] ibid s 39(3)(b).
[117] ibid s 46(7).
[118] ibid s 46(5), (7), (9).
[119] ibid s 46(7)(h).
[120] ibid s 46(7)(f).

and search premises in a specified area.[121] Certain powers can only be exercised for certain purposes, or when a specific threshold has been met. In particular, there are restrictions and limitations applied to the use of force. All force must be reasonable and necessary in the circumstances, and force that may cause grievous bodily harm or death is only ever exercised where reasonable and necessary to protect life.[122]

## C. The Relationship between Part IIIAAA of the *Defence Act* and Commonwealth Executive Power

The purpose of the 2018 amendments was to 'streamline the legal procedures for call out of the ADF' and to 'enhance the ability of the ADF to protect states, territories and Commonwealth interests against domestic violence including terrorism'.[123] Part IIIAAA of the *Defence Act* gives effect to that purpose by providing a comprehensive statutory regime that governs the use of the ADF in providing aid to the civil authority. As shown above, ss 33–36 confer power on the Governor-General to make an order calling out the ADF for the purpose of protecting the States and Territories against domestic violence, as recognised in s 119 of the Constitution, or to protect Commonwealth interests, as recognised in *Sharkey*. These are the recognised circumstances in which the ADF can be used in aid of the civil power in Australia. The Act also imposes conditions on the exercise of this power by the Governor-General in ss 37–38. The Act authorises the use of coercive powers by members of the ADF who are called out under a Commonwealth interests order or a State protection order and details the manner and conditions of their exercise.[124]

Australian courts have not yet had the opportunity to consider the issue, however the extensive and detailed powers conferred on the ADF by Part IIIAAA of the *Defence Act* are likely to have abrogated or displaced executive powers with respect to the use of the ADF for internal security operations. In Australia, as in the United Kingdom, an important limitation on prerogative powers is that they are subject to abrogation or displacement by statute. The relationship between the prerogative and statute is governed by the principle that was laid down in the important and influential decision of the House of Lords in *Attorney-General v De Keyser's Royal Hotel Ltd*.[125] That principle is that 'when a prerogative power of the Executive Government is directly regulated by statute, the Executive can no longer rely on the prerogative power but must act in accordance with the statutory

[121] ibid s 51A.
[122] ibid s 51N.
[123] Explanatory Memorandum to the Defence Amendment (Call Out of the Australian Defence Force) Bill 2018 (Cth), 2 para 3.
[124] *Defence Act 1903* (Cth) Part IIIAAA, div 3, div 4, div 5.
[125] *Attorney-General v De Keyser's Royal Hotel Ltd* [1920] UKHL 1; [1920] AC 508.

regime laid down by the Parliament'.[126] In these circumstances, the prerogative is to be regarded as abrogated, abridged or 'displaced' by the statute.[127] The statutory displacement of the prerogative may occur by express words or by necessary implication.[128]

The *De Keyser* principle has been imported into the Australian constitutional jurisprudence.[129] Australian courts have, however, adapted this common law principle to the Australian constitutional context. This is evident in the decision in *Ruddock v Vadarlis*,[130] discussed in the next chapter of this book, where the majority applied the *De Keyser* principle to determine whether Commonwealth legislation had abrogated or displaced non-statutory executive powers of 'significance' to national sovereignty, rather than the prerogative.[131]

Australian courts have generally been reluctant to find that legislation has abrogated or displaced executive powers that are 'important' to national sovereignty or the functioning of the Executive Government.[132] Some judges have applied a strong presumption against displacement and have found that the power 'is not

[126] This is the statement of principle that was approved by a plurality of the High Court of Australia in *Jarratt v Commissioner of Police (NSW)* (2005) 224 CLR 44, 69–70 [85] (McHugh, Gummow and Hayne JJ), quoting *Re Residential Tenancies Tribunal (NSW) and Henderson; Ex parte Defence Housing Authority* (1997) 190 CLR 410, 459 (McHugh J) (*Henderson's case*), and a majority of the High Court in *Northern Territory v Arnhem Land Aboriginal Land Trust* (2008) 236 CLR 24, 58 [27] (Gleeson CJ, Gummow, Hayne and Crennan JJ) (*Arnhem Land Trust case*). See also *De Keyser* (n 125) 526 (Lord Dunedin), 539–40 (Lord Atkinson), 554 (Lord Moulton), 561–62 (Lord Sumner), 575 (Lord Parmoor).

[127] This book refers to 'displacement' of the prerogative by statute. 'Displacement' has been used interchangeably with terms such as 'abrogation', 'abridgement' or 'ouster' of the prerogative: see, eg, J Goldring, 'The Impact of Statutes on the Royal Prerogative: Australasian Attitudes as to the Rule in Attorney-General v De Keyser's Royal Hotel Ltd' (1974) 48 *Australian Law Journal* 434, 438; Winterton, 'The Relationship' (n 23) 43; B Saunders, 'Democracy, Liberty and the Prerogative: The Displacement of Inherent Executive Power by Statute' (2013) 41 *Federal Law Review* 363. In *Oates v Attorney-General (Cth)* (2001) 181 ALR 559, 569 [40], Lindgren J interpreted 'displaced' as 'including the notion of partial displacement, that is, confinement, restriction or limitation' of the prerogative. This wider conception of displacement will be adopted in this book.

[128] *De Keyser* (n 125) 576 (Lord Parmoor). See also *Laker Airways Ltd v Department of Trade* [1977] 1 QB 643, 719–21 (Roskill LJ); *R v Secretary of State for the Home Department; Ex parte Fire Brigades Union* [1995] 2 AC 513, 552 (Lord Browne-Wilkinson); *R (Miller) v Secretary of State for Exiting the European Union* [2017] UKSC 5; [2018] AC 61 [48].

[129] *Re Richard Foreman & Sons Pty Ltd; Uther v Federal Commissioner of Taxation* (1947) 74 CLR 508, 514 (Latham CJ); *Barton v Commonwealth* (1974) 131 CLR 477, 488 (Barwick CJ), 501 (Mason J); *Brown v West* (1990) 169 CLR 195, 202, 205 (Mason CJ, Brennan, Deane, Dawson and Toohey JJ); *Ling v Commonwealth* (1994) 51 FCR 88, 92 (Gummow, Lee and Hill JJ); *Henderson's case* (n 126) 459 (McHugh J); *Ruddock v Vadarlis* (2001) 110 FCR 491 (*Tampa case*), 501 [33] (Black CJ), 539–40 [181]–[182] (French J, Beaumont J agreeing at 514 [95]); *Oates v Attorney-General (Cth)* 2003 214 CLR 496, 511 [37] (Gleeson CJ, McHugh, Gummow, Kirby, Hayne and Heydon JJ); *Jarratt* (n 126) 69–70 [85] (McHugh, Gummow and Hayne JJ), 84–85 [129] (Callinan J); *Arnhem Land Trust case* (n 126) 58 [27] (Gleeson CJ, Gummow, Hayne and Crennan JJ); *CPCF v Minister for Immigration and Border Protection* (2015) 255 CLR 514, 600–01 [279] (Kiefel J); *Cadia Holdings Pty Ltd v New South Wales* (2010) 242 CLR 195, 204 [14] (French CJ), 228 [94] (Gummow, Hayne, Heydon and Crennan JJ).

[130] *Tampa case* (n 129).

[131] ibid 540 [185] (French J).

[132] See especially *Barton* (n 129) 488 (Barwick CJ), 491 (McTiernan and Menzies JJ), 501 (Mason J), 506–08 (Jacobs J); *Ling* (n 129) 94, 97 (Gummow, Lee and Hill JJ); *Tampa case* (n 129) 544–46 [199]–[204] (French J, Beaumont J agreeing at 514 [95]); *Oates* (n 129) 511 [37]–[40], 512–13 [45]–[46] (Gleeson CJ, McHugh, Gummow, Kirby, Hayne and Heydon JJ).

displaced except by a clear and unambiguous' provision.[133] This will generally require a direct inconsistency between the provisions of the statute and the exercise of executive power. There may be a direct inconsistency where the statutory provisions impose conditions on the power that could be avoided by the inherent executive power.[134] Other judges have taken the view that once the Parliament has enacted legislation that comprehensively regulates a subject, such that it 'covers the field', it is the legislation that applies and the executive power ceases to operate.[135]

In ascertaining whether an executive power has been impliedly abrogated by statute, Australian courts have also considered the significance of provisions in the statute that purport to preserve the existence of the prerogative. For example, Part IIIAAA of the *Defence Act* includes s 51ZD, which is entitled 'Effect on other Defence Force utilisation and powers'. It states that 'This Part does not affect any utilisation of the Defence Force that would be permitted or required, or any powers that the Defence Force would have, if this part were disregarded'.[136]

The meaning of a similar provision in the *Maritime Powers Act 2013* (Cth) was considered in *CPCF v Minister for Immigration and Border Protection*.[137] Section 5 of the *Maritime Powers Act 2013* (Cth) is entitled 'Effect on executive power' and expressly states that 'This Act does not limit the executive power of the Commonwealth'. In their respective judgments, French CJ, Hayne and Bell JJ, and Kiefel J considered the effect of s 5 of the *Maritime Powers Act* on Commonwealth executive power. The Commonwealth argued that these express words made it clear that it was the Parliament's intention that the *Maritime Powers Act* operate in addition to non-statutory executive power.

It is significant that all of the judges who considered the issue in *CPCF* rejected this argument.[138] Chief Justice French considered that the *Maritime Powers Act* conferred a range of powers on Executive officers and imposed conditions on their exercise. Accordingly, s 5 could not be construed as 'preserving unconstrained an executive power the exercise of which is constrained by the *MPA* [*Maritime Powers Act*]'.[139] Justices Hayne and Bell reached a similar conclusion in their joint judgment.[140] Their Honours thought that it was 'probable' that s 5 of the MPA should be 'read as saying no more than that no negative inference should be drawn about the ambit of executive power from the enactment of the MP Act' but did not consider it necessary to resolve this issue.[141]

[133] See, eg, *Barton* (n 129) 488 (Barwick CJ), 491 (McTiernan and Menzies JJ), 501 (Mason J), 506–08 (Jacobs J); *Tampa case* (n 129) 540–41 [184]–[185], 545 [201] (French J, Beaumont J agreeing at 514 [95]).

[134] See, eg, *Jarratt* (n 126) 69 [81], 69–70 [85] (McHugh, Gummow and Hayne JJ), 84–85 [129] (Callinan J); *CPCF* (n 129) 600 [277], 601–02 [283] (Kiefel J).

[135] See, eg, *Tampa case* (n 129) 501 [34] (Black CJ); *CPCF* (n 129) 600–01 [279] (Kiefel J).

[136] Similar provisions appear in the *Migration Act 1958* (Cth), s 7 and the *Maritime Powers Act 2013* (Cth), s 5.

[137] *CPCF* (n 129).

[138] ibid 538 [41] (French CJ), 564–65 [141] (Hayne and Bell JJ), 601–02 [283] (Kiefel J).

[139] ibid 538 [41].

[140] ibid 564–65 [141].

[141] ibid.

In particular, Kiefel J cited with approval an observation in *John Holland Pty Ltd v Victorian Workcover Authority* that 'such a statement is only a statement of intention which informs the construction of the Act as a whole. It must be an intention which the substantive provisions of the Act are capable of supporting'.[142] Justice Kiefel reaffirmed that the 'relevant "intention" of a statute is that which is revealed to the court by ordinary processes of statutory construction'.[143] In this respect, it was significant that the *Maritime Powers Act* 'authorise[d] a decision that the relevant powers be exercised in a particular way and detail[ed] the manner and conditions of their exercise'.[144] Justice Kiefel concluded that the *Maritime Powers Act* did not support an intention that the Commonwealth Executive is to retain a complete discretion as to how powers of detention and removal of non-citizens from Australia are to be exercised. Section 5 was 'better understood as preserving such other … executive powers as may be exercised conformably' with the *Maritime Powers Act* provisions.[145] It would appear from the judgments in *CPCF* that express statements of intention in legislation may not be effective in preserving an unconstrained non-statutory executive power in circumstances where the statute also contains detailed provisions that impose conditions and limitations on the exercise of executive power.

In light of the authority in *CPCF* it is difficult to see how the enactment of the comprehensive statutory regime in Part IIIAAA of the *Defence Act*, which places conditions on the exercise of the power to call out the ADF in aid of the civil authority, would be consistent with a legislative intention to preserve the inherent executive power on the same topic. The source of the power to call out the ADF to protect Commonwealth interests or the States and Territories against domestic violence, then, appears to be Part IIIAAA of the *Defence Act* and the exercise of this power is subject to its conditions. This interpretation coheres with the approach adopted in *CPCF*. However, the use of the ADF by the Commonwealth to respond to non-violent civil emergencies, such as natural disasters or pandemics, is not authorised under Part IIIAAA.[146] As is shown below, the Commonwealth Executive Government relied on its non-statutory executive power to support the deployment of the ADF to respond to the Black Summer bushfires and COVID-19 pandemic.

## III. Use of the ADF During Civil Emergencies in Australia

There are two different types of assistance that can be provided by the ADF when it is deployed internally within Australia.[147] This chapter is primarily concerned with

[142] ibid 601 [282], quoting *John Holland Pty Ltd v Victorian Workcover Authority* (2009) 239 CLR 518, 527 [20] (French CJ, Gummow, Hayne, Heydon, Crennan, Kiefel and Bell JJ).

[143] *CPCF* (n 129) 601 [282], citing *Momcilovic v The Queen* (2011) 245 CLR 1, 74 [111]–[112] (Gummow J), 133–34 [315], 141 [341] (Hayne J), 235 [638] (Crennan and Kiefel JJ).

[144] *CPCF* (n 129) 601–02 [283].

[145] ibid.

[146] See also Twomey, 'The Prerogative and the Courts' (n 4) 71.

[147] White (n 7) 447. As White notes, these are reflected in Defence Instructions but they are not available to the public: *Defence Instruction (General) OPS 01-1 Defence Force Aid to the Civil Authority*.

the utilisation of the ADF to provide Defence Assistance to the Civil Community (DACC) in emergencies, for which the civilian community lacks the necessary resources or equipment to adequately respond, such as natural disasters, or search and rescue operations.[148] The use of the ADF in this capacity is to be distinguished from the provision of Defence Force Aid to the Civil Authority, which is now regulated by Part IIIAAA of the *Defence Act*, as discussed above, because it does not involve the use or potential use of force against the civilian population.[149] 'Force', in this context, includes intrusive or coercive acts as well as any restriction of freedom of movement of the civil community, irrespective of whether there is physical contact.[150]

Until December 2012, the provision of DACC was governed by the *Defence Instructions (General) OPS 05-1: Defence Assistance to the Civil Community – policy and procedures*. The *Defence Instructions* were replaced by the *Defence Assistance to the Community Manual* and the *Defence Assistance to the Civil Community Policy*.[151] The *DACC Manual* sets out the procedures by which the Department of Defence provides and coordinates the provision of defence assistance to the civil community in both emergency and non-emergency situations.[152] The *DACC Policy* 'articulates the main principles that guide the appropriate provision of DACC'.[153]

There are two categories of DACC, namely 'emergency' and 'non-emergency' assistance.[154] Emergency assistance is further divided into three categories according to the type and duration of assistance.[155] During the Black Summer bushfires and COVID-19 pandemic, the ADF provided 'emergency recovery assistance' in accordance with the DACC framework[156] and the Australian Government Disaster Response Plan (COMDISPLAN).[157] While these policy frameworks provide important guidance on the tasks that can be undertaken by the ADF in providing DACC, they are not the source of the Commonwealth's power to use the ADF for these purposes. The utilisation of the ADF to provide DACC during emergencies is an exercise of non-statutory executive power.

For a discussion of the legal basis of the Defence Instructions see Letts and McLaughlin, 'Call-Out Powers' (n 12). The DACC was covered by *Defence Instruction (General) OPS 05-1 Defence Assistance to the Civil Community* until it was replaced in December 2012 with the *Defence Assistance to the Civil Community Manual and Policy.*

[148] White (n 7) 446–47. See also D Letts and R McLaughlin, 'Military Aid to the Civil Power' in R Creyke, D Stephens and P Sutherland (eds), *Military Law in Australia* (Alexandria, Federation Press, 2019) 115, 128–29.

[149] Australian Department of Defence, *Defence Assistance to the Civil Community Manual* (17 August 2020) [1.1] (*DACC Manual*); Australian Department of Defence, *Defence Assistance to the Civil Community Policy* (17 August 2020) [1.4], [1.11] (*DACC Policy*).

[150] *DACC Manual* (n 149) [1.1], [6.1]; *DACC Policy* (n 149) [1.4].

[151] *DACC Policy* (n 149).

[152] *DACC Manual* (n 149) [1.1].

[153] ibid [1.1].

[154] ibid [2.4]; *DACC Policy* (n 149) [1.10].

[155] *DACC Policy* (n 149) [1.10]; *DACC Manual* (n 149) [2.4].

[156] See *DACC Manual* (n 149) Ch 3, DACC Category 3.

[157] Australian Government, *COMDISPLAN 2020: Australian Government Disaster Response Plan* (Department of Home Affairs, 2020).

## A. Operation Bushfire Assist

In the summer of 2019–20 Australia was confronted with 'unprecedented' bushfires that created crises on multiple fronts across each of the States and Territories.[158] While there was recognition that the State and Territory governments have primary responsibility for emergency and disaster management, the scale and nature of the Black Summer bushfires created community expectations that the Commonwealth should play a more prominent role in responding to national emergencies and disasters, given that it has unique capabilities and resources, including the ADF, at its disposal.[159] Between September 2019 and March 2020 the ADF provided significant emergency assistance to the States and Territories in the response to, and recovery from, the Black Summer bushfires. 'Operation Bushfire Assist' was established on 31 December 2019.[160] At its peak, more than 6,500 members of the ADF, including 3,000 ADF reserves, provided resources and logistical support, including transportation of personnel and equipment, engineering assistance, bases for firefighting aircraft, large-scale evacuations, search and rescue operations, and surveillance of fire fronts.[161] The ADF also assisted the response and recovery efforts by clearing roads and firebreaks, repairing fences, providing drinking water to Kangaroo Island and Bega, and catering to emergency services personnel and evacuees.[162]

On 4 January 2020, during the height of the bushfire crisis, the Governor-General issued a compulsory call out order of the ADF reserves under s 28(1) of the *Defence Act*.[163] Three thousand army reserve members from Forces Command were called out for continuous full-time service 'to provide civil aid, humanitarian assistance, medical or civil emergency or disaster relief'.[164] The Order was revoked on 7 February 2020. In addition to the ADF reserves, the Commonwealth Executive Government exercised its non-statutory executive power and deployed 3,500 regular full-time members of the ADF to provide assistance and support to State and Territory authorities during Operation Bushfire Assist.[165]

[158] Royal Commission into National Natural Disaster Arrangements, *Royal Commission into National Natural Disaster Arrangements Report* (28 October 2020) 5 (Royal Commission Report).

[159] ibid 6.

[160] Australian Department of Defence, 'Operation Bushfire Assist concludes' (Joint Media Release of Prime Minister of Australia Hon Scott Morrison MP and Senator Hon Linda Reynolds CSC, 26 March 2020) www.minister.defence.gov.au/minister/lreynolds/media-releases/operation-bushfire-assist-concludes.

[161] Royal Commission Report (n 158) 188–89.

[162] ibid 190.

[163] See also *Defence Act 1903* (Cth) s 28(4)(b), which provided that an order could be made on the advice of the Minister.

[164] See *Defence Act 1903* (Cth) s 28(3)(g).

[165] Australian Department of Defence, 'Defence Support to firefighting effort' (Media release of Senator Hon Linda Reynolds CSC, 11 November 2019) www.minister.defence.gov.au/minister/lreynolds/media-releases/defence-support-firefighting-effort.

Part IIIAAA of the *Defence Act* did not support the call out of the ADF reserves, nor the deployment of regular members of the ADF, because there was no domestic violence. As such, members of the ADF and reserves that were deployed during Operation Bushfire Assist were not authorised to exercise coercive powers. Furthermore, while provision was made in the *Defence Act* for the Governor-General to call out the reserves to provide assistance to the civil community, it did not set out powers, rights and obligations of members of the reserves when they are so engaged. Accordingly, once the ADF reserves were called out, they were exercising non-statutory executive power in accordance with the DACC framework.

While the ADF had been utilised to respond to and assist with recovery from natural disasters in the past, the Australian Prime Minister expressed concern that, during Operation Bushfire Assist, the ADF was operating in a 'constitutional grey zone'.[166] In particular, there was some uncertainty about whether the use by the Commonwealth Executive Government of the ADF to respond to emergencies was authorised under the Constitution, and the scope and limits of the powers that the ADF could exercise in the course of undertaking disaster relief and recovery actions. There were also concerns that ADF personnel were not afforded adequate legal protection from civil and criminal liability during Operation Bushfire Assist, such as for trespass or damage to property.[167]

In the wake of the Royal Commission into National Natural Disaster Arrangements ('Bushfires Royal Commission'), the Commonwealth Parliament enacted the *Defence Legislation Amendment (Enhancement of Defence Force Response to Emergencies) Act 2020* (Cth). This Act amended the *Defence Act* by providing immunity from civil and criminal liability for ADF members and personnel 'who, in the good faith performance of duties, provide assistance in the preparation for, response to and recovery from a natural disaster or other emergency' in circumstances where the assistance was provided at the direction of the Minister.[168] However, these amendments did not fully resolve questions about the source and limits of the Commonwealth's executive power to use the ADF during civil emergencies, which is discussed below.

## B. Operation COVID-19 Assist

After having endured the Black Summer bushfires, Australia was then confronted with the emergence of the COVID-19 pandemic. On 18 March 2020 the

[166] Prime Minister of Australia, 'National Royal Commission into Black Summer Bushfires established' (Media release of Prime Minister of Australia Hon Scott Morrison MP, 20 February 2020) www.pm.gov.au/media/national-royal-commission-black-summer-bushfires-established.

[167] Royal Commission Report (n 158) 200. See also Twomey, 'The Prerogative and the Courts' (n 4) 73.

[168] Explanatory Memorandum to the Defence Legislation Amendment (Enhancement of Defence Force Response to Emergencies) Act 2020 (Cth), s 123AA.

Governor-General made a declaration that a 'human biosecurity emergency' existed.[169] Declarations of an emergency and a public health emergency were made by State and Territory governments under their public health and emergency legislation,[170] which enlivened the exercise of emergency powers.[171] The Commonwealth Executive Government has asserted a prominent role in coordinating the response to the COVID-19 pandemic through the creation of the National Cabinet[172] and financial assistance to individuals and businesses adversely affected by COVID-19.[173]

An important feature of the Commonwealth's response to the COVID-19 pandemic has been the deployment of the ADF to provide assistance to State and Territory authorities in responding to the pandemic. On 1 April 2020 'Operation COVID-19 Assist' was established.[174] Through 'Operation COVID-19 Assist', ADF personnel have been utilised to support the national response to the COVID-19 pandemic by providing 'logistics support for the State and Territory police as they enforce mandatory quarantine and isolation measures', and border control measures.[175] ADF personnel have also been utilised to support the Department of Health with contact tracing, emergency clinical support, frontline swab testing support at testing facilities, and logistical support for civilian authorities.[176]

The use of the ADF to provide assistance during the COVID-19 pandemic was not authorised under Part IIIAAA of the *Defence Act* because it was not action taken to protect Commonwealth interests or the States and Territories against

[169] *Biosecurity (Human Biosecurity Emergency) (Human Coronavirus with Pandemic Potential) Declaration 2020* (Cth).

[170] See, eg, *Public Health and Wellbeing Act 2008* (Vic) s 198; *Public Health Act 2005* (SA) s 87; *Public Health Act 1997* (ACT) s 119; *Public Health Act 2005* (Qld) s 319(2); *Public and Environmental Health Act 2011* (NT) ss 48, 49; *Public Health Act 1997* (Tas) s 15; *Public Health Act 2016* (WA) s 167; *Emergency Management Act 2005* (WA) s 56.

[171] See *Public Health and Wellbeing Act 2008* (Vic), Part 10, Div 3; *Public Health Act 2005* (Qld), Ch 8, Part 7A; *Public Health Act 2016* (WA), Part 12, Div 4; *Emergency Management Act 2005* (WA), Part 6; *Public Health Act 1997* (Tas), Part 2, Div 2; *Public Health Act 1997* (ACT), Part 7; *Public and Environmental Health Act 2011* (NT), Part 5, Div 2; *Public Health Act 2011* (SA), Part 11.

[172] This is a significant development in Commonwealth–State relations in Australia but it is beyond the scope of this book to consider the National Cabinet in detail. See further A Twomey, 'Federal and State Powers to Deal with Pandemics: Cooperation, Conflict and Confusion' in B Bennett and I Freckelton (eds), *Pandemics, Public Health Emergencies and Government Powers: Perspectives on Australian Law* (Annandale, Federation Press, 2021); C Saunders, 'The National Cabinet Has Worked. Can it Last?' (2020) *Pursuit*, pursuit.unimelb.edu.au/articles/the-national-cabinet-has-worked-can-it-last.

[173] *Coronavirus Economic Response Package (Payments and Benefits) Act 2020* (Cth).

[174] Australian Department of Defence, 'Expansion of ADF support to COVID-19 Assist' (Media release of Senator Hon Linda Reynolds CSC, 1 April 2020) www.minister.defence.gov.au/minister/lreynolds/media-releases/expansion-adf-support-covid-19-assist.

[175] Australian Department of Defence, 'Defence Support to Mandatory Quarantine Measures Commences' (Media release of Senator Hon Linda Reynolds CSC, 29 March 2020) www.minister.defence.gov.au/minister/lreynolds/media-releases/defence-support-mandatory-quarantine-measures-commences; Australian Department of Health, 'Defence support the vaccine rollout in aged care' (Media Release of Hon Greg Hunt MP, 3 March 2021) www.health.gov.au/ministers/the-hon-greg-hunt-mp/media/defence-support-the-vaccine-rollout-in-aged-care.

[176] Australian Department of Health, 'Defence support the vaccine rollout in aged care' (n 175). See also Australian Department of Defence, 'Operation COVID-19 Assist' (Web page, 25 March 2022) www.defence.gov.au/operations/opcovid19-assist.

'domestic violence'. Furthermore, there was no call out of the ADF reserves. While ADF personnel can be made 'human biosecurity officers' under the *Biosecurity Act 2015* (Cth),[177] and can exercise coercive powers conferred on them by that Act,[178] the deployment of the ADF for 'Operation COVID-19 Assist' was not supported by this legislation.

The deployment of the ADF for Operation COVID-19 Assist was undertaken in accordance with the DACC framework and COMDISPLAN as an exercise of the Commonwealth's non-statutory executive power.[179] The Minister announced that 'ADF members have no coercive enforcement powers'.[180] However, ADF personnel have been deployed alongside the State and Territory police to provide assistance in the enforcement of mandatory hotel quarantine and isolation measures and State border closures, which necessarily restrict the freedom of movement of individuals.[181]

Important questions have been raised in the literature about whether, and on what basis, the Commonwealth's use of the ADF to provide emergency assistance in relation to the Black Summer bushfires and COVID-19 pandemic was authorised under the Constitution.[182] The next section of this chapter considers the scope of the Commonwealth's executive power to use the ADF during civil emergencies in Australia.

## IV. Scope of Commonwealth Executive Power to Use the ADF During Emergencies

The foregoing demonstrated that the use of the ADF for Operation Bushfire Assist and Operation COVID-19 Assist was not action taken pursuant to Part IIIAAA of the *Defence Act*, nor other Commonwealth legislation. While assistance was provided in accordance with the DACC framework and COMDISPLAN, these administrative policy frameworks do not provide the source of power to use the ADF to provide assistance during a civil emergency. They assume that the power exists; they are not the source of it.

As discussed above, s 68 of the Constitution vests the command of the armed forces of the Commonwealth in the Governor-General. In so doing, the prerogative relating to the control and disposition of the armed forces, which is exercisable by the Governor-General on ministerial advice, is given a constitutional source.[183]

[177] *Biosecurity Act 2015* (Cth) s 563 (meaning of 'human biosecurity officer' under the Act).

[178] ibid ss 60, 566.

[179] Australian Department of Defence, 'Defence support to mandatory quarantine measures commences' (n 175).

[180] ibid.

[181] See also Twomey, 'The Prerogative and the Courts' (n 4) 74–75.

[182] See especially Twomey, 'The Prerogative and the Courts' (n 4); Gray (n 68).

[183] See also Twomey, 'The Prerogative and the Courts' (n 4) 76.

While s 68 of the Constitution is the source of the executive power relating to the control and disposition of the armed forces, the prerogative informs its content. As such, it is necessary to have regard to the common law to determine the nature and scope of the power.[184] The existence of the prerogative relating to the control and disposition of the armed forces has long been recognised in the United Kingdom. In *China Navigation Company Ltd v Attorney-General*[185] Lord Lawrence remarked:

> It is unnecessary to specify the various powers relating to the army which Parliament has thus tacitly left to the unfettered control of the Crown, it is sufficient to state that they undoubtedly include the organisation, armament, maintenance, disposition and use of the standing army in time of peace ... In my opinion, therefore, the powers which the Crown exercises as to the disposition and use of the standing army in time of peace are powers vested in the Crown by prerogative right at common law.[186]

In *Chandler v Director of Public Prosecutions*[187] Viscount Radcliffe confirmed that 'the disposition, armament and direction of the defence forces of the State are matters decided upon by the Crown and are within its jurisdiction as the executive power of the State'.[188] In that same case, Lord Hodson remarked that

> the Crown has, and this is not disputed, the right as head of the State to decide in peace and war the disposition of its armed forces and has purported to exercise this right for the safety and interests of the State.[189]

In Australia, the prerogative relating to the control and disposition of the armed forces permits the Crown 'to determine the organisation, structure, placement, arming and equipment of the ADF'.[190] As such, parliamentary authorisation is not required to move the ADF to different places within Australia.[191] The scope of the prerogative is, however, limited by Australia's federal constitutional context. Section 119 of the Constitution operates as a limit on the exercise of this prerogative, to the extent that a request for assistance is required before the Commonwealth can deploy the ADF to protect the States and Territories from domestic violence.[192]

While the prerogative for the control and disposition of the ADF gives the Commonwealth the authority to place the ADF in a State or Territory and to control its conduct, it does not empower the ADF to provide assistance during natural disasters or emergencies.[193] In Australia, another source of power is required to support executive action undertaken by the Commonwealth to respond to emergencies, including the use of the ADF for this purpose. In the

[184] Sapienza (n 4) 22.
[185] *China Navigation Company Ltd v Attorney-General* [1932] 2 KB 197.
[186] ibid 228 (Lawrence LJ).
[187] *Chandler v Director of Public Prosecutions* [1964] AC 763.
[188] ibid 796 (Viscount Radcliffe).
[189] ibid 800 (Lord Hodson); see also 791 (Lord Reid), 807 (Lord Devlin). See also *Burmah Oil Co (Burmah Trading) Ltd v Lord Advocate* [1965] AC 75, 100 (Lord Reid).
[190] Moore (n 6) 89.
[191] ibid 168–70.
[192] See also Twomey, 'The Prerogative and the Courts' (n 4) 76.
[193] ibid 77; Moore (n 6) 168–70.

absence of authorisation by legislation or by a specific constitutional provision, the issue is whether the use of the ADF to respond to non-violent civil emergencies falls within the scope of the inherent executive power under s 61 of the Constitution.

## A. Prerogative Powers for the Preservation of Public Safety and the Maintenance of the Peace

There is a judicially recognised prerogative for the preservation of public safety in the United Kingdom. In the 1965 decision of the House of Lords in *Burmah Oil*,[194] Lord Hodson accepted the existence of a prerogative to respond to emergencies, which was not limited to war but could be invoked in circumstances giving rise to 'a national emergency, an urgent necessity for taking extreme steps for the protection of the realm'.[195] Viscount Radcliffe observed in the same case that certain powers in the nature of the prerogative were derived from duties that 'were vested in the Sovereign as the leader of the people and the chief executive instrument for protecting the public safety'.[196] The exercise of this prerogative was not confined to 'the imminence or outbreak of war' but could also be invoked to respond to civil emergencies that threatened public safety or public order, such as 'riot, pestilence and conflagration'.[197] In commenting on the scope of the prerogative, Viscount Radcliffe explained that the types of executive acts that could be authorised by this prerogative were not amenable to categorisation because the scope of the prerogative depended 'on the necessity of the occasion'.[198]

There has also been relatively recent judicial recognition in the United Kingdom of a prerogative to keep the peace within the realm. This power was described as the 'sister' of the war prerogative in the 1989 decision in *R v Secretary of State for the Home Department; Ex parte Northumbria Police Authority* ('*Northumbria case*').[199] In that case, the Home Secretary had, by Circular No 40/1986, authorised the Home Office to maintain and supply certain equipment to the police, including 'plastic baton rounds and C.S. gas'. The Court of Appeal accepted that the power to engage in these activities was conferred on the Home Secretary by the *Police Act 1964* (UK). Nevertheless, it proceeded to investigate the existence and scope of the Crown's prerogative to maintain the

[194] *Burmah Oil* (n 189).

[195] ibid 136 (Lord Hodson), quoting with approval *Crown of Leon (Owners) v Admiralty Commissioners* [1921] 1 KB 590, 603–04 (Earl of Reading CJ); J Chitty, *A Treatise on the Law of the Prerogatives of the Crown and the Relative Duties and Rights of the Subject* (London, J Butterworth, 1820) 50.

[196] *Burmah Oil* (n 189) 115 (Viscount Radcliffe).

[197] ibid 114–15 (Viscount Radcliffe).

[198] ibid 115.

[199] *R v Secretary of State for the Home Department; Ex parte Northumbria Police Authority* [1989] 1 QB 26, 58A (Nourse LJ).

peace on the basis that there had 'probably never been a comparable occasion for investigating a prerogative of keeping the peace within the realm'.[200]

On this particular issue, the Court confirmed the decision of the Divisional Court that the supply of equipment to the police forces was supported by the prerogative power to meet an actual or apprehended threat to the Queen's peace.[201] Lord Justice Croom-Johnson, for example, found that the prerogative extended to 'maintaining the Queen's peace and keeping law and order'.[202] His Honour had 'no doubt that the Crown does have a prerogative power to keep the peace, which is bound up with its undoubted right to see that crime is prevented and justice administered'.[203] Lord Justice Purchas agreed, finding that the prerogative extended to 'all that is reasonably necessary to preserve the peace of the realm',[204] and this included the provision of equipment to the police.

The decision in the *Northumbria case* has caused some disquiet among scholars, not least because the Court did not define the limits of the prerogative to maintain the peace.[205] There was little historical evidence to support the existence of such a prerogative, other than in an actual emergency or crisis. A reference to a prerogative to maintain the peace was conspicuously absent from the catalogue of prerogative powers set out by Chitty in his *Treatise on the Law of the Prerogatives of the Crown*.[206] It was suggested that the finding of this prerogative to maintain the peace contradicted Lord Diplock's observation in *British Broadcasting Corporation v Johns* that 'it is 350 years and a civil war too late for the Queen's courts to broaden the prerogative'.[207] In his judgment, Nourse LJ appeared to anticipate these concerns. He did not attribute significance to the fact that references to a prerogative of keeping the peace in reported cases and authoritative texts were 'scarce'.[208] Nourse LJ reasoned that it had never been 'practicable to identify all the prerogative powers of the Crown'[209] and suggested that there was 'no historical or other basis for denying to the war prerogative a sister prerogative of keeping the peace within the realm'.[210]

[200] ibid 56F (Nourse LJ).

[201] ibid 34A (Mann J), 44A–B (Croom-Johnson LJ), 53G, 54A, 55A–B, G–H (Purchas LJ), 58A, 58H–59A, 59C–E (Nourse LJ).

[202] ibid 44B.

[203] ibid.

[204] ibid 53G–54A.

[205] See, eg, HJ Beynon, 'Prerogative to Supply Plastic Baton Rounds and CS to the Police' [1987] *Public Law* 146; AW Bradley, 'Police powers and the prerogative' [1988] (Autumn) *Public Law* 298; R Ward, 'Baton Rounds and Circulars' (1988) 1 *Cambridge Law Journal* 155; L Zines, 'The Inherent Executive Power of the Commonwealth' (2005) 16 *Public Law Review* 279, 286–90; M Cohn, 'Medieval Chains, Invisible Inks: On Non-Statutory Powers of the Executive' (2005) 25 *Oxford Journal of Legal Studies* 97, 108.

[206] Chitty (n 195). See also Bradley (n 205) 301; Ward (n 205) 156–57; Zines (n 205) 287–88; Cohn (n 205) 108.

[207] *British Broadcasting Corporation v Johns* [1965] Ch 32, 79. See also T Poole, 'United Kingdom: The Royal Prerogative' (2010) 8 *International Journal of Constitutional Law* 146, 148.

[208] *Northumbria case* (n 199) 56E.

[209] ibid 58A (Nourse LJ).

[210] ibid.

Chapter 2 demonstrated that the executive power of the Commonwealth in s 61 derives some content from the royal prerogative. While recent judicial observations confirm that the executive power of the Commonwealth 'cannot be treated as a species of the royal prerogative', the prerogative continues to inform its content.[211] However, the High Court has also emphasised in its recent decisions that the Australian Constitution created a different legal system from that which exists in the United Kingdom. In particular, the Commonwealth and State governments are constituent parts of a federal system of government established by the Australian Constitution. As such, the prerogative powers enjoyed by the Commonwealth Executive Government under s 61 are not coextensive with the prerogative in the United Kingdom.[212] The High Court has recognised that s 61 comprises 'only such of the prerogatives of the Crown as are properly attributable to the Commonwealth'.[213]

While the Australian Constitution sets out the subject matters over which the legislative power of the Commonwealth can be exercised in ss 51 and 52, it does not address the distribution of prerogative powers between the Commonwealth and State governments. As the majority explained in *Cadia Holdings Pty Ltd v New South Wales*,[214]

> the creation of the federation presented issues still not fully resolved of the allocation between the Commonwealth and States of prerogatives which pre-federation had been divided between the Imperial and colonial governments, and of their adaptation to the division of executive authority in the federal system established by the *Constitution*.[215]

In ascertaining the allocation of the prerogatives between the Commonwealth and the States, courts have generally been guided by the distribution of legislative powers effected by the Australian Constitution.[216] There can, however, be difficulties in adapting prerogative powers from the United Kingdom to the federal structure of the Australian Constitution. The exercise of prerogative powers to preserve public safety and to maintain the peace exposes some of these difficulties.

The power to respond to 'a national emergency, an urgent necessity for taking extreme steps for the protection of the realm'[217] appears to fall within the scope of the prerogative. Renfree was of the view that the prerogative regarding the

[211] See, eg, *Tampa case* (n 129) 540 [183] (French J); *Re Ditfort; Ex parte Deputy Commissioner of Taxation* (1988) 19 FCR 347, 369 (Gummow J); *Pape* (n 65) 60 [127] (French CJ). See also Sapienza (n 4) 22; C Saunders, 'The Concept of the Crown' (2015) 38 *Melbourne University Law Review* 873, 891–92.

[212] See also Saunders, 'The Concept of the Crown' (n 211) 891.

[213] *Williams v Commonwealth [No 1]* (2012) 248 CLR 156, 186 [25] (French CJ), 343–44 [488] (Crennan J); *Cadia* (n 129) 226 [86] (Gummow, Hayne, Heydon and Crennan JJ).

[214] *Cadia* (n 129).

[215] ibid 226 [87] (Gummow, Hayne, Heydon and Crennan JJ).

[216] See, eg, *Federal Commissioner of Taxation v Official Liquidator of E O Farley Ltd (in liq)* (1940) 63 CLR 278, 320 (Evatt J); *Cadia* (n 129) 210 [31] (French CJ).

[217] *Burmah Oil* (n 189) 136 (Lord Hodson), quoting with approval *Crown of Leon* (n 195) 603–04 (Earl of Reading CJ); Chitty (n 195) 50.

preservation of public safety, described by the maxim *salus populi suprema lex*, was inherited by the Crown in right of the Commonwealth of Australia and was capable of being exercised by the Commonwealth to deal with 'attack from abroad and domestic violence within'.[218]

Such a power could also be seen as arising directly from s 61, which states that the executive power of the Commonwealth extends to the 'maintenance of this Constitution'.[219] In the *Communist Party case* Williams J defined this phrase to mean 'the protection and safeguarding of something immediately prescribed or authorized by the Constitution without the intervention of Federal legislation'.[220] The notion of 'maintaining' the Constitution contemplates the exercise of executive power to protect the Constitution and the system of government that it establishes.[221] As Gummow, Crennan and Bell JJ observed in *Pape*, it 'conveys the idea of the protection of the body politic or nation of Australia'.[222]

It is not clear whether the prerogative to maintain the peace or deal with 'riot, pestilence and conflagration', as it exists in the United Kingdom, would be regarded by the High Court as being 'attributable to the Commonwealth' rather than the States. The prerogative to maintain the peace in the United Kingdom was understood as being associated with 'keeping law and order'[223] and the Crown's 'undoubted right to see that crime is prevented and justice administered'.[224] These are functions that are not allocated to the Commonwealth by the Australian Constitution. The State governments in Australia have presumptive responsibility for the maintenance of internal law and order, as recognised by s 119 of the Constitution.[225]

While s 119 contemplates circumstances requiring Commonwealth intervention in matters of internal security, it also operates as a limit on the prerogative.[226] By stipulating that the Commonwealth must receive a request from a State before it can intervene in domestic violence occurring within a State, s 119 preserves an important area of responsibility for the States relating to internal security.[227]

The prerogative power to maintain the peace is one that would ordinarily be exercisable by the governments of the States. However, Dixon J recognised

[218] HE Renfree, *The Executive Power of the Commonwealth of Australia* (Sydney, Legal Books, 1984) 466. The Latin phrase *salus populi est suprema lex* translates to 'the welfare of the people, or of the public, is supreme law'.

[219] See also A Twomey, 'Pushing the Boundaries of Executive Power: *Pape*, the Prerogative and Nationhood Powers' (2010) 34 *Melbourne University Law Review* 313, 331, 336; Twomey, 'The French Court' (n 23) 52–53.

[220] *Communist Party case* (n 1) 230 (Williams J).

[221] Sapienza (n 4) 21; Twomey, 'The French Court' (n 23) 52–53; G Winterton, 'The Limits and Use of Executive Power by Government' (2003) 31 *Federal Law Review* 421, 425.

[222] *Pape* (n 65) 83 [215] (Gummow, Crennan and Bell JJ).

[223] *Northumbria case* (n 199) 44B (Croom-Johnson LJ).

[224] ibid.

[225] ibid. See also Zines (n 205) 287, 289–90.

[226] *Sharkey* (n 27) 150–51 (Dixon J); *Thomas* (n 28) 394–95 [247]–[249] (Kirby J). See also Stephenson, 'Fertile Ground' (n 16) 295.

[227] Stephenson, 'Fertile Ground' (n 16) 295. See also White (n 7) 444.

in *Sharkey* that it could be exercised by the Commonwealth, in the absence of a request for assistance from a State, where the domestic violence interfered with the operations of the Commonwealth Government.[228] Therefore, executive action undertaken by the Commonwealth for the purpose of protecting itself or its interests, including the use of the ADF for this purpose, would appear to fall within the breadth of the prerogative to maintain the peace enjoyed by the Commonwealth, rather than the States. As demonstrated above, Part IIIAAA of the *Defence Act* governs the use of the ADF to protect Commonwealth interests and the States and Territories against domestic violence. Therefore, the prerogative with respect to the maintenance of the peace has been partially abrogated or displaced by statute.

Part IIIAAA does not cover the use of the ADF to provide assistance in relation to non-violent civil emergencies. To the extent that an emergency has some connection with an area of Commonwealth responsibility, which includes the subject matters of legislative power in ss 51, 52 and 122 of the Constitution and matters 'appropriate to its position under the Constitution',[229] the Commonwealth may be able to exercise a prerogative to respond to it. However, there has not been any judicial consideration of the issue because the High Court has held that the nationhood power is capable of being exercised to respond to emergencies, as demonstrated by the decision in *Pape*. This raises the question of whether the nationhood power could support the use of the ADF by the Commonwealth Executive Government to respond to civil emergencies in Australia.

## B. The Nationhood Power and National Emergencies

In the decision in *Pape*,[230] examined in Chapter 3, a majority of the High Court accepted that the Commonwealth Executive Government enjoyed, under s 61 of the Constitution, the power to respond to a national financial emergency.[231] In reaching this conclusion, the majority did not appear to consider whether the prerogative powers for the preservation of public safety were available to the Commonwealth, nor whether such powers could be adapted to suit the novel challenges of a national financial emergency.[232] Rather, they derived the power from the character and status of the Commonwealth as the national government of a federal polity. This was evident where French CJ observed that

> [t]he collection of statutory and prerogative powers and non-prerogative capacities form part of, but do not complete, the executive power. They lie within the scope of

[228] Quick and Garran (n 28) 964–65 endorsed in *Sharkey* (n 27) 151 (Dixon J); *Thomas* (n 28) 394 [248] (Kirby J).
[229] *Cadia* (n 129) 226 [86] (Gummow, Hayne, Heydon and Crennan JJ).
[230] *Pape* (n 65).
[231] ibid 23–24 [8]–[9], 63–64 [133]–[134] (French CJ), 91–92 [241]–[243] (Gummow, Crennan and Bell JJ).
[232] See also Twomey, 'Pushing the Boundaries' (n 219) 315.

> s 61, which is informed by history and the common law relevant to the relationship between the Crown and the Parliament. That history and common law emerged from what might be called an organic evolution. Section 61 is an important element of a written constitution for the government of an independent nation. While history and the common law inform its content, it is not a locked display cabinet in a constitutional museum. It is not limited to statutory powers and the prerogative. It has to be capable of serving the proper purposes of a national government.[233]

In similar vein, Gummow, Crennan and Bell JJ stated that

> [t]he conduct of the executive branch of government includes, but involves much more than, enjoyment of the benefit of those preferences, immunities and exceptions which are denied to the citizen and are commonly identified with 'the prerogative'; the executive power of the Commonwealth enables the undertaking of action appropriate to the position of the Commonwealth as a polity created by the Constitution and having regard to the spheres of responsibility vested in it.[234]

Their Honours went on to explain that

> [t]he Executive Government is the arm of government capable of and empowered to respond to a crisis be it war, natural disaster or a financial crisis on the scale here. This power has its roots in the executive power exercised in the United Kingdom up to the time of the adoption of the Constitution but in form today in Australia it is a power to act on behalf of the federal polity.[235]

Chief Justice French accepted that the expenditure of public funds for the purpose of 'avoiding or mitigating the large scale adverse effects' of a global financial crisis on the Australian economy was a 'proper purpose' of national government.[236] The Commonwealth's position was 'peculiar' because the States and Territories did not have the capacity or the resources to implement, within a short time frame, measures that were 'rationally adjudged' as 'avoiding or mitigating' the adverse effects of a national economic crisis in Australia.[237]

For Gummow, Crennan and Bell JJ, on the other hand, the critical feature of the case was the acceptance by the parties that the global financial crisis posed a significant threat to the national economy.[238] This was evident where their Honours remarked that 'this case may be resolved without going beyond the notions of national emergency and the fiscal means of promptly responding to that situation'.[239] In these circumstances, they considered that the determination by the Commonwealth Executive Government of the need for an immediate fiscal stimulus to the national economy was 'somewhat analogous to determining

[233] *Pape* (n 65) 60 [127].
[234] ibid 83 [214].
[235] ibid 89 [233].
[236] ibid 63 [133].
[237] ibid.
[238] ibid 89 [233] (Gummow, Crennan and Bell JJ).
[239] ibid 91 [241].

a state of emergency in circumstances of a natural disaster'.[240] Justices Gummow, Crennan and Bell concluded that the measures in *Pape* were 'peculiarly adapted' to the national government because 'only the Commonwealth has the resources available to respond promptly to the present financial crisis on the scale exemplified by the *Bonus Act*'.[241]

Justices Hayne and Kiefel criticised this aspect of the majority judgment. While they accepted that the Commonwealth Executive Government had power to engage in executive action appropriate to its character and status as a national government, to be ascertained by the application of Mason J's 'peculiarly adapted' test,[242] they did not accept that this power could support the implementation of any measures that the Commonwealth Executive Government deemed necessary to respond to a national crisis or emergency. According to their Honours, the approach adopted by the majority conflated 'distinct questions about ends and means'.[243]

Thus, the majority of the High Court in *Pape* accepted that the nationhood power could, in the circumstances of what was agreed to be a global financial crisis, be invoked by the Commonwealth Executive Government to support the administration of 'short-term fiscal measures to meet adverse economic conditions affecting the nation as a whole'.[244] There are judicial statements in subsequent decisions that suggest that the nationhood power 'arises under the Constitution and has been held capable of responding to events such as a national emergency'.[245]

*Pape*, however, demonstrates that there are limits on the nationhood power, even when it is being exercised to respond to an emergency. In particular, in his judgment in *Pape* French CJ cautioned that the nationhood power could not be equated to 'a general power to manage the national economy'[246] or address problems of 'national concern'.[247] The majority judgments in *Pape* demonstrate that, for the nationhood power to be enlivened to support executive action undertaken in an emergency, the emergency must affect the nation as a whole, such that only the Commonwealth has the resources and capacities to respond to it, as ascertained through the application of Mason J's 'peculiarly adapted' test.

In *Pape* the majority also approved the statement of Mason CJ and Deane and Gaudron JJ in *Davis v Commonwealth* that 'the existence of Commonwealth executive power in areas beyond the express grants of legislative power will ordinarily be clearest where Commonwealth executive or legislative action involves no

[240] ibid 89 [233].
[241] ibid 91 [241].
[242] ibid 116 [328]–[329].
[243] ibid 122 [349].
[244] ibid 63 [133] (French CJ), 91 [241] (Gummow, Crennan and Bell JJ).
[245] *CPCF* (n 129) 568 [150] (Hayne and Bell JJ), 596 [260] (Kiefel J).
[246] *Pape* (n 65) 63 [133].
[247] ibid 24 [10], 63 [133] (French CJ); see also 124–25 [359] and 125 [363]–[364] (Hayne and Kiefel JJ) and 176–77 [509], 192–93 [550]–[552] (Heydon J).

real competition with State executive or legislative competence'.[248] Furthermore, as Brennan J stated in *Davis*, the 'peculiarly adapted' test 'invites consideration of the sufficiency of the powers of the States to engage effectively in the enterprise or activity in question and of the need for national action (whether unilateral or in co-operation with the States) to secure the contemplated benefit'.[249]

In ascertaining whether the nationhood power could support the use by the Commonwealth Executive Government of the ADF to respond to these emergencies, it is significant that the States and Territories have requested assistance under the COMDISPLAN and DACC frameworks. The threshold that must be met to make a request for assistance under COMDISPLAN is that

> all government, community and commercial resources are exhausted or are likely to be exhausted; the jurisdiction is unable to mobilise its own resources (or community and commercial resources) in time; or the Australian Government has a capability that the State or Territory does not have.[250]

The threshold under the *DACC Manual* is in similar terms, namely,

> where the scale of the emergency or disaster exceeds or exhausts the response capacity and capabilities of the State or Territory (government, community and/or commercial) or where resources cannot be mobilised in sufficient time, they may seek Australian Government non-financial assistance, including from Defence.[251]

Where the Commonwealth utilises the ADF to provide assistance to the States and Territory authorities in responding to natural disasters or emergencies, the federal distribution of powers is unaffected by the exercise of Commonwealth executive power.

While the 'peculiarly adapted' test can be applied to determine whether the executive action falls within the subject matters with respect to which the Commonwealth Executive Government may act, where those subject matters are not expressly referred to in the constitutional division of responsibilities between the Commonwealth and the States, it does not clarify the types of executive action the Commonwealth is empowered to undertake in relation to those subject matters, which is a question of the 'depth' of the executive power. This issue did not arise in *Pape*. The executive action undertaken in *Pape*, namely the expenditure of public funds, was an exercise of the Commonwealth's capacity to act as a legal person. Unlike the prerogative, which is capable of being exercised so as to alter or interfere with the rights, duties and status of individuals, an act done in the execution of a capacity 'involves nothing more than the utilisation of a bare capacity or

[248] *Davis v Commonwealth* (1988) 166 CLR 79, 93–94 approved in *Pape* (n 65) 62–63 [131]–[133] (French CJ), 90–91 [239] (Gummow, Crennan and Bell JJ).

[249] *Davis* (n 248) 111.

[250] Australian Government, *COMDISPLAN 2020* (n 157) 5 [1.4.6].

[251] *DACC Manual* (n 149) 1A-3.

permission, which can also be described as ability to act or as a "faculty"'.[252] While the exercise of a capacity may still have legal effects, this is not because the act is 'uniquely that of the Executive Government' but because of the application of the general law to all persons.[253]

As discussed above, the deployments of the ADF for Operation Bushfire Assist and Operation COVID-19 Assist were undertaken in accordance with the DACC framework and COMDISPLAN.[254] The use of the ADF in this capacity does not involve the use or potential use of force against the civilian population, which includes 'any restriction of freedom of movement in the civil community'.[255] However, in responding to natural disasters, ADF members may be required to enter private property without permission and undertake other tasks, such as clearing firebreaks, that may be regarded as coercive activities. Similarly, for Operation COVID-19 assist, ADF personnel have been deployed alongside the State and Territory police to provide assistance in the enforcement of mandatory hotel quarantine and isolation measures and State border closures, which necessarily restrict the freedom of movement of individuals.

The High Court has recognised that there are limitations to the 'depth' of the nationhood power that relate to the capacity of the Commonwealth to undertake executive action that interferes with the legal rights and duties of individuals.[256] Courts have been reluctant to find that s 51(xxxix) can support coercive legislation as incidental to the execution of the nationhood power. In *Pape* French CJ warned that

> [f]uture questions about the application of the executive power to the control or regulation of conduct or activities under coercive laws, absent authority supplied by a statute made under some head of power other than s 51(xxxix) alone, are likely to be answered conservatively.[257]

*Pape* did not resolve the question of whether the nationhood power is, like the prerogative, 'capable of interfering with legal rights of others'[258] or whether it is a 'facultative' capacity to 'engage in enterprises and activities peculiarly adapted to the government of a nation and which cannot otherwise be carried on for the benefit of the nation'.[259] Therefore, while the nationhood power may be capable

[252] *Plaintiff M68/2015 v Minister for Immigration and Border Protection* (2016) 257 CLR 42, 98 [135] (Gageler J).
[253] ibid 98 [135] (Gageler J). See also Twomey, 'The Prerogative and the Courts' (n 4) 81–82.
[254] Australian Department of Defence, 'Defence support to mandatory quarantine measures comments' (n 175); Australian Department of Defence, 'Operation COVID-19 Assist' (Web page, 25 March 2022) news.defence.gov.au/national/latest-updates-operation-covid-19-assist.
[255] *DACC Manual* (n 149) [1.1]; *DACC Policy* (n 149) [1.4], [1.11].
[256] See also Twomey, 'Pushing the Boundaries' (n 219) 339–42; Twomey, 'The Prerogative and the Courts' (n 4) 65–67, 85; Zines (n 205) 280; Moore (n 6) 72–73; P Stephenson, 'Nationhood and Section 61 of the Constitution' (2018) 43 *University of Western Australia Law Review* 149, 164.
[257] *Pape* (n 65) 24 [10] (French CJ).
[258] *Plaintiff M68* (n 252) 98 [135] (Gageler J).
[259] *Victoria v Commonwealth and Hayden* (1975) 134 CLR 338, 397 (Mason J) (*AAP case*). See also Twomey, 'The Prerogative and the Courts' (n 4) 85; Twomey, 'Pushing the Boundaries' (n 219) 339–42.

of being exercised to respond to a national emergency or disaster, it is not clear whether a court would accept that it is capable of supporting coercive executive action undertaken by the ADF to respond to a national emergency in the absence of statutory authorisation.

## V. Conclusion

This chapter has examined the executive power to use the ADF for internal security operations and emergencies in Australia. It demonstrated that Part IIIAAA of the *Defence Act* has put on a statutory footing the use of the ADF to protect a Commonwealth interest or the States and Territories against domestic violence; however, the use of the ADF for non-violent civil emergencies remains an exercise of non-statutory executive power. This chapter exposed the uncertainty about the scope of the nationhood power to support executive action undertaken by the ADF during emergencies that is capable of interfering with the legal rights of individuals.

The next chapter of this book critically examines the reasoning of the majority of the Full Court of the Federal Court of Australia in finding that the nationhood power provided the constitutional basis for coercive action undertaken by the Commonwealth to the entry of non-citizens into Australia. It is demonstrated that this decision sits uncomfortably with the judicial statements that have been considered in this book about the scope and limitations of the nationhood power and, therefore, should not detract from the weight of authority that suggests that there are limits to the 'depth' of the nationhood power.

# 5

# The Nationhood Power and Border Protection

> The power to determine who may come into Australia is so central to its sovereignty that it is not to be supposed that the Government of the nation would lack under the power conferred upon it directly by the Constitution, the ability to prevent people not part of the Australian community, from entering.
>
> Justice Robert French, 2001[1]

The preceding chapters of this book have demonstrated that there are limitations on the scope of the nationhood power. In addition to limits on the 'breadth' of the power, derived from the principle of federalism, Australian courts have recognised that there are limits on the types of executive action that the Commonwealth is empowered to undertake pursuant to the nationhood power. These limits to the 'depth' of the executive power relate to the capacity of the Commonwealth to undertake executive action that interferes with the legal rights and duties of individuals. There is, however, one anomaly: a decision which suggests that the nationhood power *has* added depth to the executive power of the Commonwealth. This decision is *Ruddock v Vadarlis* ('*Tampa case*')[2] and is the focus of this chapter.

In the *Tampa case*, a majority of the Full Court of the Federal Court held that the Commonwealth could, in the absence of supporting legislation, exercise its executive power to detain non-citizens on board a vessel for the purpose of excluding and expelling them from Australian territorial waters, and deploy officers from the Australian Special Air Service Regiment (SAS) for this purpose. The power was described by French J as being 'central' to Australia's status as a sovereign nation.

[1] *Ruddock v Vadarlis* (2001) 110 FCR 491 (*Tampa case*). Reproduced with permission of Thomson Reuters (Professional) Australia Limited, legal.thomsonreuters.com.au.

[2] ibid. Some of the material in this chapter is drawn from the following works and has been reproduced with the permission of the publishers: P Stephenson, 'Nationhood and Section 61 of the Constitution' (2018) 43 *University of Western Australia Law Review* 149; P Stephenson, 'Statutory Displacement of the Prerogative in Australia' in Janina Boughey and Lisa Burton Crawford (eds), *Interpreting Executive Power* (Alexandria, Federation Press, 2020) 203; P Stephenson, 'The Relationship between the Royal Prerogative and Statute in Australia' (2021) 44 *Melbourne University Law Review* 1001.

However, the decision of French J (with whom Beaumont J agreed) has been criticised by scholars as significantly expanding the depth of the executive power of the Commonwealth.[3]

This chapter argues that the majority in the *Tampa case* erred in finding that the nationhood power supported the executive action that was undertaken by the Commonwealth to prevent the entry of non-citizens into Australia. It begins by setting out the political context which gave rise to the *Tampa* litigation in the Federal Court of Australia. It then critically examines the reasoning relied on by French J in finding that the nationhood power supported the activities of exclusion, detention and expulsion. It concludes by demonstrating that French J's judgment in the *Tampa case* sits uncomfortably with statements that have been made by the High Court about the nature and scope of the nationhood power. It is argued that the majority decision in the *Tampa case* should not detract from the weight of authority that suggests that there are limits to the 'depth' of the nationhood power.

## I. The *Tampa Case*

On 26 August 2001, at the request of the Australian Maritime Safety Authority, a Norwegian container ship, the *MV Tampa*, diverted its course from Fremantle to Singapore to render assistance to a sinking Indonesian fishing boat, the *Palapa*, in the Indian Ocean, about 75 nautical miles north of Christmas Island.[4] The Captain of the *Tampa*, Arne Rinnan, rescued 433 people from the sinking vessel.[5] He then proceeded to head towards the Indonesian port of Merak on the

[3] See, eg, B Selway, 'All at Sea – Constitutional Assumptions and "the Executive Power of the Commonwealth"' (2003) 31 *Federal Law Review* 495; E Willheim, 'MV Tampa: The Australian Response' (2003) 15 *International Journal of Refugee Law* 159; S Evans, 'The Rule of Law, Constitutionalism and the MV Tampa' (2002) 13 *Public Law Review* 94; L Zines, 'The Inherent Executive Power of the Commonwealth' (2005) 16 *Public Law Review* 279; G Winterton, 'The Limits and Use of Executive Power by Government' (2003) 31 *Federal Law Review* 421; G Winterton, 'The Relationship between Commonwealth Legislative and Executive Power' (2004) 25 *Adelaide Law Review* 21; P Gerangelos, 'Parliament, the Executive, the Governor-General and the Republic: The George Winterton Thesis' in HP Lee and P Gerangelos (eds), *Constitutional Advancement in a Frozen Continent: Essays in Honour of George Winterton* (Annandale, Federation Press, 2009) 189, 193–98; P Gerangelos, 'The Executive Power of the Commonwealth of Australia: Section 61 of the Commonwealth Constitution, "Nationhood" and the Future of the Prerogative' (2012) 12 *Oxford University Commonwealth Law Journal* 97; D Rothwell, 'The Law of the Sea and the MV Tampa Incident: Reconciling Maritime Principles with Coastal State Sovereignty' (2002) 13 *Public Law Review* 118; H Pringle and E Thompson, 'The Tampa Affair and the Role of the Australian Parliament' (2002) 13 *Public Law Review* 128; P Mathew, 'Australian Refugee Protection in the Wake of the Tampa' (2002) 96 *American Journal of International Law* 661; G Duke, 'Popular Sovereignty and the Nationhood Power' (2017) 45 *Federal Law Review* 415.

[4] *Tampa case* (n 1) 522 [131] (French J). See also Senate Select Committee on A Certain Maritime Incident, 'Inquiry into A Certain Maritime Incident' (Main Report, Parliament of Australia, 23 October 2002) 1 [1.2] ('Maritime Incident Report').

[5] *Tampa case* (n 1) 522 [131] (French J).

southern coast of Java, but subsequently changed course towards the Australian Territory of Christmas Island because the rescued passengers threatened to harm themselves if he did not.[6]

The following day, when the *Tampa* was approximately 13.5 nautical miles off Christmas Island, the Secretary of the Department of Immigration and Multicultural Affairs, Neville Nixon, advised Captain Rinnan that 'the Australian Government at the highest level formally requests that you not approach Christmas Island'.[7] The Administrator of Christmas Island, Bill Taylor, was also advised by the Cabinet Office to prohibit the *Tampa* from entering Australian territorial waters and directed the Harbour Master to close the Christmas Island port at Flying Fish Cove. On 27 August 2001 an order came into effect prohibiting 'all boat movements in and out of the Cove'.[8]

Captain Rinnan had reported concerns to Australian authorities about the medical condition of the rescued persons and welfare of his crew, and issued several distress calls, but had not received any assistance. Accordingly, on the morning of 29 August 2001, contrary to the orders given by Australian officials, Rinnan steered the *Tampa* into Australian territorial waters, stopping about four nautical miles off Christmas Island.[9] Two hours later, the Commonwealth deployed 45 SAS officers from the ADF to seize control of the *Tampa*.[10] The officers rendered medical assistance to the rescued persons and provided security for the crew of the vessel. The presence of the SAS officers also ensured that Captain Rinnan would not make any attempt to move the *Tampa* into the port at Christmas Island.[11] The rescued persons had no access to external communications while on board the *Tampa*.[12]

The *Migration Act 1958* (Cth) conferred extensive powers on the Commonwealth relating to expulsion and detention[13] that could be exercised where 'unlawful non-citizens'[14] had entered the 'migration zone'.[15] Crucially, the port at Christmas Island was within Australia's migration zone for the purposes of the *Migration Act*. Accordingly, had the *Tampa* entered the port, the Commonwealth Government would have been required to determine the status of the rescued persons pursuant

[6] ibid 522–23 [132].

[7] ibid 523 [134].

[8] ibid 523 [133]. The order was an exercise of the Harbour Master's powers conferred by the *Shipping and Pilotage Act 1967* (WA) s 5.

[9] *Tampa case* (n 1) 524 [136].

[10] ibid.

[11] ibid 529 [150].

[12] ibid.

[13] *Migration Act 1958* (Cth) ss 189, 198–99.

[14] An 'unlawful non-citizen' for the purpose of ss 13 and 14 of the *Migration Act 1958* (Cth) is a person that does not hold a visa entitling them to enter Australia.

[15] *Migration Act 1958* (Cth) s 189. Section 5 of the *Migration Act 1958* (Cth) defined 'migration zone' as 'the area consisting of the States, the Territories, Australian resource installations and Australian sea installations and, to avoid doubt, includes: (a) land that is part of a State or Territory at mean low water; and (b) sea within the limits of both a State or a Territory and a port; and (c) piers, or similar structures, any part of which is connected to such land or to ground under such sea; but does not include sea within the limits of a State or Territory but not in a port'.

to the *Migration Act*.[16] However, in keeping with its political commitment to protect Australia's sovereignty and the integrity of its borders from the 'rising flood of unauthorised arrivals',[17] the Commonwealth Government wanted to preclude the rescued persons from having access to the procedures for protection visas under the *Migration Act*.[18] Accordingly, the Commonwealth argued instead that it could exercise its inherent executive power to prevent non-citizens from entering Australia.

On the evening of 29 August 2001 – the same day that the *Tampa* had entered Australian territorial waters contrary to the request of government officials – the Prime Minister, John Howard, introduced the *Border Protection Bill 2001* (Cth) ('the Bill') in the House of Representatives. The Bill was a drastic piece of legislation that purported to retrospectively validate the actions taken by the Commonwealth in responding to the *Tampa* affair.[19] It conferred wide discretion on Commonwealth officers to use coercive force and exercise powers[20] that were unreviewable by Australian courts.[21] It also granted Commonwealth officers immunity from civil or criminal proceedings in respect of any action taken.[22]

In his second reading speech for the Bill, the Prime Minister invoked the 'national interest' in an attempt to justify the Bill being rushed through the Parliament. Prime Minister Howard presented the *Tampa* affair as posing a real and unprecedented threat to Australia's sovereignty, describing the Bill as 'an unusual bill for unusual circumstances'.[23] The *Tampa* affair had, in the Prime Minister's view, created

> an unusual situation, but it does require a very quick, comprehensive and unambiguous response from the representatives of the Australian people. It is in the national interest that this vessel not be allowed to remain in Australian territorial waters. It is in our national interest that this vessel be returned to international waters. It is in the national interest that we have the power to prevent beyond any argument people infringing the sovereignty of this country. One of the great enduring responsibilities of a government is to protect the integrity of its borders. There is no doubt that the integrity of the borders of Australia has been under increasing threat from the rising flood of unauthorised arrivals ...[24]

[16] *Migration Act 1958* (Cth) s 15. A similar point was made in M Crock, B Saul and A Dastyari, *Future Seekers II: Refugees and Irregular Migration in Australia* (Annandale, Federation Press, 2006) 22–23, 109–10.

[17] Commonwealth, *Parliamentary Debates*, House of Representatives, 29 August 2001, 30517–18, 30569–70 (John Howard, Prime Minister).

[18] See also Willheim (n 3) 180. It is generally understood that the Commonwealth is not free to choose to exercise the prerogative where statute exists that covers the same field as that occupied by the prerogative: T Poole, 'United Kingdom: The Royal Prerogative' (2010) 8 *International Journal of Constitutional Law* 146, 148.

[19] See also Pringle and Thompson (n 3) 133–35; Mathew (n 3) 661–63; Evans (n 3) 99–101.

[20] Border Protection Bill 2001 (Cth) ss 4(1), 4(3), 5.

[21] ibid ss 4(2), 8, 7, 10.

[22] ibid s 7.

[23] Commonwealth, *Parliamentary Debates*, House of Representatives, 29 August 2001, 30570 (John Howard, Prime Minister).

[24] ibid.

Similar rhetoric was adopted by other members of the Howard Government. There were references made to stopping the 'insidious trade of smuggling'[25] and 'illegal conspiracy to breach the laws of Australia'.[26] Ruddock spoke of the 'growing threats to our borders', citing the increase in unauthorised arrivals by boat from 921 in 1988–99 to 4,141 in 2000–01.[27] In a radio interview, Prime Minister Howard declared that he would 'draw a line on what is increasingly becoming an uncontrollable number of illegal arrivals in this country'.[28] The *Tampa* affair was characterised as a 'crisis' that warranted a swift and determined legislative response.[29]

Nevertheless, the Bill was defeated in the Senate. Several members of the Opposition criticised the Bill on the basis that the 'draconian' measures in it were unnecessary in the circumstances. Anthony Albanese remarked that 'this is not a refugee crisis – 400 people on a boat do not represent a crisis'.[30] The Leader of the Opposition, Kim Beazley, did not accept that the *Tampa* affair was a 'national catastrophe of some description that required a piece of legislation to put beyond doubt … the capacity of the Commonwealth to respond to it'.[31] He was of the view that a call out of the ADF

> is for extreme circumstances arising with a possible threat to the security of the nation, the survival of the government or the possibility of riot and revolution on the streets, in circumstances in which it is necessary to call out the military to save social cohesion and to save the operation of government and, in some circumstances, to save people who are the subject of terrorist threat – an order of issue and problem miles higher than the problems that we happen to be dealing with here, important though they are.[32]

The Prime Minister, however, was adamant that the rescued persons on board the *Tampa* would not be allowed to enter the port at Christmas Island. In Prime Minister Howard's view, it was Australia's sovereign right 'to effectively control its borders and to decide who comes here and under what circumstances and Australia has no intention of surrendering or compromising that right'.[33]

It was in this highly politicised environment that the *Tampa* litigation took place. On 31 August 2001 proceedings were commenced in the Federal Court

[25] ibid 30685 (Philip Ruddock, Minister for Immigration and Multicultural Affairs).

[26] Commonwealth, *Parliamentary Debates*, Senate, 30 August 2001, 27095 (Robert Hill, Minister for Defence).

[27] Commonwealth, *Parliamentary Debates*, House of Representatives, 18 September 2001, 30869 (Philip Ruddock, Minister for Immigration and Multicultural Affairs). See also Commonwealth, *Parliamentary Debates*, House of Representatives, 19 September 2001, 30968 (De-Anne Kelly).

[28] N Mitchell, Interview with John Howard, Prime Minister of Australia (Radio 3AW, Melbourne, 31 August 2001) quoted in Maritime Incident Report (n 4).

[29] The government has been described as 'manufacturing a crisis' in Crock, Saul and Dastyari (n 16) 5. See further T Poole, 'The Law of Emergency and Reason of State' in E Criddle (ed), *Human Rights in Emergencies* (New York, Cambridge University Press, 2016).

[30] Commonwealth, *Parliamentary Debates*, House of Representatives, 30 August 2001, 30729 (Anthony Albanese).

[31] ibid 29 August 2001, 30571 (Kim Beazley).

[32] ibid 30 August 2001, 30680–81 (Kim Beazley).

[33] ibid 29 August 2001, 30517–18 (John Howard, Prime Minister).

of Australia by the Victorian Council for Civil Liberties and Mr Eric Vadarlis against the Minister for Immigration and Multicultural Affairs, Attorney-General, Minister for Defence and the Commonwealth.[34] The applications were heard together by North J. The applicants claimed relief in the nature of mandamus, habeas corpus and injunction.

## A. The Decision of North J at First Instance

The applicants also sought, and were granted, an interlocutory injunction restraining the respondents from removing the *Tampa* from Australian territorial waters until the commencement of the hearing on 1 September 2001. On that date the Australian government had concluded agreements with New Zealand and Nauru for the rescued persons on the *Tampa* to be processed in these countries.[35] The rescued persons were to be transferred from the *Tampa* to an Australian troopship, the *HMAS Manoora*, which would sail to Port Moresby in Papua New Guinea, and from there they would be flown to either New Zealand or Nauru.[36] The parties to the proceedings agreed on 3 September 2001 that the interlocutory injunction would be lifted, provided that the rescued persons remained on the *Manoora* until the determination of the proceedings.[37]

Justice North handed down his decision on 11 September 2001. He found that the applicants lacked standing to seek relief in the nature of an injunction or mandamus. However, North J held that the rescued persons had been unlawfully detained on the *Tampa* and made the order of relief in the nature of a writ of habeas corpus to secure their release. In finding for the applicants, North J ordered that the rescued persons be released from the *Tampa* and brought to the Australian mainland.

Justice North found that the Commonwealth respondents had exercised complete control of the rescued persons, as evidenced by the closure of the port at Christmas Island, the prohibition of communication with the rescued persons and the lack of consultation with them about the agreements with Nauru and New Zealand.[38] Having concluded that there was total restraint on the freedom of the rescued persons, North J then considered whether the detention was lawful. As the Commonwealth had chosen not to exercise powers conferred on it under the *Migration Act*, the Commonwealth Solicitor-General argued that the actions

[34] *Victorian Council for Civil Liberties v Minister for Immigration and Multicultural Affairs* (2001) 110 FCR 452 (*VCCL case*).

[35] ibid 464–65 [40]. See also Department of the Prime Minister and Cabinet, 'Joint Press Conference with the Minister for Immigration the Hon Philip Ruddock MP' (Transcript 11753, Sydney, 1 September 2001).

[36] *VCCL case* (n 34) 466–67 [42].

[37] ibid.

[38] ibid 473–74 [81]–[82].

taken by the Commonwealth were a valid exercise of the prerogative to expel aliens. On this question, North J found that the comprehensive regime in the *Migration Act* relating to the exclusion and deportation of aliens had abrogated the prerogative power in this area.[39]

In North J's view, the role of the Court in this case was to ensure that the Commonwealth Executive was exercising its power lawfully. Justice North therefore rejected the Commonwealth Solicitor-General's contention that 'the Court should not stand in the way of the exercise by the Executive of its attempt to protect the borders of Australia'.[40] His Honour pointed out that the Executive had chosen not to exercise the powers conferred on it by the *Migration Act*, electing instead to rely on inherent executive power to exclude, detain and expel the rescued persons.[41] Justice North concluded that the rescued persons had, therefore, been unlawfully detained by the Commonwealth and ordered that the Commonwealth release them and have them brought to a place on the Australian mainland.[42]

## B. The Decision of the Full Court of the Federal Court of Australia on Appeal

The Commonwealth successfully appealed the decision of North J to the Full Court of the Federal Court, consisting of Black CJ, and French and Beaumont JJ. The subsequent application for special leave to appeal the Federal Court's decision was refused by the High Court.

The Federal Court was required to consider two important constitutional questions, namely whether the executive power of the Commonwealth included a power to exclude, detain and expel non-citizens in the absence of statutory authorisation and, secondly, if it did, whether this power had been abrogated or displaced by the *Migration Act*.

Justice French (with whom Beaumont J agreed) delivered the main majority judgment, finding that the actions taken by the Commonwealth to effect the exclusion and expulsion of the rescued persons were within the scope of the executive power, and there had been no detention of the rescued persons by the Commonwealth Government. Furthermore, the *Migration Act* had not displaced the inherent executive power. Chief Justice Black dissented. In his view, the Commonwealth did not possess any non-statutory or prerogative powers to detain the rescued persons on board the *Tampa* and, even if it did, those powers had been abrogated by the *Migration Act*.

[39] ibid 481 [120], 482 [122].
[40] ibid 477 [102].
[41] ibid. *cf* Poole, 'The Law of Emergency' (n 29) 148.
[42] *VCCL case* (n 34) 473 [81], 474 [86], 482 [122].

## II. The *Tampa Case:* Expanding the 'Depth' of the Executive Power?

The majority in the *Tampa case* found that the Commonwealth could, in the absence of statutory authorisation, exercise an inherent executive power to prevent the entry of non-citizens into Australia. This included detaining non-citizens on board a vessel in order to effect their exclusion and expulsion from Australian territorial waters and the deployment of officers from the SAS for this purpose.[43] The power was described by French J as being 'central' to Australia's status as a sovereign nation. While French J eschewed any reference to the nationhood power in his judgment in the *Tampa case*, his reliance on the reasoning of Jacobs J in *Victoria v Commonwealth and Hayden* ('*AAP case*')[44] and Brennan J in *Davis v Commonwealth*[45] suggested that the nationhood power provided the constitutional basis for the executive action undertaken by the Commonwealth, and there is support for this view in the academic literature.[46]

In the *Tampa case* French J seemingly rejected the proposition that the depth of the executive power of the Commonwealth is limited to the prerogative powers of the Crown, quoting with approval remarks made by Gummow J in *Re Ditfort; Ex parte Deputy Commissioner of Taxation*[47] that 'in Australia … one looks not to the content of the prerogative in Britain, but rather to s 61 of the Constitution, by which the executive power of the Commonwealth was vested in the Crown'.[48] Justice French elaborated on this statement where he explained:

> The Executive power of the Commonwealth under s 61 cannot be treated as a species of the royal prerogative … While the Executive power may derive some of its content by reference to the royal prerogative, it is a power conferred as part of a negotiated federal compact expressed in a written *Constitution* distributing powers between the three arms of government reflected in Chs I, II and III of the *Constitution* and, as to legislative powers, between the polities that comprise the federation. The power is subject, not only to the limitations as to subject matter that flow directly from the *Constitution* but also to the laws of the Commonwealth made under it.[49]

In his examination of the executive power of the Commonwealth, French J approved the remarks of Jacobs J in the *AAP case* and Brennan J in *Davis* that s 61

[43] The majority concluded that the executive action taken by the Commonwealth could not 'constitute a restraint upon their liberty': *Tampa case* (n 1) 547–48 [212], 548 [214] (French CJ), 514 [95] (Beaumont J). This is arguable, especially as the rescued persons on board the *MV Tampa* had no access to external communications while on board the vessel and could not leave it. See further ibid 511 [75], 511–12 [80] (Black CJ); Willheim (n 3) 181–88.

[44] *Victoria v Commonwealth and Hayden* (1975) 134 CLR 338 (*AAP case*).

[45] *Davis v Commonwealth* (1988) 166 CLR 79.

[46] See especially Winterton, 'The Limits' (n 3) 428–33; Winterton, 'The Relationship' (n 3) 29–36; Zines (n 3).

[47] *Re Ditfort; Ex parte Deputy Commissioner of Taxation* (1988) 19 FCR 347.

[48] ibid 369 (Gummow J), quoted with approval in the *Tampa case* (n 1) 538–39 [179].

[49] *Tampa case* (n 1) 540 [183].

imports 'the idea of Australia as a nation' and assigns to the Executive functions relating generally to 'the protection and advancement of the Australian nation'.[50] According to French J, the depth of the executive power conferred by s 61 was 'to be measured by reference to Australia's status as a sovereign nation and by reference to the terms of the *Constitution* itself'.[51]

The majority decision in the *Tampa case* has been criticised by scholars as significantly expanding the scope of the executive power of the Commonwealth.[52] As Ernst Willheim has observed, 'issues of external sovereignty are legally distinct from issues as to the internal distribution of powers as between the executive and the legislative branches of government'.[53] It may be that in international law the Commonwealth, as a sovereign polity, possesses the 'right' to determine who may enter its territory.[54] That fact alone does not resolve the question of which branch of government, namely the Parliament or the Executive, should be conferred with the power to exercise that right.[55]

Justice French reasoned that Australia's acquisition of sovereignty had assigned 'the gatekeeping function' to the Commonwealth Executive.[56] The 'gatekeeping function' – which was described as the power to determine who may enter Australian territory and the Australian community – was reflected in the conferral of powers on the Commonwealth Parliament to make laws with respect to naturalisation and aliens (s 51(xix)), immigration and emigration (s 51(xxvii)) and the influx of criminals (s 51(xxviii)).[57] Justice French was satisfied that the executive power of the Commonwealth extended to these subject matters, which were, in his opinion, 'central to the expression of Australia's status and sovereignty as a nation'.[58]

The question as to whether the executive power of the Commonwealth extended to the subject matters of 'aliens' and 'immigration' is a question of *breadth*.[59] There was no dispute in the *Tampa case* that these subject matters fell within an area of responsibility allocated to the Commonwealth by the Constitution. The main issue in the *Tampa case* was whether the Commonwealth Executive could undertake coercive activities of exclusion, detention and expulsion without statutory

[50] *Davis* (n 45) 110, citing *AAP case* (n 44) 406 (Jacobs J), quoted in *Tampa case* (n 1) 539 [180] (French J).

[51] *Tampa case* (n 1) 542 [191].

[52] See, eg, Selway (n 3); Zines (n 3); Willheim (n 3); Evans (n 3); Winterton, 'The Limits' (n 3); Winterton, 'The Relationship' (n 3); Gerangelos, 'Parliament' (n 3) 193–98; Rothwell (n 3); Pringle and Thompson (n 3); Mathew (n 3).

[53] Willheim (n 3) 186–87. See also Zines (n 3) 291–92. Similar observations were made in *CPCF v Minister for Immigration and Border Protection* (2015) 255 CLR 514, 597 [265] (Kiefel J).

[54] *CPCF* (n 53) 597 [264] (Kiefel J).

[55] See also Evans (n 3) 97; Willheim (n 3) 186–87.

[56] *Tampa case* (n 1) 541.

[57] ibid 542–43 [192].

[58] ibid 542 [192].

[59] G Winterton, *Parliament, the Executive and the Governor-General: A Constitutional Analysis* (Melbourne, Melbourne University Press, 1983) 27–47. See also Zines (n 3) 281; Evans (n 3) 97.

authorisation.[60] It was, therefore, a question of *depth* that required an analysis of the existence and scope of the prerogative powers incorporated in s 61.[61]

Chief Justice Black adopted this approach in his dissent. His Honour confined his analysis to a consideration of the existence and scope of the prerogative power relating to aliens. At the beginning of his judgment, Black CJ stated that it was a general principle of law that the Commonwealth Executive could not, in the absence of statutory authority, subject anyone in Australia to detention. In particular, he referred to the following statement in *Chu Kheng Lim v Minister for Immigration, Local Government and Ethnic Affairs* ('*Lim*')[62] that

> [s]ince the common law knows neither letter de cachet nor other executive warrant authorising arbitrary arrest or detention, any officer of the Commonwealth who purports to authorise or enforce the detention in custody of such an alien without judicial mandate will be acting lawfully only to the extent that his or her conduct is justified by valid statutory provision.[63]

Chief Justice Black carefully analysed the cases cited by the Commonwealth Solicitor-General in support of a Crown prerogative to expel aliens.[64] The cases did not, in his Honour's view, resolve the question of whether this particular prerogative had been extinguished, either because legislation had abrogated it, or because the continued existence of the prerogative was incompatible with modern constitutional jurisprudence.[65] The Chief Justice concluded that 'it is, at best, doubtful that the asserted prerogative continues to exist at common law'.[66] The depth of the executive power, then, was measured by Black CJ according to the prerogative powers of the Crown. Indeed, his Honour observed that

> [i]t would be a very strange circumstance if the at best doubtful and historically long-unused power to exclude or expel should emerge in a strong modern form from s 61 of the *Constitution* by virtue of general conceptions of 'the national interest'. That is all the more so when according to English constitutional theory new prerogative powers cannot be created …[67]

Chief Justice Black concluded that even if the Commonwealth had possessed a prerogative or other non-statutory executive power to expel non-citizens, it had been abrogated by Parliament through the enactment of the *Migration Act*.[68]

[60] Simon Evans observed that French J did not distinguish between the subject matters of executive power and the activities which can be undertaken in relation to those subject matters in Evans (n 3) 97.

[61] Winterton, *Parliament* (n 59) 115–17; Zines (n 3) 281; Evans (n 3) 97.

[62] *Chu Kheng Lim v Minister for Immigration, Local Government and Ethnic Affairs* (1992) 176 CLR 1.

[63] ibid 19 (Brennan Deane and Dawson JJ); see also 13 (Mason CJ), 63 (McHugh J), quoted with approval in the *Tampa case* (n 1) 495 [5] (Black CJ).

[64] See especially *Musgrove v Toy* [1891] UKPC 16; [1891] AC 272; *Ex parte Lo Pak* (1888) 9 LR (NSW) 221; *Ex parte Leong Kum* (1888) 9 LR (NSW) 251; *Robtelmes v Brenan* (1906) 4 CLR 395; *Attorney-General (Canada) v Cain* [1906] UKPC 55; [1906] AC 542.

[65] *Tampa case* (n 1) 498 [19]–[20].

[66] ibid 500–01 [29].

[67] ibid 501 [30].

[68] *VCCL case* (n 34) 481 [120], 482 [122].

The *Migration Act* provided 'a comprehensive regime for the control of Australia's borders'.[69] Accordingly, there could be 'no parallel Executive right in the area expressly covered' by this legislation.[70]

The approach adopted by Black CJ in the *Tampa case* took account of the British constitutional history and context that had traditionally informed the content and scope of s 61, and cohered with earlier decisions of the High Court.[71] In particular, *Barton v Commonwealth*[72] was a decision of the High Court that raised a similar issue to the *Tampa case*, namely whether the Commonwealth could exercise its executive power to make a request for extradition from Brazil. As Australia did not have an extradition treaty with Brazil, the *Extradition (Foreign States) Act 1966–1973* (Cth) ('*Extradition Act*') did not apply. The Court accepted that the Crown prerogative to seek and accept the detention of a fugitive pending extradition[73] and surrender of a fugitive[74] from a non-treaty state was incorporated in s 61 of the Constitution and exercisable by the Commonwealth in the absence of statutory authorisation.

Furthermore, in *Johnson v Kent*[75] the Court considered the depth of the executive power of the Commonwealth. In that case, the Commonwealth Government proposed to establish a communications tower, as well as a restaurant and viewing facilities, on Black Mountain in Canberra. The issue in that case was whether the Commonwealth Executive could, in the absence of statutory authorisation, undertake these activities. The case did not raise the issue of breadth because the subject matter of the executive power fell within the territories power in s 122 of the Constitution.[76] In considering the depth of the executive power, the Court found that the prerogative supported the Commonwealth developing its own land.[77] Furthermore, there was no intention in the *Post and Telegraph Act 1901–1970* (Cth), *Wireless Telegraphy Act 1905–1966* (Cth) or *Broadcasting and Television Act 1942–1969* (Cth) to limit or confine the exercise of the prerogative in the Australian Capital Territory.[78]

In the *Tampa case*, however, French J gave short shrift to any discussion about the continued existence of the prerogative to expel aliens. Writing extra-curially, the late Justice Bradley Selway suggested that French J adopted an approach that was premised on an assumption that s 61 should be interpreted in the same way as Article 2(1) of the US Constitution.[79] However, the powers of the US Executive,

[69] *Tampa case* (n 1) 507 [60], 509 [64].
[70] ibid 507 [61].
[71] See also Zines (n 3) 281; Winterton, 'The Relationship' (n 3) 30–31; Gerangelos, 'The Executive Power' (n 3) 105–12.
[72] *Barton v Commonwealth* (1974) 131 CLR 477.
[73] ibid 489–90 (McTiernan and Menzies JJ).
[74] ibid 485–86 (Barwick CJ).
[75] *Johnson v Kent* (1975) 132 CLR 164.
[76] See also Winterton, 'The Relationship' (n 3) 30.
[77] *Johnson* (n 75) 169–70 (Barwick CJ), 174 (Jacobs J).
[78] ibid 170 (Barwick CJ).
[79] Selway (n 3) 498–501.

in contrast to the Commonwealth, do not include the prerogative powers of the Crown. The US Constitution confers on the US Executive all powers and functions necessary to carry out its constitutional responsibilities.[80] Therefore, while it is unnecessary for the US Supreme Court to consider the extent to which the prerogatives may be incorporated in the US Constitution, the same cannot be said of Australian courts when interpreting the Australian Constitution. Indeed, French J relied on the inherent executive nationhood power, rather than the prerogative powers of the Crown, to support the executive action in the *Tampa case*. Justice French reasoned that

> the Executive power of the Commonwealth, absent statutory extinguishment or abridgement, would extend to a power to prevent the entry of non-citizens and to do such things as are necessary to effect such exclusion … The power to determine who may come into Australia is so central to its sovereignty that it is not to be supposed that the Government of the nation would lack under the power conferred upon it directly by the *Constitution*, the ability to prevent people not part of the Australia[n] community, from entering.[81]

In the *Tampa case* then, the nationhood power provided the constitutional basis for the detention of non-citizens on board the *Tampa* by SAS officers. The majority denied that there was detention, concluding that 'the executive action taken by the Commonwealth could not "constitute a restraint upon their liberty"'.[82] In French J's view, the rescued persons on board the *Tampa* 'had no right to land'.[83] This finding that there was no detention in the *Tampa case* is clearly arguable. There were a number of factors, referred to by both North J at first instance and later by Black CJ, which suggested that the Commonwealth was 'committed to retaining control of the fate of the rescuees in all respects'.[84] The rescued persons had no access to external communications and could not leave the vessel. Furthermore, their movements on board the vessel were controlled by the SAS officers.[85] As Black CJ concluded in his dissent, the rescued persons on board the *Tampa* were 'in a real and practical sense, detained by the Commonwealth'.[86]

It is a principle of the common law that the Executive cannot, through the exercise of its prerogative power alone, deprive an individual of liberty.[87] The majority's finding in the *Tampa case* that the nationhood power supported the impugned executive action sits uncomfortably with the statements that have been made by the High Court about its nature and scope. It was demonstrated in Chapters 3 and 4 of this book that the nationhood power has found judicial support to the extent that it is a facultative capacity to 'engage in enterprises and

[80] ibid 499.
[81] *Tampa case* (n 1) 543 [193].
[82] ibid 547–48 [212], 548 [214] (French CJ), 514 [95] (Beaumont J).
[83] ibid 547–48 [212] (French J).
[84] ibid 511 [78] (Black CJ), referring to *VCCL case* (n 34) 472–73 [77]–[81] (North J).
[85] *Tampa case* (n 1) 511–12 [80].
[86] ibid 511 [77].
[87] *Lim* (n 62) 19 (Brennan, Deane and Dawson JJ) affirmed in the *Tampa case* (n 1) 495 [5] (Black CJ).

activities peculiarly adapted to the government of a nation and which cannot otherwise be carried on for the benefit of the nation'.[88] However, the executive action undertaken by the Commonwealth in the *Tampa case* involved coercive action that was denied to the Executive by the common law. Chief Justice Black made a similar observation in his judgment in the *Tampa case*:

> The Australian cases in which the Executive power has had an 'interest of the nation' ingredient can be contrasted with those in which such a power has been asserted for coercive purposes. Thus, this Executive power has been validly used to set up the Australian Bicentennial Authority … and the CSIRO, but has been held not to be available to sustain deportation; detention or extradition of a fugitive; the arrest of a person believed to have committed a felony abroad; the arbitrary denial of mail and telephone services; or compulsion to attend to give evidence or to produce documents in an inquiry.[89]

This statement of Black CJ recognises that, apart from the majority decision in the *Tampa case*, the authorities do not support the finding that the nationhood power extends to the coercive activities of exclusion, detention and expulsion of non-citizens in the absence of statutory authorisation. In the cases where the nationhood power has provided the constitutional basis for the impugned executive action, the legality of the enterprise or activity was not in dispute because they involved the exercise of the capacities of the Commonwealth shared with legal persons and therefore fell within the depth of the executive power.[90] The statements made by members of the Court in those earlier decisions certainly appear to reject the notion that the nationhood power would be capable of supporting coercive action undertaken by the Commonwealth Executive without statutory authorisation. It will be recalled that in *Davis*, for example, Brennan J held that 'where the Executive Government engages in [an] activity in order to advance the nation – an essentially facultative function – the execution of executive power is not the occasion for a wide impairment of individual freedom'.[91]

Two recent decisions of the High Court concerning the Commonwealth's controversial border protection policy, 'Operation Sovereign Borders', cast further doubt on whether the nationhood power could support coercive executive action taken to prevent the entry of non-citizens in Australia.

## A. *CPCF v Minister for Immigration and Border Protection*

*CPCF v Minister for Immigration and Border Protection*[92] concerned the constitutional validity of the Commonwealth's detention of asylum seekers on board an

[88] A Twomey, 'Pushing the Boundaries of Commonwealth Executive Power: *Pape*, the Prerogative and Nationhood Powers' (2010) 34 *Melbourne University Law Review* 313, 339.
[89] *Tampa case* (n 1) 501 [31] (references omitted).
[90] See also Twomey, 'Pushing the Boundaries' (n 88) 339; Zines (n 3) 280.
[91] *Davis* (n 45) 112–13 (Brennan J). See also Twomey, 'Pushing the Boundaries' (n 88) 327.
[92] *CPCF* (n 53).

Australian vessel but outside Australia's territorial waters.[93] On 29 June 2014 an Australian border protection vessel intercepted an Indian flagged vessel approximately 16 nautical miles off the coast of Christmas Island. The Indian vessel became unseaworthy after it caught fire, and the 156 passengers, including the plaintiff, were transferred to the Australian vessel.[94] Following a decision of the National Security Committee of Cabinet on 1 July 2014, the Commonwealth detained the passengers on board the Australian vessel, while they were transported to India pursuant to the *Maritime Powers Act 2013* (Cth) ('*MPA*').[95] Australia and India did not, however, have an agreement whereby India would receive asylum seekers. Accordingly, the Australian vessel remained in waters near India for about 12 days, from 10 July 2014 until 22 July 2014, while diplomatic negotiations between the two countries took place. It subsequently became apparent that Australia would not be able to reach an agreement with India within a reasonable time.[96] The Minister for Immigration and Border Protection then directed the Australian vessel to sail to Australian territory, namely the Cocos (Keeling) Islands, where the passengers disembarked and were taken into immigration detention.[97]

The plaintiff claimed that he had been unlawfully detained on the Australian border protection vessel for a period of 27 days, from 1 July 2014 to 27 July 2014. The detention which gave rise to the claim had occurred outside of Australia's territorial waters. The High Court was required to determine whether the steps taken by the Commonwealth for the purpose of preventing the plaintiff entering Australia, as well as the detention, were authorised by the *MPA* or, alternatively, non-statutory executive power. The majority, consisting of French CJ, and Crennan, Gageler and Keane JJ (Hayne and Bell JJ, and Kiefel J dissenting) concluded that the action taken by the Commonwealth, including the detention, was authorised by legislation, namely the *MPA*. Nevertheless, five members of the Court considered the scope of the Commonwealth's non-statutory executive power in s 61 of the Constitution.

Chief Justice French and Keane J reiterated that the Commonwealth possessed this inherent power, but only Keane J accepted that it would have supported the Commonwealth's actions in this case.[98] Justice Keane cited French J's judgment in the *Tampa case* with approval. He concluded that it 'can hardly be controversial' that the executive power conferred by s 61 extended to 'the compulsory removal

[93] For a critical analysis of this decision see P Billings, 'Operation Sovereign Borders and Interdiction at Sea: *CPCF v Minister for Immigration and Border Protection*' (2016) 23 *Australian Journal of Administrative Law* 76; J Stellios, *Zines's The High Court and the Constitution*, 6th edn (Annandale, Federation Press, 2015) 400–01.

[94] *CPCF* (n 53) 524–25 [2] (French CJ).

[95] ibid.

[96] ibid 525 [3].

[97] ibid.

[98] ibid 648–49 [482]–[484], 650 [489] (Keane J).

from Australia's contiguous zone of non-citizens who would otherwise enter Australia contrary to the *Migration Act*'.[99]

Justices Hayne, Bell and Kiefel issued strong dissents on this point. Their Honours held that neither the common law prerogatives, nor the nationhood power, could support the actions taken by the Commonwealth, including the transportation of the plaintiff to India, or the detention of the plaintiff on the Commonwealth vessel.[100] Their Honours concluded that positive statutory authority was required to support the detention of an alien both within, and beyond, Australia's borders.

In their joint judgment, Hayne and Bell JJ held that the nationhood power could not be invoked in the present case to support the actions taken by the Commonwealth, including the transportation of the plaintiff to India, or the detention of the plaintiff on the Commonwealth vessel, without statutory authorisation.[101] Justices Hayne and Bell formed the view that

> [r]eference to the so-called non-statutory executive power of the Commonwealth provides no answer to that question. Reference to the royal prerogative provides no answer. Reference to 'the defence and protection of the nation' is irrelevant, especially if it is intended to invoke echoes of the power to declare war and engage in war-like operations. Reference to an implied executive 'nationhood power' to respond to national emergencies is likewise irrelevant. Powers of those kinds are not engaged in this case.[102]

Justice Kiefel similarly held that the nationhood power was not enlivened in this case. Her Honour drew an important distinction between issues of state sovereignty in international law and questions about the distribution and extent of powers in the Australian Constitution.[103] In this regard, Kiefel J stated:

> [T]he executive power to which the Commonwealth defendants refer is one which resides in every nation State, as an aspect of its sovereignty. That being the case, it should not be confused with what has sometimes been described as the nationhood power, which arises under the *Constitution* and has been held capable of responding to events such as a national emergency. This case does not involve such a power, nor those powers relevant to conditions of war or the protection of Australia as nation.[104]

*CPCF* is highly significant because, of the five judges who considered the scope of the non-statutory executive power of the Commonwealth, three held that the detention and removal of non-citizens to a place outside Australia could not be supported by the nationhood power.

[99] ibid 648–49 [484].
[100] ibid 568 [150] (Hayne and Bell JJ), 596 [260] (Kiefel J).
[101] ibid 568 [150].
[102] ibid.
[103] ibid 597 [264]–[265].
[104] ibid 596 [260].

## B. *Plaintiff M68/2015 v Minister for Immigration and Border Protection*

The second challenge to 'Operation Sovereign Borders' was *Plaintiff M68*.[105] At issue in *Plaintiff M68* was the legality of the Commonwealth's detention of the plaintiff in a Regional Processing Centre on Nauru. At the time, the Commonwealth Government had a contract with Transfield Services Pty Ltd for the provision of offshore detention services on Nauru and Manus Island. When the plaintiff's case was commenced in the High Court, the only legislative authorisation for Commonwealth expenditure under the Transfield contract were one-line descriptions of the programmes in Schedule 1AA of the *Financial Framework (Supplementary Powers) Regulations 1997* (Cth) ('Regulations'). Accordingly, the case had initially raised questions concerning the scope of the Commonwealth's power to contract and spend and the validity of Schedule 1AA of the Regulations.

However, on 30 June 2015, several months after the commencement of the case in the High Court, the Commonwealth passed retrospective legislation that introduced a new s 198AHA into the *Migration Act*. The effect of this amendment was to provide retrospective and prospective legislative support for executive action, including the making of payments, in relation to regional processing functions of a country. This shifted the focus of the case away from the scope of non-statutory executive power to the limits on extra-judicial detention identified in the case of *Lim*[106] and derived from Chapter III of the Constitution.

Justice Gageler was the only member of the Court to address the non-statutory executive power of the Commonwealth to procure or enforce a deprivation of liberty. It was not strictly necessary for him to do so, given that he concluded that s 198AHA was constitutionally valid. Accordingly, the plaintiff's detention by the Commonwealth for the purpose of regional processing was authorised under this legislation. Unlike *CPCF*, *Plaintiff M68* did not raise questions concerning the existence and scope of any prerogative power to prevent aliens from entering Australia.[107] Justice Gageler reasoned that the constraints on extra-judicial detention were not derived from Chapter III of the Constitution but were 'the consequence of an inherent constitutional incapacity which is commensurate with the availability, long settled at the time of the establishment of the Commonwealth, of habeas corpus to compel release form any executive detention not affirmatively authorised by statute'.[108] Furthermore, this 'inherent constitutional incapacity' could not be removed by legislation. As Gageler J explained,

> [t]hat inherent constitutional incapacity of the Executive Government of the Commonwealth to authorise or enforce a deprivation of liberty is a limitation on the

[105] *Plaintiff M68/2015 v Minister for Immigration and Border Protection* (2016) 257 CLR 42.
[106] *Lim* (n 62).
[107] *Plaintiff M68* (n 105) 106 [164].
[108] ibid 105 [159].

> depth of the non-prerogative non-statutory executive power of the Commonwealth conferred by s 61 of the Constitution. As such, it cannot be removed by a law enacted by the Parliament of any State … Nor can the inherent constitutional incapacity be removed by a law enacted by the Commonwealth Parliament under s 51(xxxix) of the Constitution; it is not 'incidental to the execution' of executive power to change an inherent characteristic of that power.[109]

This aspect of Gageler J's reasoning in *Plaintiff M68* warrants further critical analysis but it is beyond the scope of this book to undertake that task.[110] However, Gageler J's recognition of an inherent constitutional incapacity of the Executive Government to 'authorise or enforce a deprivation of liberty' suggests that there are limits on the types of executive action that can be supported by the nationhood power, which are derived from the common law but adapted to the Australian constitutional context.

## III. The Relationship between Commonwealth Executive Power and the *Migration Act 1958* (Cth)

The second issue for the Court's consideration in the *Tampa case* concerned the relationship between the *Migration Act* and the inherent executive power. It is a constitutional principle that a prerogative power of the Crown may be abrogated, curtailed or displaced by a validly enacted statute. In the leading twentieth-century case on this topic, *Attorney General v De Keyser's Royal Hotel Ltd* ('*De Keyser*'),[111] the House of Lords confirmed that a prerogative power will be displaced by a statute that confers, or directly regulates, a power that is equivalent to the prerogative. In these circumstances, the Executive Government derives its authority from the statutory regime, rather than the prerogative, and must observe the conditions, limitations and restrictions placed on the exercise of its power by the Parliament.

The *De Keyser* principle has been imported into the Australian constitutional jurisprudence.[112] It operates as a limitation on the prerogative. It is an important

[109] ibid 105–06 [162].

[110] ibid 96–101 [130]–[146]. See further P Gerangelos, 'Section 61 of the Commonwealth Constitution and an "Historical Constitutional Approach": An Excursus on Justice Gageler's Reasoning in the *M68* Case' (2018) 43 *University of Western Australia Law Review* 103.

[111] *Attorney-General v De Keyser's Royal Hotel Ltd* [1920] UKHL 1; [1920] AC 508.

[112] See especially *Re Richard Foreman & Sons Pty Ltd; Uther v Federal Commissioner of Taxation (Cth)* (1947) 74 CLR 508, 514 (Latham CJ); *Barton* (n 72) 501 (Mason J); *Brown v West* (1990) 169 CLR 195, 202 (Mason CJ, Brennan, Deane, Dawson and Toohey JJ); *Ling v Commonwealth* (1994) 51 FCR 88, 92 (Gummow, Lee and Hill JJ); *Re Residential Tenancies Tribunal (NSW) and Henderson; Ex parte Defence Housing Authority* (1997) 190 CLR 410, 459 (McHugh J); *Tampa case* (n 1) 501 [33] (Black CJ), 539 [181]–[182] (French J); *Jarratt v Commissioner of Police (NSW)* (2005) 224 CLR 44, 69–70 [85] (McHugh, Gummow and Hayne JJ); *Northern Territory v Arnhem Land Aboriginal Land Trust* (2008)

mechanism for ensuring that the Executive remains responsible and accountable to the Parliament in the exercise of its powers and reflects fundamental constitutional values of parliamentary sovereignty and responsible government that are common to both the United Kingdom and Australia. The principle also gives expression to an aspect of the rule of law, namely certainty. It is important in those areas where a prerogative power exists, alongside equivalent executive powers that are conferred by statute, that individuals know what the law is and, in particular, whether executive officers are acting in accordance with the rights, obligations and powers conferred on them by statute, or whether they are exercising the prerogative or non-statutory executive power, without the attendant limits imposed by the statutory regime.[113]

Very few Australian cases have squarely considered the question of statutory displacement of the prerogative. The *Tampa case* afforded the Full Court of the Federal Court an opportunity to engage in a detailed consideration of this issue. The Court was required to determine whether the *Migration Act* had abrogated or displaced the inherent executive power to exclude non-citizens from Australia. The majority found that the executive power survived. It had not been displaced by the detailed statutory regime in the *Migration Act* that regulated the exclusion, detention and expulsion of unlawful non-citizens.

It is significant that, in his examination of the relationship between the *Migration Act* and the nationhood power, French J considered whether an intention to abrogate or displace the executive power could be discerned from the statute.[114] Even though French J thought that the executive power extended beyond the prerogative, he nevertheless applied the *De Keyser* principle – a common law principle – to determine whether the *Migration Act* had abrogated or displaced inherent executive powers of 'significance' to national sovereignty, rather than the prerogative.[115] Cheryl Saunders has suggested that this is an example of Australian courts adapting common law principles to the Australian constitutional context.[116]

In the *Tampa case* the majority appeared to accept that the nationhood power, like the prerogative, is subject to control by the Parliament. However, the *De Keyser* principle did not operate as a practical limit on the nationhood power because of the way that it was applied in the *Tampa case*. As is shown below, the majority adopted the same interpretive approach that was employed by the High Court in the 1974 decision of *Barton*. This approach has set a very high threshold for the displacement of the prerogative by statute in Australia.

236 CLR 24, 58 [27] (Gleeson CJ, Gummow, Hayne and Crennan JJ); *Cadia Holdings Pty Ltd v New South Wales* (2010) 242 CLR 195, 204 [14] (French CJ); *CPCF* (n 53) 600–01 [279] (Kiefel J).

[113] See also Evans (n 3) 99.

[114] *Tampa case* (n 1) 545 [201]–[202].

[115] See also B Saunders, 'Democracy, Liberty and the Prerogative: The Displacement of Inherent Executive Power by Statute' (2013) 41 *Federal Law Review* 363, 367–68.

[116] C Saunders, 'Separation of Legislative and Executive Power' in C Saunders and A Stone (eds), *The Oxford Handbook of the Australian Constitution* (Oxford, Oxford University Press, 2018) 632.

## A. Strong Presumption against Displacement of Important Executive Powers

Central to the majority judgment in the *Tampa case* was the finding that the executive power of the Commonwealth extended beyond the prerogative and included an inherent power derived from Australia's status as an independent, sovereign nation.[117] This power was understood by French J as being important to the expression of Australia's sovereignty.[118] The importance of the power was relevant to French J's consideration of whether it had been displaced by the *Migration Act*.[119] As the power to exclude non-citizens from Australia was an 'essential' power, French J applied a strong presumption against its displacement. This presumption could only be rebutted if the statute disclosed a 'clearly expressed'[120] or 'clear and unambiguous'[121] intention to displace the executive power.

This aspect of French J's judgment in the *Tampa case* closely resembled the approach adopted by the majority in *Barton*, except that *Barton* concerned the prerogative, rather than the nationhood power. As mentioned above, the issue in *Barton* was whether the *Extradition Act* had displaced the prerogative power to request the surrender and extradition of a fugitive from Brazil, a country with which Australia did not have an extradition treaty. The Court unanimously held that the *Extradition Act* only regulated extradition requests from foreign states with which Australia had an extradition treaty. The *Extradition Act* did not, therefore, have the effect of displacing the prerogative to request the surrender of a fugitive from a non-treaty state, such as Brazil. Accordingly, the prerogative to request extradition from non-treaty states survived and the request for extradition was valid.[122]

In *Barton* all of the judges applied a presumption against displacement. It was accepted that a statute will not be held to have abrogated or displaced a prerogative of the Crown unless it does so by 'express words or necessary implication'.[123] Three judges, however, considered that the power to request extradition was important to the Australian government, and applied a stronger presumption against its displacement in their construction of the *Extradition Act*. Chief Justice Barwick described the presumption as 'extremely strong' and declared that a statute will not displace a prerogative power of the Crown unless it does so by 'a clear and unambiguous provision'.[124] Justice Mason stated that 'the decisive consideration' in his analysis was that the prerogative power to seek and accept extradition of a fugitive was 'an important power essential to a proper vindication and an effective

[117] *Tampa case* (n 1) 540–41 [185], 543 [193], 545 [202].
[118] ibid 543 [193].
[119] ibid 540–41 [184]–[185].
[120] *Barton* (n 72) 501 (Mason J), 508 (Jacobs J).
[121] ibid 488 (Barwick CJ). See also *Tampa case* (n 1) 545 [201] (French J).
[122] *Barton* (n 72) 488 (Barwick CJ), 491 (McTiernan and Menzies JJ), 501 (Mason J), 507–08 (Jacobs J).
[123] ibid 491 (McTiernan and Menzies JJ), 501 (Mason J).
[124] ibid 488 (Barwick CJ).

enforcement of Australian municipal law'.[125] It was not, therefore, 'to be supposed that Parliament intended to abrogate the power in the absence of a clearly expressed intention to that effect'.[126] In that regard, not only was there a 'conspicuous absence of express words', but because the Act did not extend to cover extradition of fugitive offenders from non-treaty states, Mason J concluded that there was nothing in the Act which evinced a sufficiently clear intention on the part of the Parliament to displace the prerogative.[127] Justice Jacobs similarly reasoned that 'the free right of the Australian Government to communicate at will with a foreign government is an essential attribute of this country as a sovereign nation'.[128] It followed that 'an intention to withdraw or curtail a prerogative power must be clearly shown'.[129] According to Jacobs J, there was 'nothing in the Act which suggested that the executive power stemming from the prerogative [was] intended wholly to be replaced by the statutory power'.[130]

In the *Tampa case* French J characterised the power to exclude non-citizens from Australia as an 'essential' power. Accordingly, it attracted the strong presumption against displacement. Justice French observed, in this respect, that 'the greater the significance of a particular Executive power to national sovereignty, the less likely it is that, absent clear words or inescapable implication, the parliament would have intended to extinguish the power'.[131] In the absence of express words, the relevant question was whether the *Migration Act* evidenced a 'clear and unambiguous intention' to deprive the Executive of its power to prevent non-citizens from entering Australia. In his dissent, Black CJ conceded that 'if a power is well used, well-established and important to the functioning of the Executive Government, a very clear manifestation of an intention to abrogate will be required'.[132] However, Black CJ then went on to observe that

> where an asserted power is at best doubtful, and where, if it exists at all, it does so in a field that has been the concern of the Parliament for a very long time, a less stringent view of the intention necessary to abrogate such a power is appropriate.[133]

Beyond these statements, the Court did not explain the process or criteria by which it came to classify a prerogative power as 'important'. Judges may reasonably disagree on whether a prerogative power is sufficiently important to Australian sovereignty or the continued functioning of the Executive Government to attract the application of this strong presumption against displacement, as illustrated by the different opinions on this matter set out by Black CJ and French J in their

[125] ibid 501.
[126] ibid.
[127] ibid.
[128] ibid 505, 508.
[129] ibid 508.
[130] ibid 507–08.
[131] *Tampa case* (n 1) 540–41 [185].
[132] ibid 504 [40].
[133] ibid.

judgments in the *Tampa case*.[134] Indeed, there may be judicial disagreement on whether the prerogative has survived. Cases concerning the prerogative often require 'extensive historical and archival research'.[135] Chief Justice Black concluded that it was, at best, 'doubtful' whether the prerogative relating to the entry of non-citizens into Australia had survived, given that it had been regulated by legislation for such a long time.[136]

In its analysis of the royal prerogative in *R (Miller) v Secretary of State for Exiting the European Union* ('*Miller*') the majority explained that 'a prerogative power however well established may be curtailed or abrogated by statute'.[137] It remains unclear why it should be presumed that, because a power is important to national sovereignty, the Parliament did not intend to regulate it.[138] Australian courts have not provided a convincing justification or rationale for the adoption of the strong presumption against displacement of important prerogative powers. In circumstances where the Parliament has passed legislation setting out a detailed statutory regime that confers and regulates the exercise of executive powers, and especially coercive powers, the more appropriate inference to draw is that the Parliament intended to displace the equivalent prerogative powers, irrespective of whether they are 'important' to national sovereignty.[139] Constitutional scholars have expressed their preference for executive powers to be conferred and regulated by statute.[140] As Simon Evans has explained,

> [n]otwithstanding the dominance of the executive in Parliament, enacting legislation requires greater openness, scrutiny and democratic deliberation than the exercise of prerogative powers, and the exercise of powers under statute is susceptible to more effective channels of judicial review than the exercise of prerogative powers.[141]

The identification of a power as an 'important' prerogative has interpretative significance. In the absence of 'clear and unambiguous' language to the contrary, it will be assumed that the Parliament did not intend to displace the prerogative. The application of this presumption may operate to limit the otherwise clear meaning and scope of a statute, as evidenced by the majority decision in the *Tampa case*. Even though the *Migration Act* provided a comprehensive regime for the exclusion and expulsion of non-citizens from Australia and conferred extensive powers

[134] See also Willheim (n 3) 186–88; Zines (n 3) 291–93; Evans (n 3) 98–99; B Saunders (n 115) 382.
[135] Winterton, 'The Relationship' (n 3) 33–34.
[136] *Tampa case* (n 1) 504 [40]. See also *CPCF* (n 53) 600–01 [277], [280]. Justice Callinan did not consider it necessary to explore the extent of the 'current vitality' of the Crown's right to dismiss 'at pleasure' in *Jarratt* (n 112) 87–88 [135]–[137].
[137] *R (Miller) v Secretary of State for Exiting the European Union* [2017] UKSC 5; [2018] AC 61, 139 [48].
[138] See also B Saunders (n 115) 382–83; Willheim (n 3) 187–88.
[139] See also B Saunders (n 115) 382; Willheim (n 3) 187; Zines (n 3) 292–93.
[140] See, eg, G Lindell, 'Further Reflections on the Date of the Acquisition of Australia's Independence' in R French, G Lindell and C Saunders (eds), *Reflections on the Australian Constitution* (Annandale, Federation Press, 2003) 49; Evans (n 3) 99; Winterton, 'The Relationship' (n 3) 35–36; B Saunders (n 115) 382.
[141] Evans (n 3) 99.

on executive officers, the majority was not able to find that this was evidence of a sufficiently clear intention to displace the inherent executive power to exclude non-citizens from Australia.

## B. The Requirement of an Inconsistency between Statute and the Exercise of Executive Power

In his judgment in the *Tampa case* French J summarised the relationship between legislative intention and inconsistency as follows: 'the term "intention" of course is a fiction. What must be asked is whether the Migration Act operates in a way that is necessarily inconsistent with the subsistence of that Executive power described'.[142] In the *Tampa case* the majority found that the *Migration Act* did not operate in a way that was 'necessarily inconsistent' with the executive power. The majority reasoned that the provisions of the *Migration Act* were 'facultative' in nature and did not purport to diminish the executive power.[143] According to the majority, the object of the Act was control of entry. It did not confer rights on non-citizens seeking to enter Australia that would have been taken away by the exercise of the executive power.[144] There was, therefore, no inconsistency between the provisions of the statute and the exercise of executive power, so far as it related to the control of entry of non-citizens.[145]

Chief Justice Black disagreed. In his construction of the statute, the Chief Justice ascribed particular significance to the express statement of the object in the *Migration Act*, being to 'regulate, in the national interest, the coming into, and presence in, Australia of non-citizens'[146] and the detailed mechanisms governing visas, self-identification, removal and deportation that were designed to advance the object of the Act.[147] The Act conferred wide-ranging, coercive powers on executive officers and created offences and imposed penalties.[148] The fact that the *Migration Act* comprehensively regulated the field of border protection and conferred on executive officers extensive powers to act, which were equivalent to the prerogative but subject to conditions and limitations on their exercise, was sufficient evidence of the Parliament's intention to exclude the prerogative. Chief Justice Black was of the view that the conclusion to be drawn from the comprehensive regime in the *Migration Act* was 'that the Parliament intended that in the field of exclusion, entry and expulsion of aliens the Act should operate to the exclusion of any Executive

[142] *Tampa case* (n 1) 545 [202].
[143] ibid 545 [202].
[144] ibid.
[145] ibid. For a detailed analysis of French J's reasoning in the *Tampa case* see P Stephenson, 'Statutory Displacement of the Prerogative in Australia' (n 2); P Stephenson, 'The Relationship between the Royal Prerogative and Statute in Australia' (n 2).
[146] *Tampa case* (n 1) 504 [42].
[147] ibid 504 [42]–[43].
[148] ibid 505 [49].

power derived otherwise than from powers conferred by the Parliament'.[149] This conclusion was, in Black CJ's view, 'all the more readily drawn' given that there was uncertainty about whether the prerogative continued to exist at all.[150]

The different approaches adopted by French J and Black CJ in the *Tampa case* demonstrate that an inconsistency between the statute and the executive power can arise in different ways. However, as a result of the application of the strong presumption against displacement of 'important' prerogative powers, the requisite intention needs to be expressed with unmistakable clarity. The prevailing approach in the Australian case law seems to suggest that, in the absence of clear words, only a direct inconsistency will be sufficient to demonstrate that the Parliament intended to deprive the Executive of the prerogative by enacting the statutory regime.[151] As French J noted in the *Tampa case*, 'close scrutiny will be required of any contention that a statute, without express words to that effect, has displaced the operation of the Executive power by virtue of "covering the field" of the subject matter'.[152]

In the High Court's most recent decision on this topic, *CPCF*, Keane J agreed with the judgment of French J in the *Tampa case* and held that the non-statutory executive power to prevent non-citizens from entering Australia had not been abrogated by the *MPA* or the *Migration Act*, and indeed, the continued existence of this power was 'consistent' with the provisions of the *Migration Act*.[153] On the other hand, Kiefel J adopted a similar approach to that of Black CJ in her dissenting judgment.

At issue in *CPCF* as discussed above was the constitutional validity of the Commonwealth's detention of asylum seekers on board an Australian vessel but outside Australia's territorial waters. In considering whether the *MPA* displaced any non-statutory executive power, Kiefel J did not apply any presumption against displacement in her judgment. Her Honour reiterated that it was a constitutional principle that

> any prerogative power is to be regarded as displaced, or abrogated, where the Parliament has legislated on the same topic. When a matter is directly regulated by statute, the Executive Government derives its authority from the Parliament and can no longer rely on a prerogative power. Where the Executive Government exercises such authority, it is bound to observe the restrictions which the Parliament has imposed.[154]

In this respect, Kiefel J reasoned that the enactment of detailed legislation such as the *MPA*, which imposed conditions on the exercise of coercive powers of expulsion and detention, was not consistent with 'an intention that the Commonwealth Executive is to retain a complete discretion as to how such powers are to be

[149] ibid 508 [64].
[150] ibid.
[151] See also Evans (n 3) 98.
[152] *Tampa case* (n 1) 540–41 [185].
[153] *CPCF* (n 53) 651 [492].
[154] ibid 600–01 [279] (citations omitted).

exercised'.[155] Justice Kiefel was not prepared to find that the prerogative survived in circumstances where the Commonwealth Parliament had legislated extensively on topics relating to immigration and border protection since federation, and had made provision for the manner and conditions of the exercise of coercive powers of expulsion and detention in the *MPA*.[156]

The approach to displacement of the prerogative adopted by Black CJ in the *Tampa Case* and Kiefel J in *CPCF* coheres with the approach taken by a majority of the UK Supreme Court in *Miller*.[157] In that case, their Lordships were satisfied that 'a prerogative power will be displaced in a field which becomes occupied by a corresponding power conferred or regulated by statute'.[158] In contrast to the view expressed by French J in the *Tampa case*, it was not a requirement for the majority in *Miller* that the relevant statute express a 'clear and unambiguous intention' to displace the prerogative. It was sufficient that it occupied the same field as the prerogative.[159] Indeed, their Lordships rejected the argument made by Counsel for the Attorney-General in *Miller* that prerogative powers can be abrogated by statute only in express terms or by necessary implication.[160] According to the Court, the provisions of the *European Communities Act 1972* (UK) were not compatible with the continued existence of a prerogative that allowed ministers to unilaterally withdraw from the EU Treaties to which it applied.[161]

The requirement of a 'clear and unambiguous' intention to rebut the presumption has set a high threshold for statutory displacement of the prerogative and the nationhood power in Australia. As the *Tampa case* demonstrates, the majority effectively sanctioned the exercise of the nationhood power by the Commonwealth as a means of avoiding the operation of the *Migration Act* and the conditions that it placed on the exercise of executive power. As a result of this decision, the rescued persons were deprived of their right to be processed in accordance with the provisions of the *Migration Act*. It is difficult to reconcile the approach adopted by French J in ascertaining whether the executive power to exclude non-citizens from Australia had been displaced by the statute with the principle in *De Keyser*. The House of Lords was clear in that case that where the Parliament has intervened by imposing conditions, restrictions and limitations on the exercise of powers that also fell within the scope of the prerogative, the Executive derives its power from the statute and must exercise it in accordance with the statute.

[155] ibid 601–02 [283].
[156] ibid 600–01 [277], [280].
[157] *Miller* (n 137). For critical analysis of this case see, eg, T Poole 'Devotion to Legalism: On the Brexit Case' (2017) 80 *Modern Law Review* 696; N Aroney '*R (Miller) v Secretary of State for Exiting the European Union*: Three Competing Syllogisms' (2017) 80 *Modern Law Review* 726; A Twomey, 'Relevance to Australia of the UK Supreme Court's Brexit Decision' (2017) 91 *Australian Law Journal* 177.
[158] *Miller* (n 137) [48] endorsing *De Keyser* (n 111) 575 (Lord Parmoor); *Burmah Oil Co (Burma Trading) Ltd v Lord Advocate* [1964] SC (HL) 117; [1965] AC 75, 101 (Lord Reid).
[159] *Miller* (n 137) 16–17 [47]–[49], 29 [85], 30 [88].
[160] ibid 29 [85].
[161] ibid 30–31 [88]–[89].

In the *Tampa case* the majority found that the inherent executive power had not been displaced by the detailed statutory regime in the *Migration Act* that regulated the exclusion, detention and expulsion of unlawful non-citizens. The *De Keyser* principle did not operate as a *practical* limit on the executive power because of the way that it was applied by the majority in the *Tampa case*. However, it is significant that, in his examination of the relationship between the *Migration Act* and the nationhood power in the *Tampa case*, French J considered whether an intention to abrogate or displace the executive power could be discerned from the statute. Even though French J thought that the executive power extended beyond the prerogative and included the nationhood power, he nevertheless adopted the same approach to the question of displacement that Australian courts have taken in cases concerning the displacement of the prerogative. This aspect of French J's judgment in the *Tampa case* suggests that the nationhood power could be vulnerable to abrogation by legislation. This is another important limit on the depth of the nationhood power.

## IV. Conclusion

When the majority judgment in the *Tampa case* was handed down, it attracted considerable criticism from scholars. There was some concern that the nationhood power would, in the future, support coercive action taken by the Commonwealth without statutory authorisation. This chapter has argued that the majority decision in the *Tampa case* should not detract from the weight of authority that suggests that there are limitations to the depth of the nationhood power. The authorities examined in this book do not support the finding that the nationhood power is capable of supporting executive action that is capable of affecting the legal rights, duties and status of individuals, in the absence of statutory authorisation. The judgments of the dissenting Justices of the High Court in *CPCF* and Gageler J's recognition of an inherent constitutional incapacity of the Executive Government to 'authorise or enforce a deprivation of liberty' in *Plaintiff M68* lend further support to this contention. This is an important limit on the nationhood power. The High Court has, however, also ascertained the limits on the nationhood power by reference to the federal character of the Commonwealth. The next chapter of this book explores how the High Court has employed the principle of federalism to condition and limit the scope of the nationhood power.

# PART III

# Limitations on the Nationhood Power

# 6

# Federalism as a Limit on the Nationhood Power

> The growth of the Commonwealth to nationhood did not have the effect of destroying the distribution of powers carefully effected by the Constitution.
>
> Sir Harry Gibbs, 1975[1]

This chapter explains the significance of the findings of the preceding chapters for our understanding of the scope of the nationhood power. This book has demonstrated that, with the exception of the majority decision in *Ruddock v Vadarlis*,[2] Australian courts have been reluctant to find that the nationhood power is capable of supporting executive action that can interfere with the legal rights, duties and status of individuals, in the absence of statutory authorisation. The nationhood power finds its strongest support as a 'facultative' capacity to 'engage in enterprises and activities peculiarly adapted to the government of a nation and which cannot otherwise be carried on for the benefit of the nation'.[3]

This book has also demonstrated that the federal character of the Commonwealth has been an influential factor for the High Court in determining the scope of the nationhood power. This chapter examines the strong federal themes that have emerged from the judgments of the High Court that have been considered in this book. It is demonstrated that the High Court has employed a particular conception of federalism – one that affords primacy to the continued existence of the States as independent entities – to constrain the scope of the nationhood power. This conception of federalism underpinned the implied limitation on the legislative power of the Commonwealth in *Melbourne Corporation v Commonwealth*.[4]

This chapter shows that the Court has, in ascertaining whether an executive act is supported by the nationhood power, consistently applied Mason J's

[1] *Victoria v Commonwealth and Hayden* (1975) 134 CLR 338, 378 (Gibbs J) (*AAP case*). Reproduced with permission of Thomson Reuters (Professional) Australia Limited, legal.thomsonreuters.com.au.

[2] *Ruddock v Vadarlis* (2001) 110 FCR 491.

[3] *AAP case* (n 1) 397 (Mason J). See also P Stephenson, 'Nationhood and Section 61 of the Constitution' (2018) 43 *University of Western Australia Law Review* 149; A Twomey, 'The Prerogative and the Courts in Australia' (2021) 3 *Journal of Commonwealth Law* 55, 89–99; A Twomey, 'Pushing the Boundaries of Executive Power: *Pape*, the Prerogative and Nationhood Powers' (2010) 34 *Melbourne University Law Review* 313, 339–42.

[4] *Melbourne Corporation v Commonwealth* (1947) 74 CLR 31.

'peculiarly adapted' test, which was set out in *Victoria v Commonwealth and Hayden* ('*AAP case*').[5] This test is helpful in determining whether a sufficient connection exists between the impugned executive action and that area of responsibility appropriate to the 'character and status of the Commonwealth as a national government'. The chapter concludes by demonstrating that the 'peculiarly adapted' test incorporates federalism to condition and limit the nationhood power. This is evidenced by the High Court's consideration of the following factors in applying the second limb of the test, namely:

1. whether the exercise of the nationhood power involved *competition* with State executive competence;
2. whether there were other constitutional mechanisms that gave the States the opportunity to *consent* to the exercise of Commonwealth executive power.

# I. Substantive Conception of Federalism Underpinning the Nationhood Power Cases

The principle of federalism has operated to limit the scope of the nationhood power. The High Court's willingness to rely on federal considerations to constrain the scope of the nationhood power and, indeed, executive power more generally, represents a small but significant counterbalance to the centralising trend that we have witnessed in the High Court's interpretation of Commonwealth legislative heads of power since the decision in *Amalgamated Society of Engineers v Adelaide Steamship Co Ltd* ('*Engineers' case*').[6] The High Court has consistently found that the nationhood power cannot be exercised in a way that interferes with, or undermines, the continued existence of the States as independent entities in the federation, or the exercise of powers and functions within their spheres of responsibility. It is contended in this chapter that the factors considered by the Court in limiting the nationhood power are manifestations of a broader conception of federalism that underpinned the decision of the High Court in *Melbourne Corporation*.

## A. The Conception of Federalism Underpinning the *Melbourne Corporation* Principle

On 1 January 1901 the colonies united 'in one indissoluble Federal Commonwealth under the Crown'.[7] While the colonies acquired a 'new title of States' under the Constitution, they were not 'established' by it. Australian federation was premised

[5] *AAP case* (n 1).
[6] *Amalgamated Society of Engineers v Adelaide Steamship Co Ltd* (1920) 28 CLR 129 ('*Engineers' case*').
[7] ibid.

on the 'continuing' status of the colonies in a new legal and political form.[8] The Constitution and the *Commonwealth of Australia Constitution Act 1900* (UK) ('*Constitution Act*') assume the 'continuing' status of the States as independent, self-governing political entities.[9] Covering clause 3 of the *Constitution Act* refers to the 'establishment' of a 'Federal Commonwealth' and, by the operation of covering clause 6, the colonies that existed at the establishment of the Commonwealth acquired a new constitutional status. They became 'States', namely 'original States' of the Commonwealth.[10]

The 'continuing' status of the States was secured by Chapter V of the Constitution, dealing with 'The States', and ss 106, 107 and 108 in particular. These provisions stipulate that the colonial constitutions and powers of the colonial parliaments, other than those powers exclusively vested in the Commonwealth Parliament or withdrawn from the State Parliaments, and prior colonial laws, 'continue as at the establishment of the Commonwealth'. Furthermore, the States were not 'subordinate' to the Commonwealth.[11] Justice Evatt described the status of the States as being

> equal to, or co-ordinate with, that of the Commonwealth itself. Sovereignty is not attributable to one authority more than to the others; it is divided between them in accordance with the demarcation of functions set out in the Commonwealth Constitution.[12]

Australian federation, then, was predicated on the assumption that the States would, subject to the Constitution, 'continue' as autonomous, self-governing bodies politic. However, the Constitution also established the Commonwealth as the national government and conferred on it legislative, executive and judicial powers that were necessary for effecting self-government and capable of being exercised independently of the States. This fundamental principle was expressed in the first resolution moved by Henry Parkes at the 1891 Sydney Convention, which stated

> that the powers and privileges and territorial rights of the several existing colonies shall remain intact, except in respect to such surrenders as may be agreed upon as necessary and incidental to the power and authority of the National Federal Government.[13]

[8] *Melbourne Corporation* (n 4) 82 (Dixon J); *New South Wales v Commonwealth* (1975) 135 CLR 337, 446 (Stephen J) (*Seas and Submerged Lands case*); J Quick and RR Garran, *The Annotated Constitution of the Australian Commonwealth* (Sydney, Angus & Robertson, 1901) 927. See also N Aroney, *The Constitution of a Federal Commonwealth: The Making and Meaning of the Australian Constitution* (Cambridge, Cambridge University Press, 2009) 247; N Aroney, P Gerangelos, J Stellios and SL Murray (eds), *The Constitution of the Commonwealth of Australia: History, Principle and Interpretation* (Port Melbourne, Cambridge University Press, 2015) 265–66. See also *Official Report of the National Australasian Convention Debates*, Sydney, 4 March 1891, 31 (Samuel Griffith) (*Convention Debates*).

[9] Aroney et al (n 8) 255.

[10] The States have been described as having a hybrid 'continuing' and 'original' status in ibid 606.

[11] *Melbourne Corporation* (n 4) 50 (Latham CJ); *Federal Commissioner of Taxation v Official Liquidator of E O Farley Ltd (in liq)* (1940) 63 CLR 278, 312 (Dixon CJ).

[12] *Broken Hill South Ltd v Commissioner of Taxation (NSW)* (1937) 56 CLR 337, 378, quoted with approval in *Seas and Submerged Lands case* (n 8) 446 (Stephen J).

[13] *Convention Debates* (n 8) Sydney, 4 March 1891, 23–24.

Alfred Deakin observed, in similar vein, that

> [t]he federal government is to have a strictly limited power; it is not to range at will over the whole field of legislation; it is not to legislate for all conceivable circumstances of national life. On the contrary, its legislation is to be strictly limited to certain definite subjects. The states are to retain almost all their present powers, and should be quite able to protect their own rights.[14]

The 'continuing' status of the States and their coexistence as constituent entities with the Commonwealth underpinned the early High Court's approach to constitutional interpretation. In the decades following federation, the Court developed and applied the doctrine of the immunity of government instrumentalities. Under this doctrine, the Commonwealth and State governments were understood as being 'sovereign' within their respective spheres of authority and mutually independent in the exercise of their legislative and executive powers and functions. This gave rise to an implied limitation on the power of the Commonwealth and the States to interfere with or control the activities of each other.[15]

The implied immunities doctrine was rejected in the *Engineers' case*. The decision 'marked a turning point in Australian constitutional interpretation'.[16] The Court also rejected the doctrine of reserve powers and acknowledged the supremacy of Commonwealth laws arising from s 109 of the Constitution.[17] The legislative powers conferred on the Commonwealth Parliament were understood as being 'plenary' in nature and their content and exercise could not be limited by the implied immunities doctrine. The Court accepted that, subject to limited exceptions, the Commonwealth Parliament could enact laws within its areas of legislative competence that may incidentally affect the operations of the States and their agencies.[18]

In *Melbourne Corporation* the Court identified an implied limitation on the power of the Commonwealth to make laws that were intended to control, restrict or burden the States in a discriminatory manner.[19] In *Melbourne Corporation* s 48 of the *Banking Act 1945* (Cth) was held to be a discriminatory law. The effect of s 48 was to compel the States and their authorities to bank with the Commonwealth Bank. The Court invalidated the law because it placed a particular burden or disability on a State and interfered with the exercise of its governmental functions.[20]

[14] ibid, 5 March 1891, 79 (Alfred Deakin).

[15] See, eg, *Austin v Commonwealth* (2003) 215 CLR 185, 277 [212] (McHugh J); *D'Emden v Pedder* (1904) 1 CLR 191; *Deakin v Webb* (1904) 1 CLR 585; *Lyne v Webb* (1904) 1 CLR 585; *Commonwealth v New South Wales* (1906) 3 CLR 807 (Commonwealth immunity); *Federated Amalgamated Government Railway and Tramway Service Association v New South Wales Railway Employés Association* (1906) 4 CLR 488; *Baxter v Commissioners of Taxation (NSW)* (1907) 4 CLR 1087 (State immunity).

[16] *Austin* (n 15) 212 [18] (Gleeson CJ).

[17] *Queensland Electricity Commission v Commonwealth* (1985) 159 CLR 192, 212 (Mason J).

[18] *Melbourne Corporation* (n 4) 78 (Dixon J).

[19] ibid 81–82 (Dixon J).

[20] ibid 55–56, 60 (Latham CJ), 67 (Rich J), 74–75 (Starke J), 81–82 (Dixon J), 99–100 (Williams J).

While there have been different formulations of the *Melbourne Corporation* principle in the High Court over time,[21] it is generally understood that it operates as an implied limitation on the ability of the Commonwealth Parliament to enact legislation that imposes a special disability or burden on the exercise of the powers and functions of the States which curtails their capacity to function as governments.[22] The implication established in *Melbourne Corporation* was premised on a particular conception of federalism, described by Dixon J as 'that of a central government and a number of State governments separately organized. The Constitution predicates their continued existence as independent entities'.[23]

It is not the point of this chapter to examine the operation of the *Melbourne Corporation* principle as a limitation on the legislative power of the Commonwealth. Nor does it contend that the *Melbourne Corporation* principle constitutes a positive limitation on Commonwealth executive power.[24] The aim of this chapter is to demonstrate that the conception of federalism that underpinned the *Melbourne Corporation* principle has also been employed by the High Court to constrain the scope of the nationhood power.[25]

## B. Federal Considerations in the Nationhood Power Cases

This book has demonstrated in Chapter 3 that the High Court has applied the principle of federalism to limit the 'breadth' of the nationhood power. As mentioned above, the High Court's willingness to rely on federal considerations to constrain the scope of the nationhood power represents a small but significant counterbalance to the centralising trend that we have witnessed in the High Court's interpretation of Commonwealth legislative heads of power since the decision in the *Engineers' case*.[26] The High Court has consistently ascertained the limits of the nationhood power by reference to the federal character of the Commonwealth.

This was evident in the *AAP case*, where Barwick CJ, and Gibbs and Mason JJ were not prepared to find that the nationhood power could be exercised to interfere with or undermine the federal distribution of powers for which the Constitution provides. Indeed, the principle of federalism was employed by the three dissentients in the *AAP case* to confine the scope of the nationhood power. The federal

[21] See, eg, *Austin* (n 15) 249 [124] (Gaudron, Gummow and Hayne JJ).

[22] *Melbourne Corporation* (n 4) 81–82 (Dixon J); *Spence v Queensland* (2019) 268 CLR 355, 421 [108] (Kiefel CJ, Bell, Gageler and Keane JJ); *Clarke v Federal Commissioner of Taxation* (2009) 240 CLR 272, 289–90 [16], 295 [26] (French CJ), 304 [54] (Gummow, Heydon, Kiefel and Bell JJ); *Austin* (n 15) 249 [124] (Gaudron, Gummow and Hayne JJ); *Fortescue Metals Group Ltd v Commonwealth* (2013) 250 CLR 548 [130] (Hayne, Bell and Keane JJ).

[23] *Melbourne Corporation* (n 4) 82 (Dixon J).

[24] See also D Hume, A Lynch and G Williams, 'Heresy in the High Court? Federalism as a Constraint on Commonwealth Power' (2013) 41 *Federal Law Review* 71, 84.

[25] See also ibid 83–92.

[26] *Engineers' case* (n 6).

character of the polity formed part of their conception of nationhood. While it was accepted that the Commonwealth was conferred with power as a result of its acquisition of national status, it also had the 'character' of a central government in a federal polity.[27] Accordingly, the Commonwealth could not exercise the nationhood power in a manner that undermined, or unduly interfered with, the States in the exercise of their executive powers and functions. Chief Justice Barwick remarked, in this regard, that

> [t]hough some power of a special and limited kind may be attracted to the Commonwealth by the very setting up and existence of the Commonwealth as a polity, no power to deal with matters because they may conveniently and best be dealt with on a national basis is similarly derived. However desirable the exercise by the Commonwealth of power in affairs truly national in nature, the federal distribution of power for which the Constitution provides must be maintained.[28]

Justice Gibbs similarly observed that 'the growth of the Commonwealth to nationhood did not have the effect of destroying the distribution of powers carefully effected by the Constitution'.[29]

The importance ascribed to the federal system of government is also evident in Mason J's judgment, where, in discussing the scope of Commonwealth executive power, he remarked that it 'is not unlimited'[30] and that it

> does not reach beyond the area of responsibilities allocated to the Commonwealth by the Constitution, responsibilities which are ascertainable from the distribution of powers, more particularly the distribution of legislative powers, effected by the Constitution itself and the character and status of the Commonwealth as a national government.[31]

This passage was subsequently endorsed in *Duncan* and again by six members of the High Court in *Hughes*.[32] The scope of the nationhood power, as an aspect of executive power, needed to be consistent with the federal character of the polity from which it was derived. As Mason J explained,

> [i]t would be inconsistent with the broad division of responsibilities between the Commonwealth and the States achieved by the distribution of legislative powers to concede to this [nationhood] aspect of the executive power a wide operation effecting a radical transformation in what has hitherto been thought to be the Commonwealth's area of responsibility under the *Constitution*, thereby enabling the Commonwealth to

[27] This point was also noted in *Pape v Federal Commissioner of Taxation* (2009) 238 CLR 1, 181 [519] (Heydon J).

[28] *AAP case* (n 1) 362 (Barwick CJ).

[29] ibid 378 (Gibbs J).

[30] ibid 396.

[31] ibid 396, endorsed in *R v Duncan; Ex parte Australian Iron & Steel Pty Ltd* (1983) 158 CLR 535, 560 (Mason J); *Davis v Commonwealth* (1988) 166 CLR 79, 93–94 (Mason CJ, Deane and Gaudron JJ); *R v Hughes* (2000) 202 CLR 535, 554–55 [38] (Gleeson CJ, Gaudron, McHugh, Gummow, Hayne and Callinan JJ); *Pape* (n 27) 114 [323], 115–16 [327], 124 [357] (Hayne and Kiefel JJ); *Williams v Commonwealth [No 1]* (2012) 248 CLR 156, 188 [29] (French CJ), 156 [133] (Gummow and Bell JJ), 251 [197] (Hayne J), 356–57 [539] (Crennan J), 364 [564], 371 [586] (Kiefel J).

[32] *Duncan* (n 31) 560; *Hughes* (n 31) 554–55.

> carry out within Australia programmes standing outside the acknowledged heads of legislative power merely because these programmes can be conveniently formulated and administered by the national government.[33]

This approach to determining the scope and limits of the nationhood power was given effect by the High Court in decisions following the *AAP case*, where there is evidence of federalism being used by the High Court to constrain the scope of the nationhood power, and executive power more generally. In *Pape v Commissioner of Taxation* several members of the Court endorsed Mason J's observation in the *AAP case* that the scope of the executive power of the Commonwealth needed to be ascertained 'from the distribution of powers, more particularly the distribution of legislative powers, effected by the Constitution itself and the character and status of the Commonwealth as a national government'.[34] Chief Justice French found that the nationhood power 'has to be capable of serving the proper purposes of a national government' but stressed that it could not 'be invoked to set aside the distribution of powers between the Commonwealth and the States'.[35]

In *Pape* Gummow, Crennan and Bell JJ stated that the executive power of the Commonwealth needed to be ascertained having regard to 'the position of the Executive Governments of the States'.[36] In similar vein, Hayne and Kiefel JJ described the executive power of the Commonwealth as 'the executive power of a polity of limited powers'[37] and were of the view that a wide spending power could have 'consequences that follow for the continued existence of separate polities, separately organised'.[38]

In *Williams v Commonwealth [No 1]* Hayne J referred to these judgments and confirmed that 'these limits reflect considerations of the kind expressed by Dixon J in *Melbourne Corporation.* They reflect the distribution of powers between the Commonwealth and the States'.[39] Federal considerations also featured prominently in the reasoning of the Court in *Williams v Commonwealth [No 1]* to limit the scope of Commonwealth executive power more generally.[40] Chief Justice French was of the view that a wide spending power would have 'consequences for the Federation'.[41] His Honour considered the effect of a wide spending power on the capacity of the States to exercise their constitutional powers and functions and concluded that it could 'diminish the authority of the States in their

[33] *AAP case* (n 1) 398, endorsed in *Davis* (n 31) 103 (Wilson and Dawson JJ); *Pape* (n 27) 50 [96] (French CJ), 117 [330], 124 [357] (Hayne and Kiefel JJ), 181 [519], 187 [533] (Heydon J); *Williams [No 1]* (n 31) 303–04 [363] (Heydon J), [504] 348 (Crennan J), 371 [584], 372 [587] (Kiefel J).

[34] *Pape* (n 27) 63 [132] (French CJ), 114 [323], 115–16 [327], 124 [357] (Hayne and Kiefel JJ), 188–89 [537] (Heydon J), endorsing *AAP case* (n 1) 396–97 (Mason J).

[35] *Pape* (n 27) 60 [127] (French CJ).

[36] ibid 85 [220].

[37] ibid 118–19 [335].

[38] ibid 120 [339].

[39] *Williams v Commonwealth [No 1]* (n 31) 248 [192] (citation omitted), 252 [198], 270 [248] (Hayne J).

[40] ibid 252 [199] (Hayne J).

[41] ibid 192–93 [37].

fields of operation' in a real and practical way.[42] In a similar vein, Kiefel J found that a wide spending power 'may enable the Commonwealth to encroach upon areas of State operation and thereby affect the distribution of powers between the Commonwealth and States'.[43] Justices Gummow and Bell also attributed significance to 'the position of the States in the federal system established by the *Constitution*' in assessing the ambit of Commonwealth executive power.[44]

In *Williams v Commonwealth [No 2]* the majority joint judgment described the federal distribution of powers and functions between the Commonwealth and the States as being a 'basal consideration'[45] in determining the ambit of the executive power of the Commonwealth. It was acknowledged that the Commonwealth must 'possess all the powers that it needs in order to function as a polity'.[46] The character of the Commonwealth was that of a 'central polity of a federation in which independent governments exist in the one area and exercise powers in different fields of action carefully defined by law'.[47]

The next section of this chapter demonstrates that the High Court incorporated federalism as a limit on the nationhood power through its application of Mason J's 'peculiarly adapted' test. In determining the scope of the power of the Commonwealth Executive Government to 'engage in enterprises and activities peculiarly adapted to the government of a nation and which cannot otherwise be carried on for the benefit of the nation', there was judicial consideration of whether there was any *competition* with State executive competence and whether there were other constitutional mechanisms that gave the States the opportunity to *consent* to the exercise of Commonwealth executive power. The importance ascribed to these factors reflects some concern to prevent the unmitigated expansion of the breadth of Commonwealth executive power. The Court was not prepared to accept that the nationhood power could be exercised by the Commonwealth to interfere with, or undermine, the continued existence of the States as independent entities in the federation, or the capacity of the States to exercise powers and functions within their spheres of responsibility.

## II. Competition with State Executive Competence

In his application of the 'peculiarly adapted' test in the *AAP case*, Mason J expressed some concern that the Regional Councils would be 'operating not under the aegis of the States, but independently of and perhaps in competition with them and

[42] ibid.
[43] ibid 370 [581].
[44] ibid 218 [89], 237–38 [155].
[45] *Williams v Commonwealth [No 2]* (2014) 252 CLR 416, 469 [83] (French CJ, Hayne, Kiefel, Bell and Keane JJ).
[46] ibid 467–68 [78].
[47] ibid 469 [83]. See also *AAP case* (n 1) 396–97 (Mason J).

their institutions'.[48] The effect of the Australian Assistance Plan was to reconfigure the Australian community into regions for the purpose of coordinating and providing a wide range of social welfare services. The Regional Councils would be established to provide these services, which extended to child care, parent education, family counselling and housekeeping services and were also conferred with 'a very wide discretion'[49] to determine how the money they received from the direct grants would be spent.

There was, therefore, real competition with the legislative or executive competence of the States. The activities associated with the Australian Assistance Plan largely fell outside the legislative competence of the Commonwealth in ss 51(xxiii) and 51(xxiiiA), but could have been implemented by the States, had a conditional grant been made to them pursuant to s 96 of the Constitution. The Commonwealth established the Regional Councils, which it directly funded and controlled, in order to more effectively achieve its policy objectives in relation to social welfare, without needing to obtain the agreement of the State governments.

In determining the scope of Commonwealth executive power in *Davis*, the majority of the High Court considered whether the activities associated with the commemoration of the Bicentenary involved any competition with the executive competence of the States. As Mason CJ, and Deane and Gaudron JJ explained, 'the existence of Commonwealth executive power in areas beyond the express grants of legislative power will ordinarily be clearest where Commonwealth executive or legislative action involves no real competition with State executive or legislative competence'.[50] In similar vein, Brennan J observed that Mason J's 'peculiarly adapted' test

> invites consideration of the sufficiency of the powers of the States to engage effectively in the enterprise or activity in question and of the need for national action (whether unilateral or in co-operation with the States) to secure the contemplated benefit.[51]

In their application of the 'peculiarly adapted' test in *Davis*, then, several members of the Court conceptualised the States as having presumptive responsibility over areas of legislative and executive competence that could not be interfered with by the exercise of Commonwealth power. Similarly, in both *Davis* and *Pape* the Court considered whether there was any intrusion by the Commonwealth on the executive competence of the States and concluded that there was not. However, it is significant that in applying the 'peculiarly adapted' test, the Court considered whether the States had the real and practical capacity to carry out the activities in question or, indeed, whether that capacity was already being exercised.[52]

[48] *AAP case* (n 1) 400.
[49] ibid 376 (Gibbs J).
[50] *Davis* (n 31) 92 (Mason CJ, Deane and Gaudron JJ).
[51] ibid 111.
[52] ibid 93–94 (Mason CJ, Deane and Gaudron JJ), 111 (Brennan J); *Pape* (n 27) 62 [131], 63 [133] (French CJ), 90–91 [239] (Gummow, Crennan and Bell JJ).

The Court was careful to ensure that the nationhood power was not being exercised by the Commonwealth in a way that would interfere with the capacity of the States to function in their sphere of responsibility.

It has been argued that the majority in *Davis* uncritically accepted that it was more appropriate for the Commonwealth, rather than the States, to organise and commemorate the Bicentenary. In this regard, Anne Twomey has observed that the actual event being celebrated was the settlement of the colony of New South Wales, rather than federation.[53] The majority of the Court did not give, in Twomey's view, any compelling reason as to why the Bicentenary needed to be celebrated by the Commonwealth, rather than the States and they made no attempt to even pay 'lip-service' to the second limb of the 'peculiarly adapted' test.[54]

It is, however, significant that in their joint judgment, Mason CJ, and Deane and Gaudron JJ considered whether the States could have effectively organised and commemorated the Australian Bicentenary. The plurality noted that while the States had a 'part to play, whether as part of an exercise in co-operative federalism or otherwise',[55] this could not be allowed 'to obscure the plain fact that the commemoration of the Bicentenary is pre-eminently the business and the concern of the Commonwealth as the national government'.[56] The interest of the States in the commemoration of the Bicentenary was 'of a more limited character'.[57] Justice Brennan also observed that the second limb of the 'peculiarly adapted' test invited 'consideration of the sufficiency of the powers of the States to engage effectively in the enterprise or activity in question and of the need for national action (whether unilateral or in co-operation with the States) to secure the contemplated benefit'.[58]

There seems to be judicial acceptance that the nationhood power may operate in relation to matters associated with Australia's national identity because it does not involve any interference with the federal distribution of powers.[59] *Davis* demonstrated that the nationhood power supported executive action associated with the organisation and commemoration of the bicentenary of European settlement of Australia. In addition to the celebration of events of national significance, it has been suggested that the nationhood power may provide the authority to determine and manage national symbols, including the national flag, emblems and anthem, and the establishment of an Australian honours system, the Order of Australia, and the conferral of those honours.[60] Twomey has explained that these matters also fall within a prerogative power that was inherited by the Crown in

[53] Twomey, 'Pushing the Boundaries' (n 3) 328.
[54] ibid 329.
[55] *Davis* (n 31) 94.
[56] ibid.
[57] ibid.
[58] ibid 111.
[59] ibid 93 (Mason CJ, Deane and Gaudron JJ), 111 (Brennan J).
[60] ibid. See also L Zines, *The High Court and the Constitution*, 5th edn (Annandale, Federation Press, 2008) 414.

right of the Commonwealth of Australia, and within the executive power in s 61 of the Constitution.[61] As these matters attach to Australia's national status, the exercise of power in this area does not interfere with the legislative and executive competence of the States.[62]

The nationhood power may also support activities associated with Australia's national heritage and culture. This may include the establishment of national institutions, such as national art galleries, museums and orchestras, as well as national sport institutes.[63] It has been suggested that the nationhood power may also support the Commonwealth purchasing and operating historical places and buildings that form 'part of the heritage distinctive of the Australian nation'[64] for the benefit of the public.[65] It would, presumably, also support Commonwealth contracting and spending for these purposes, although the extent to which this could be done in the absence of supporting legislation is not clear following the two *Williams* decisions.[66]

The influence of federalism as a limit on the 'breadth' of the nationhood power is also evident in *Pape*. In *Pape* the majority accepted that 'short-term fiscal measures to meet adverse economic conditions affecting the nation as a whole' were, in the circumstances of what was agreed to be a significant global financial crisis, 'peculiarly within the capacity and resources of the Commonwealth'.[67] Chief Justice French appeared to ascribe particular significance to the short-term nature of the measures in *Pape*, noting that the exercise of Commonwealth executive power in this case would not have amounted to any permanent interference with the constitutional distribution of powers.[68]

Justices Gummow, Crennan and Bell also thought that the measures in *Pape* were 'peculiarly adapted' to the national government. According to their Honours, the case could be 'resolved without going beyond the notions of national emergency and the fiscal means of promptly responding to that situation'.[69] The judgment of

[61] Twomey suggests that the prerogative power and incidental legislative power in s 51(xxxix) supports the *Flags Act 1953* (Cth) in A Twomey, 'The French Court, the Nature of the Executive Power and its Reconciliation with the Expenditure Power' in H Jackson (ed), *Essays in Honour of Chief Justice French* (Alexandria, Federation Press, 2019) 53–54. For the grant of honours as part of the prerogative see: *Kline v Official Secretary to the Governor-General* (2013) 249 CLR 645, 653 [11] (French CJ, Crennan, Kiefel and Bell JJ). See also A Sapienza, *Judicial Review of Non-Statutory Executive Action* (Alexandria, Federation Press, 2020).

[62] Twomey (n 61) 53.

[63] Zines, *The High Court* (n 60) 414. Twomey has suggested that the establishment of national institutions would also be supported by the prerogative to establish government bodies or the territories power, where those institutions are in Canberra in Twomey (n 61) 53–54; Twomey, 'Pushing the Boundaries' (n 3) 335–38.

[64] *Commonwealth v Tasmania* (1983) 158 CLR 1, 109 (Gibbs CJ), 252–53 (Deane J), 322–23 (Dawson J), 203–04 (Wilson J).

[65] ibid.

[66] Expenditure supported by the prerogative or nationhood power was listed as an exception. It would not appear to fall within the category of 'ordinary and well recognised functions of government'.

[67] *Pape* (n 27) 63 [133] (French CJ), 91 [241] (Gummow, Crennan and Bell JJ).

[68] ibid 60 [127].

[69] ibid 91 [241] (Gummow, Crennan and Bell JJ).

Gummow, Crennan and Bell JJ in *Pape* has been criticised on the basis that the second limb of the 'peculiarly adapted' test was not applied. It has been argued that the Commonwealth could have stimulated the economy through other means, namely by enacting legislation under the taxation power in s 51(ii) or by increasing welfare payments under s 51(xxiiiA).[70] Alternatively, the Commonwealth could have made conditional grants to the States under s 96 of the Constitution.[71] However, a critical feature of the plurality's judgment was their acceptance that the global financial crisis posed an imminent threat to the national economy.[72] This invited Gummow, Crennan and Bell JJ to consider whether the States had the capacity to respond, as swiftly and urgently as was required, in order to prevent a national economic recession. The influence of federalism is, therefore, still evident in *Pape*. It is significant that the majority felt compelled to explain why the States were not capable of responding to a national economic emergency.[73]

The majority in *Pape* also ascribed significance to the fact that there was no competition, in a *practical* sense, with the executive competence and authority of the States.[74] An important factor for French CJ in finding that the nationhood power supported the executive action in *Pape* was that it did not involve competition with the executive competence of the States, partly because of its short-term nature, but also because the Commonwealth was uniquely equipped with the 'resources and capacity' to respond effectively to it.[75] Chief Justice French concluded, in this regard, that the States did not have the capacity or the resources to implement, within a short time frame, measures that were 'rationally adjudged' as 'avoiding or mitigating' the adverse effects of a national financial crisis in Australia.[76]

Justices Gummow, Crennan and Bell similarly considered that Commonwealth executive power could be limited by 'some constraint having its source in the position of the Executive Governments of the States'.[77] They also acknowledged judicial statements made in *Davis* that the executive power is clearest where it involves no competition with areas of State executive competence.[78] Their Honours reasoned that there was no such competition in this case because 'only the Commonwealth has the resources available to respond promptly to the present financial crisis on the scale exemplified by the *Bonus Act*'.[79] Both limbs of the 'peculiarly adapted' test were satisfied. The threat posed by the global financial crisis to the nation as a

[70] ibid 123–24 [355]–[356] (Hayne and Kiefel JJ). See also Twomey, 'Pushing the Boundaries' (n 3) 330.

[71] *Pape* (n 27) 178–79 [513] (Heydon J).

[72] ibid 89 [233], 91 [241] (Gummow, Crennan and Bell JJ).

[73] See also Hume, Lynch and Williams (n 24); 83–84; P Stephenson, 'Justice Mason in the Australian Assistance Plan Case (1975): Nationhood, Federalism and Commonwealth Executive Power' in A Lynch (ed), *Great Australian Dissents* (Cambridge, Cambridge University Press, 2016) 186.

[74] *Pape* (n 27) 62 [131].

[75] ibid 60 [127], 24 [9] (French CJ).

[76] ibid 63 [133].

[77] ibid 85 [220].

[78] ibid 90–91 [239].

[79] ibid 90–91 [239], 91–92 [242].

whole warranted a national response, and importantly, there were no other practical means available, either to the Commonwealth or the States, that could have been implemented within the requisite time frame. Federalism did, therefore, play an important role in informing the interpretation of the nationhood power in *Pape*. The judgments of the justices that held that the payments were supported by the nationhood power were underpinned by a conception of federalism that affords primacy to the continued autonomy of the States. This is evident from the majority's consideration of whether the States had the practical capacity and resources to respond swiftly to the threat posed by the global financial crisis.

The notion of a national 'crisis' or 'emergency' has proven to be an influential factor for the High Court in ascertaining the scope of the nationhood power. In *Williams v Commonwealth [No 1]* the majority of the High Court ascribed significance to the fact that the case did not involve 'a natural disaster or national economic or other emergency in which only the Commonwealth has the means to provide a prompt response'.[80] The majority concluded that in the absence of an emergency, or some other circumstance that meant that the Commonwealth was uniquely equipped to respond to a situation, the provision of school chaplaincy services was not 'peculiarly adapted' to a national government. The nationhood power could not support the provision of school chaplaincy services.

In *Williams v Commonwealth [No 2]* French CJ, and Hayne, Kiefel, Bell and Keane JJ confirmed the existence of 'those aspects of executive power which might be referred to loosely as the Executive's power to deal with or respond to a national emergency (considered in *Pape*) or other matters of the kind commonly grouped under the heading "nationhood"'.[81] In *CPCF v Minister for Immigration and Border Protection* Hayne and Bell JJ recognised 'an implied executive "nationhood power" to respond to national emergencies'.[82] In the same case, Kiefel J also confirmed that the nationhood power 'arises under the Constitution and has been held capable of responding to events such as a national emergency'.[83]

*Pape*, however, demonstrates that there are limits on the scope of the nationhood power, even when it is being exercised to respond to an emergency. In particular, in his judgment in *Pape*, French CJ cautioned that the nationhood power could not be equated to 'a general power to manage the national economy'[84] or address problems of 'national concern'.[85] The majority judgments in *Pape* demonstrate that, for the nationhood power to be enlivened to support executive action undertaken in an emergency, the emergency must affect the nation as a

[80] *Williams [No 1]* (n 31) 235 [146] (Gummow and Bell JJ), 250–51 [196], 267 [240] (Hayne J), 346–47 [499] (Crennan J), 362 [599] (Kiefel J).

[81] ibid 454. Quoted with approval in *Williams [No 2]* (n 45) 454 [23] (French CJ, Hayne, Kiefel, Bell and Keane JJ).

[82] *CPCF v Minister for Immigration and Border Protection* (2015) 255 CLR 514, 568 [150].

[83] ibid 596 [260].

[84] *Pape* (n 27) 63 [133].

[85] ibid 24 [10], 63 [133] (French CJ), see also 124–25 [359] and 125 [363]–[364] (Hayne and Kiefel JJ) and 176–77 [509], 192–93 [550]–[552] (Heydon J).

whole, such that only the Commonwealth has the capacity to adequately respond to it, as ascertained through the application of Mason J's 'peculiarly adapted' test.

Justice Mason's 'peculiarly adapted' test incorporates the principle of federalism to condition and constrain the scope of the nationhood power. It invites consideration of the competence and capacity of the States to undertake the activities in question. It can be, as demonstrated by the decisions discussed above, an effective constraint on the scope of the nationhood power. What is striking about the recent decision of the High Court in *Williams v Commonwealth [No 1]* is that the Court has used federalism to constrain the scope of executive power more broadly. A majority of the Court considered in that case whether the services covered by the National School Chaplaincy Program fell within an area of responsibility allocated to the Commonwealth by the Constitution.[86]

Chief Justice French opened his judgment in *Williams v Commonwealth [No 1]* by endorsing the view taken by Alfred Deakin that, as 'a general rule, wherever the executive power of the Commonwealth extends, that of the States is correspondingly reduced'.[87] Indeed, what comes through in the judgment of French CJ in *Williams v Commonwealth [No 1]* is an explanation as to why federalism has been employed as a constraint on the executive power of the Commonwealth. Chief Justice French's judgment evinces real concern to maintain the autonomy of the States in their fields of competence.

Chief Justice French spoke of an expansive Commonwealth spending power as having the potential, in a practical way, to 'diminish the authority of the States in their fields of operation' and competence.[88] Chief Justice French was of the view that if the Commonwealth spending power was afforded a wide interpretation, this would diminish the competence and capacity of the States to function in their areas of responsibility and concluded that the Commonwealth and States

> have concurrent competencies subject to the paramountcy of Commonwealth laws effected by s 109 of the *Constitution*. The character of the Commonwealth Government as a national government does not entitle it, as a general proposition, to enter into any such field of activity by executive action alone. Such an extension of Commonwealth executive powers would, in a practical sense, as Deakin predicted, correspondingly reduce those of the States and compromise what Inglis Clark described as the essential and distinctive feature of 'a truly federal government'.[89]

Justices Gummow and Bell referred approvingly to the observations made by Mason J on this point in the *AAP case* and concluded that the States had the 'legal and practical capacity to provide for a scheme such as the NSCP'.[90]

[86] The relationship between federalism and Commonwealth executive power more broadly has been discussed in Hume, Lynch and Williams (n 24); G Appleby and S McDonald, 'Looking at the Executive Power through the High Court's New Spectacles' (2013) 35 *Sydney Law Review* 253.

[87] *Williams [No 1]* (n 31) 178 [1].

[88] ibid 192–93 [37]; Hume, Lynch and Williams (n 24) 77, 82–83.

[89] *Williams [No 1]* (n 31) 216–17 [83].

[90] ibid 235 [146].

This consideration, in their Honours' view, reflected 'concern with the federal structure and the position of the States'.[91] Furthermore, their Honours were of the view that the conduct of the public school system in Queensland was the 'responsibility' of that State.[92] Similar observations were made by Hayne, Crennan and Kiefel JJ in their respective judgments.[93] They were of the view that the States were capable of providing the services covered by the NSCP, as underscored by Queensland's own funding scheme for school chaplaincy services.

Justice Kiefel, in particular, was reluctant to find that the Commonwealth had a wide spending power because this interpretation 'may enable the Commonwealth to encroach upon areas of State operation and thereby affect the distribution of powers as between the Commonwealth and the States'.[94] Furthermore, her Honour thought that the provision of chaplaincy services in schools involved competition between the State and Commonwealth Executives as both governments required adherence to their respective guidelines as a condition of funding.[95] Justice Kiefel concluded that not only was the Queensland government in a position to administer funding for chaplaincy services, it was already funding those services and was actively involved in the development of policy in that area.[96] There was, therefore, 'direct competition' with an area of State competence and the capacity of the executive government of the States.

## III. Availability of Other Constitutional Mechanisms and the Relevance of State Consent

The Court has, in applying the second limb of the 'peculiarly adapted' test, also considered the availability of other constitutional mechanisms that gave the States the opportunity to consent to the implementation of the impugned enterprise or activity. There is evidence of this in *R v Duncan; Ex parte Australian Iron & Steel Pty Ltd*.[97] In that case, Mason J found that the nationhood power could support the Commonwealth's entry into an intergovernmental agreement with the States on matters of joint interest, provided that 'the end to be achieved and the means by which it is to be achieved are consistent with and do not contravene the Constitution'.[98] In finding that the nationhood power supported the agreement, Mason J placed emphasis on its consensual nature.[99] The nationhood power was

[91] ibid 234–35 [144].
[92] ibid.
[93] ibid 272–73 [257] (Hayne J), 347–48 [501]–[503] (Crennan J), 373 [591] (Kiefel J).
[94] ibid 370 [581].
[95] ibid 372 [590].
[96] ibid 373 [591].
[97] *Duncan* (n 31).
[98] ibid 560.
[99] C Saunders, 'Intergovernmental Agreements and the Executive Power' (2005) 16 *Public Law Review* 294, 307.

not being used to override or circumvent the federal distribution of powers, but to facilitate joint cooperative executive (and legislative) action on certain matters that were of interest to both the Commonwealth and the States.

Several members of the Court placed varying degrees of emphasis on the 'consensual aspect' of s 96 grants in their application of the second limb of the 'peculiarly adapted' test. Section 96 confers power on the Commonwealth Parliament to 'grant financial assistance to the States on the terms and conditions as the Parliament thinks fit'.[100] The Court has employed s 96 to confine the scope of the nationhood power, and executive power more broadly, in order to preserve the autonomy of the States and their capacity to choose when, and under what conditions, they will participate in the implementation of Commonwealth policy objectives.[101] The Court, in construing s 96 in this way, appears to have conceptualised the States as having areas of executive competence or authority insulated from the unilateral interference by the Commonwealth through the exercise of its executive power.

In the *AAP case* both Barwick CJ and Mason J thought that the activities associated with the Australian Assistance Plan could have been made the subject of conditions attached to a s 96 grant and implemented by the States, instead of the Regional Councils. However, this was not consonant with the Whitlam Government's political objectives at the time. The Australian Assistance Plan was a vehicle through which the Commonwealth could more efficiently implement its policy objectives in the area of social welfare. By funding the Regional Councils directly, the Commonwealth was not required to negotiate with the States. The Commonwealth could, therefore, effectively bypass the States and exercise more control in the implementation of its social welfare reform agenda.

The Court harboured no illusions about the true nature of a s 96 grant. The Court was aware that, while often described as being 'consensual' in nature, the extent of vertical fiscal imbalance in Australia meant that, in practice, the States had little or no choice but to accept the grants and the conditions attached to them. Indeed, in his judgment in the *AAP case*, Barwick CJ acknowledged that s 96 had been used as a vehicle for the Commonwealth to 'intrude in point of policy and perhaps of administration' in areas beyond the subject matters of Commonwealth legislative power.[102] Nevertheless, Barwick CJ thought that it was important that

[100] For more on s 96 grants see, eg, AJ Myers, 'The Grants Power: Key to Commonwealth-State Financial Relations' (1970) 7 *Melbourne University Law Review* 549; C Saunders, 'Towards a Theory for Section 96 (Part I)' (1987) 16 *Melbourne University Law Review* 1; C Saunders, 'Towards a Theory for Section 96 (Part II)' (1988) 16 *Melbourne University Law Review* 699; C Saunders and K Yam, 'Government Regulation by Contract: Implications for the Rule of Law' (2004) 15 *Public Law Review* 51; J Crowe and P Stephenson, 'Reimagining Fiscal Federalism: Section 96 as a Transitional Provision' (2014) 33 *University of Queensland Law Journal* 221; S Chordia, A Lynch and G Williams, '*Williams v Commonwealth*: Commonwealth Executive Power and Australian Federalism' (2013) 37 *Melbourne University Law Review* 189, 215–18.

[101] See also Hume, Lynch and Williams (n 24) 79; Appleby and McDonald (n 86) 267.

[102] *AAP case* (n 1) 357.

the nature of a grant made under s 96 was consensual. The Chief Justice remarked, in this regard, that the

> intrusions by the Commonwealth into areas of State power which action under s 96 enables, wear a consensual aspect. Commonwealth expenditure of the Consolidated Revenue Fund to service a purpose which it is not constitutionally lawful for the Commonwealth to pursue, is quite a different matter. If allowed, it not only alters what may be called the financial federalism of the Constitution but it permits the Commonwealth effectively to interfere, without the consent of the State, in matters covered by the residue of governmental power assigned by the Constitution to the State.[103]

For the Chief Justice, the appropriate constitutional mechanism for expenditure on and engagement in policy areas beyond the areas allocated to it by the Constitution was a s 96 grant. Indeed, in his Honour's opinion, apart from s 96, the Commonwealth could not 'enter that residual area left by the Constitution to the States, either by legislative or by executive act'.[104]

Justice Mason adopted a similar view. He ultimately concluded that the Australian Assistance Plan was not supported by the nationhood power. In reaching this conclusion, he considered whether the establishment and direct financing of the Regional Councils was the only way in which the Commonwealth could have implemented the Australian Assistance Plan, and answered this in the negative. In his view, it was a scheme which could have been effectively administered by the States, had a conditional grant been made to them under s 96.[105] Justice Mason went further and found that a s 96 grant was, in fact, the appropriate way for the Australian Assistance Plan to be carried out. He observed that

> [i]n this respect s 96 has a dual significance. On the one hand it indicates that the executive power, like the appropriation power, extends to the investigation and formulation of policies to be expressed in conditions to be attached to grants made to the States. On the other hand its presence confirms what is otherwise deducible form the Constitution, that is, that the executive power is not unlimited and that there is a very large area of activity which lies outside the executive power of the Commonwealth but which may become the subject of conditions attached to grants under s 96.[106]

In *Williams v Commonwealth [No 1]* the majority found that the NSCP, like the Australian Assistance Plan, could have been made the subject of a conditional grant to the States under s 96 of the Constitution.[107] Justice Hayne placed a particular emphasis on the 'consensual nature' of s 96.[108] He noted that if the Commonwealth was afforded a wide spending power, it 'would not only give s 96

[103] ibid 357–58.
[104] ibid 358.
[105] ibid 400.
[106] *Williams [No 1]* (n 31) 235–36 [148] (Gummow and Bell JJ).
[107] ibid 348 [503] (Crennan J), 373 [591]–[593] (Kiefel J). See also 270–71 [251] (Hayne J).
[108] ibid 270 [248].

of the Constitution a place in the constitutional framework very different from the place it has hitherto been understood to occupy but also render it otiose'.[109] For Hayne J, s 96 was an 'immediate textual foundation for limiting the power to spend'.[110]

Other members of the Court reasoned that there was nothing to support or justify the bypassing of s 96 in *Williams v Commonwealth [No 1]*.[111] The NSCP was not in the same category of urgency as the direct payments made to taxpayers in *Pape*. Justice Crennan noted, in this regard, that there was no evidence to suggest that the Commonwealth was the level of government 'exclusively, best or uniquely authorised' to engage in this particular activity and was of the view that there was nothing to 'explain or justify … the bypassing of s 96'.[112] Justice Kiefel similarly observed that the funding for the NSCP could have been 'accommodated by grant on condition under s 96'.[113] Her Honour was satisfied that the NSCP fell within the 'province of the States'.[114] Accordingly, there was no justification for Commonwealth incursion into an area of State competence by executive action alone.

The significance that has been ascribed to the 'consensual aspect' of s 96 grants to States in the *AAP case* and in *Williams v Commonwealth [No 1]* reflected a conception of federalism that afforded primacy to the continued existence of the States as entities. The majority of the Court rejected an expansive interpretation of the nationhood power, on the basis that it could support executive action that could diminish the autonomy of the States in their spheres of responsibility. In the context of spending, it was important that the States had the opportunity to consent to the conditions of a grant, or the opportunity to reject it, which would have been removed by a wide spending power that could support direct grants to non-government bodies in relation to matters outside of its areas of legislative power. As Hume, Lynch and Williams have noted, '[a] state without choice lacks the independence which the Constitution predicates'.[115]

Section 119 of the Constitution, like s 96, wears a 'consensual aspect'. It preserves the autonomy of the States to choose when, and indeed whether, they require Commonwealth assistance in the form of a military intervention in an outbreak of domestic violence. It insulates the States from interference by the Commonwealth by prohibiting the Commonwealth from intervening in domestic violence in the absence of an application by the State government. If the Commonwealth's executive power to call out the military was afforded an expansive construction, this would, to use French CJ's words in *Williams v Commonwealth [No 1]*, 'diminish the authority of the States in their fields of operation'.[116]

[109] ibid 267 [243], 270 [247].
[110] ibid 270–71 [251].
[111] ibid 234 [143], 235 [146] (Gummow and Bell JJ).
[112] ibid 348 [503].
[113] ibid 373 [593].
[114] ibid.
[115] Hume, Lynch and Williams (n 24) 79.
[116] *Williams v Commonwealth [No 1]* (n 31) 192–93 [37].

The second limb of s 119 provides that the Commonwealth shall, upon the application of the Executive Government of the State, protect every State against domestic violence. This provision has been interpreted as a federal constraint on the power of the Commonwealth.[117] By stipulating that the Commonwealth must wait for an application from a State before it can intervene in domestic violence occurring within a State, s 119 preserves an important area of responsibility for the States relating to internal security. Without an application from a State government, it is beyond the power of the Commonwealth to take action to protect the State against domestic violence. Section 119, therefore, puts domestic violence beyond the reach of the legislative and executive power of the Commonwealth, unless there is a real connection with Commonwealth interests. This prohibition ensures that the States have immunity from Commonwealth interference in relation to these matters of internal concern.[118]

The consequences of a wide interpretation of the protection aspect of the nationhood power for s 119 are largely the same as a broad interpretation of the Commonwealth's spending powers for s 96. Expansive military call out powers would render s 119 redundant and would confer a wide power on the Commonwealth to call out the ADF domestically. A construction of the scope of the Commonwealth's executive power to call out the ADF should, therefore, have regard to the continuing operation of s 119 of the Constitution, particularly as s 119 is, in contrast to s 96, worded as a permanent constitutional provision.[119]

In *R v Sharkey*, discussed in Chapter 4, Dixon J relied on s 119 to limit the scope of the inherent legislative power. Section 119 was particularly relevant to Dixon J's consideration of the validity of s 24A(1)(g) of the *Crimes Act 1914–1946* (Cth) ('*Crimes Act*'). Dixon J was of the view that s 24A(1)(g) differed from the other forms of seditious intention in s 24A(1) of the *Crimes Act*, which his Honour had held to be valid because it concerned 'feelings or relations among people'.[120] Accordingly, it formed a matter of internal order and fell beyond the scope of the legislative power of the Commonwealth.[121] Dixon J reasoned that the presence of s 119 suggested that the Commonwealth's inherent legislative power could not 'authorise legislation upon matters which are prima facie within the province of the States upon grounds of a connection with Federal affairs that is only tenuous, vague, fanciful or remote'[122] and struck down s 24A(1)(g) on this basis. Justice Dixon was therefore willing to interpret s 119 as a federal constraint on the power of the Commonwealth.[123] Similarly, in the *Protective Security Review* ('Review'),[124]

117 *R v Sharkey* (1949) 79 CLR 121.

118 L Zines, 'The Inherent Executive Power of the Commonwealth' (2005) 16 *Public Law Review* 279, 289–90; P Stephenson, 'Fertile Ground for Federalism? Internal Security, the States and Section 119 of the *Constitution*' (2015) 43 *Federal Law Review* 289, 296–301.

119 For a reconceptualisation of s 96 as a transitional provision see Crowe and Stephenson (n 100).

120 *Sharkey* (n 117) 148–50.

121 ibid 150–54.

122 ibid 151.

123 ibid. See also *Thomas v Mowbray* (2007) 233 CLR 307, 394 [247], [249] (Kirby J).

124 RM Hope, *Protective Security Review (unclassified version)* (Parliamentary Paper No 397, 1979).

both Hope J and Sir Victor Windeyer considered whether the Bowral Call Out contravened s 119.[125] In the latter case, as discussed in Chapter 4, the call out was found to have been supported by the inherent executive power, which was exercised for the purpose of protecting the Commonwealth and its interests, rather than the States, as required by s 119. However, it is significant that in reaching this conclusion, Hope J and Sir Victor Windeyer had regard to s 119 of the Constitution.

These statements indicate that the nationhood power cannot be exercised in a way that interferes with, or undermines, the federal distribution of powers. The requirement in s 119 that the Commonwealth wait for an application from a State government before intervening in domestic violence is evidence of the framers' intention to preserve an area of State competence relating to the maintenance of internal law, order and security. The presence of s 119 has been interpreted as insulating the States from Commonwealth interference in this area of responsibility. Therefore, while the Commonwealth Executive Government can exercise power for the purpose of protecting itself and the Constitution, it remains subject to the federal constraints imposed by the Constitution, including express provisions such as s 119. The judicial statements examined in this book appear to reject an interpretation of the nationhood power that would authorise the Commonwealth to unilaterally intrude on that area of responsibility.

## IV. Conclusion

This chapter has demonstrated that the High Court has relied on federalism to limit the scope of the nationhood power. The High Court has, in ascertaining whether an executive act is supported by the nationhood power, consistently applied Mason J's 'peculiarly adapted' test. In its application of the second limb of this test, the High Court has considered

1. whether the exercise of the nationhood power involved *competition* with the executive competence of the States;
2. whether there were other constitutional mechanisms that gave the States the opportunity to *consent* to the exercise of Commonwealth executive power.

It was demonstrated that these factors reflected the conception of federalism that underpinned the implied limitation on the legislative power of the Commonwealth in *Melbourne Corporation*. This conception of federalism, which affords primacy to the continued existence of the States as independent entities, has underpinned the High Court's limitations on the scope of the nationhood power.

[125] ibid 30 [3.10], 32 –33 [3.18], 148–49 [10.25], 159 [10.62].

Justice Mason's 'peculiarly adapted' test strikes a balance between ensuring that the Commonwealth is equipped with the powers necessary for it to function as the national government, while preserving the federal distribution of powers effected by the Constitution. It reflects the 'character and status' of the Commonwealth as the national government of an independent and *federal* polity.

# 7

# Conclusion

> Section 61 is an important element of a written constitution for the government of an independent nation. While history and the common law inform its content, it is not a locked display cabinet in a constitutional museum. It is not limited to statutory powers and the prerogative. It has to be capable of serving the proper purposes of a national government.
>
> Justice Robert French, 2009[1]

This book has established that the High Court of Australia has recognised that the Commonwealth Executive Government enjoys 'inherent' or 'implied' power derived from its character and status as a national government.[2] This so-called nationhood power is captured by Mason J's formulation of it in *Victoria v Commonwealth and Hayden* ('*AAP case*').[3] In his judgment, Mason J stated:

> [T]here is to be deduced from the existence and character of the Commonwealth as a national government and from the presence of ss 51(xxxix) and 61 a capacity to engage in enterprises and activities peculiarly adapted to the government of a nation and which cannot otherwise be carried on for the benefit of the nation.[4]

This book has demonstrated that in the decades since the *AAP case* was decided, the Commonwealth Government has relied on the nationhood power to support a wide range of executive action undertaken to commemorate events of national significance;[5] implement controversial spending programmes[6] and intergovernmental agreements;[7] respond to national emergencies, including a national

[1] *Pape v Federal Commissioner of Taxation* (2009) 238 CLR 1. Reproduced with permission of Thomson Reuters (Professional) Australia Limited, legal.thomsonreuters.com.au.

[2] *Victoria v Commonwealth and Hayden* (1975) 134 CLR 338, 362 (Barwick CJ), 375 (Gibbs J), 397 (Mason J), 412 (Jacobs J) (*AAP case*).

[3] ibid.

[4] ibid 397.

[5] *Davis v Commonwealth* (1988) 166 CLR 79.

[6] *Pape* (n 1). Note that the High Court did not accept the Commonwealth's submissions that the nationhood power provided the constitutional basis for the spending on the NSCP in *Williams v Commonwealth [No 1]* (2012) 248 CLR 156 and *Williams v Commonwealth [No 2]* (2014) 252 CLR 416.

[7] *R v Duncan; Ex parte Australian Iron & Steel Pty Ltd* (1983) 158 CLR 535, 560 (Mason J).

fiscal emergency;[8] maintain internal security;[9] and prevent non-citizens from entering Australia.[10]

Furthermore, in some cases, the nationhood power was given legislative expression by the operation of the express incidental power in s 51(xxxix) of the Constitution.[11] Section 51(xxxix) confers power on the Commonwealth Parliament to make laws with respect to 'matters incidental to the execution of any power vested by this Constitution … in the government of the Commonwealth'. As such, where executive action is supported by the nationhood power, the Commonwealth Parliament can enact legislation to facilitate the exercise of that power under s 51(xxxix). This raised additional questions about what is 'incidental' to the exercise of the nationhood power.

This book has examined the development of the nationhood power in the Australian constitutional jurisprudence, beginning with the decision in the *AAP case*. It examined the interpretation of the nationhood power in the decision in *Davis v Commonwealth*, before turning to consider its application in the spending cases of *Pape v Federal Commissioner of Taxation*, *Williams v Commonwealth [No 1]* and *Williams v Commonwealth [No 2]*.

While some justices contemplated a wide interpretation of the nationhood power in the formative phases of its development, as extending to matters associated with 'national advancement', the cases examined in the book have demonstrated that the High Court has imposed limitations on the nationhood power. The High Court has assessed the limits of the nationhood power by reference to the federal system of government established by the Constitution. In doing so, the Court has limited any great expansion of the breadth of Commonwealth executive power.

The High Court accepted in *Davis* that the organisation and commemoration of the 1988 bicentenary of European settlement in Australia was an activity 'peculiarly adapted to the government of a nation and which cannot otherwise be carried on for the benefit of the nation'. In addition to the celebration of events of national significance, it has been suggested that the nationhood power could potentially support the management of national symbols, including the national flag, emblems and anthem, and the establishment of an Australian honours system, the Order of Australia, and the conferral of those honours.[12] As these matters attach to Australia's national status, the exercise of power in this area does not interfere with the legislative and executive competence of the States.[13]

[8] *Pape* (n 1).

[9] *R v Sharkey* (1949) 79 CLR 121; *Burns v Ransley* (1949) 79 CLR 101; *Australian Communist Party v Commonwealth* (1951) 83 CLR 1.

[10] *Ruddock v Vadarlis* (2001) 110 FCR 491, 542 [191], 543 [193] (French J, Beaumont J agreeing at 514 [95]) (*Tampa case*).

[11] See, eg, *Commonwealth v Tasmania* (1983) 158 CLR 1 ('*Tasmanian Dam Case*'); *Davis* (n 5); *Pape* (n 1).

[12] *Davis* (n 5) 93 (Mason CJ, Deane and Gaudron JJ), 111 (Brennan J). See also L Zines, *The High Court and the Constitution*, 5th edn (Annandale, Federation Press, 2008) 414.

[13] A Twomey, 'The French Court, the Nature of the Executive Power and its Reconciliation with the Expenditure Power' in H Jackson (ed), *Essays in Honour of Chief Justice French* (Alexandria, Federation Press, 2019) 53–54.

The majority also accepted in *Pape* that 'short-term fiscal measures to meet adverse economic conditions affecting the nation as a whole' were, in the circumstances of what was agreed to be a significant global financial crisis, 'peculiarly within the capacity and resources of the Commonwealth'[14] and that s 51(xxxix) of the Constitution supported the enactment of the *Tax Bonus for Working Australians Act (No 2) 2009* (Cth) ('*Tax Bonus Act*') as being incidental to the execution of the nationhood power. The Commonwealth action in *Pape* involved 'no real competition' with the State legislative or executive competence because only the Commonwealth had the resources and the capacity to respond on the scale, and within the time frame, that was necessary to address the adverse effects of a global financial crisis on the Australian economy.[15]

Thus, while the nationhood power has been held capable of responding to events such as a national emergency[16] the application of the 'peculiarly adapted' test in *Pape* operated to prevent the expansion of the breadth of executive power under 'some general rubric such as "national concern" or "national emergency"'.[17] The judgments in *Pape* demonstrate that, for the nationhood power to be enlivened to support executive action undertaken in an emergency, it must be of a national character and must be one to which the Commonwealth has a 'peculiar' capacity to respond.

In rejecting the application of the nationhood power in the *Williams* decisions, the High Court has indicated that it is not prepared to accept an interpretation of the nationhood power that would enable the Commonwealth to undertake executive action in respect of matters that it deems as being of national interest or concern. As Crennan J explained in *Williams v Commonwealth [No 1]*,

> the fact that an initiative, enterprise or activity can be 'conveniently formulated and administered by the national government', or that it ostensibly does not interfere with State powers, is not sufficient to render it one of 'truly national endeavour' or 'pre-eminently the business and the concern of the Commonwealth as the national government'.[18]

The High Court has applied Mason J's formulation of the nationhood power as a test for ascertaining whether the executive action is appropriate to the 'character and status of the Commonwealth as the national government' in circumstances where the Commonwealth is acting beyond the subject matters of its enumerated legislative powers in ss 51, 52 and 122 of the Constitution. The application of this test has operated to limit the scope of the nationhood power. In its application of this aspect of the test, the High Court has considered whether there was

[14] *Pape* (n 1) 63 [133] (French CJ), 91 [241] (Gummow, Crennan and Bell JJ).

[15] ibid 23 [8], 63 [133].

[16] *CPCF v Minister for Immigration and Border Protection* (2015) 255 CLR 514, 568 [150] (Hayne and Bell JJ), 596 [260] (Kiefel J).

[17] *Pape* (n 1) 24 [10] (French CJ), see also 124–25 [359] and 125 [363]–[364] (Hayne and Kiefel JJ) and 176–77 [509], 192–93 [550]–[552] (Heydon J).

[18] *Williams v Commonwealth [No 1]* (n 6) 348 [504] (Crennan J) (citations omitted).

any competition with State executive competence and whether there were other constitutional mechanisms that gave the States the opportunity to consent to the exercise of Commonwealth executive power.

It was demonstrated that these factors are manifestations of a particular conception of federalism that also underpinned the implication established in *Melbourne Corporation* to limit the legislative power of the Commonwealth. These factors reflect a conception of federalism described by Dixon J as 'that of a central government and a number of State governments separately organized. The Constitution predicates their continued existence as independent entities'.[19] The Court's reliance on 'federal considerations' to limit the scope of the nationhood power has prevented an expansion of the breadth of Commonwealth executive power that is capable of interfering with, or undermining, the continued existence of the States as independent entities in the federation, or the capacity of the States to exercise powers and functions within their spheres of responsibility.

In addition to limits on the breadth of the nationhood power, derived from the principle of federalism, Australian courts have also recognised that there are limits on the types of executive action that the Commonwealth is empowered to undertake 'for the benefit of the nation' pursuant to the nationhood power. These limits to the 'depth' of the executive power relate to the capacity of the Commonwealth to undertake executive action that interferes with the legal rights and duties of individuals.

This was evident in the way that the High Court has approached the question of construction of the scope of the incidental legislative power in s 51(xxxix) in *Davis* and *Pape*. The High Court has accepted that there are limits on the scope of the incidental power in s 51(xxxix), when it is used with the nationhood power, that reflect the limitations on the Executive derived from the common law. In particular, there was recognition in *Davis* that s 51(xxxix) could not be used to support a law that created criminal offences, 'except in so far as is necessary to protect the efficacy of the execution by the Executive Government of its powers and capacities'.[20] This limitation on the scope of the incidental power in s 51(xxxix) reflected the inability of the Commonwealth Executive to create an offence, derived from the common law.[21]

In *Pape* there was recognition that the Commonwealth Executive Government could not rely on the executive power to create new legal rights and liabilities that the tax bonus scheme required.[22] As such, the Commonwealth Parliament relied on s 51(xxxix) to enact the *Tax Bonus Act* to facilitate the exercise of the nationhood aspect of the executive power in s 61. The majority judgments were otherwise

[19] *Melbourne Corporation v Commonwealth* (1947) 74 CLR 31, 82 (Dixon J).
[20] *Davis* (n 5) 112–13 (Brennan J).
[21] ibid 112.
[22] *Pape* (n 1) 92 [243] (Gummow, Crennan and Bell JJ). See also C Saunders, 'Separation of Legislative and Executive Power' in C Saunders and A Stone (eds), *The Oxford Handbook of the Australian Constitution* (Oxford, Oxford University Press, 2018) 634; HP Lee, MWR Adams, C Campbell and P Emerton, *Emergency Powers in Australia*, 2nd edn (Cambridge, Cambridge University Press, 2019) 76.

reluctant to accept that s 51(xxxix) could support coercive legislation as incidental to the execution of the nationhood power. The issue did not arise in *Pape* because the *Tax Bonus Act* was not coercive in nature. Nevertheless, French CJ warned that

> [f]uture questions about the application of the executive power to the control or regulation of conduct or activities under coercive laws, absent authority supplied by a statute made under some head of power other than s 51(xxxix) alone, are likely to be answered conservatively.[23]

Thus, the decisions in *Davis* and *Pape* certainly suggest that 'the incidental power could not be used to convert a non-coercive executive power into a coercive one',[24] but this remains a live issue for future cases.[25] Chapter 4 exposed the uncertainty about the scope of the nationhood power to support the use of the ADF for internal security and civil emergencies where members of the ADF may be required to interfere with the legal rights, duties or status of individuals in the course of carrying out their duties.

It was also demonstrated that Australian courts have adapted the common law principle for the abrogation or displacement of the prerogative to the Australian constitutional context. This was evident in the decision in the *Tampa case*, where the majority applied the *De Keyser* principle to determine whether Commonwealth legislation had abrogated or displaced inherent executive powers of 'significance' to national sovereignty, rather than the prerogative.[26] This is another important limit on the depth of the nationhood power because it suggests that the nationhood power, like the prerogative, is subject to control by the Parliament.

It was demonstrated in Chapter 4 that many of the prerogative or nationhood powers with respect to the use of the ADF for internal security operations in Australia are likely to have been abrogated or displaced by the comprehensive statutory regime in Part IIIAAA of the *Defence Act 1903* (Cth), which conditions and limits the exercise of coercive powers when the ADF is called out to protect Commonwealth interests or the States and Territories against domestic violence. However, Chapter 5 demonstrated that Australian courts have generally been reluctant to find that there has been legislation that has abrogated or displaced executive powers that are 'important' to national sovereignty or the functioning of the Executive Government.[27] In its more recent decisions, however,

[23] *Pape* (n 1) 24 [10] (French CJ).

[24] A Twomey, 'Pushing the Boundaries of Executive Power: *Pape*, The Prerogative and Nationhood Powers' (2010) 34 *Melbourne University Law Review* 313, 327; P Stephenson, 'Nationhood and Section 61 of the Constitution' (2018) 43 *University of Western Australia Law Review* 149, 164.

[25] See also Saunders, 'Separation of Legislative and Executive Power' (n 22) 634; Twomey, 'Pushing the Boundaries' (n 24) 340; A Twomey, 'The Prerogative and the Courts in Australia' (2021) 3 *Journal of Commonwealth Law* 55, 66–67.

[26] See also Saunders, 'Separation of Legislative and Executive Power' (n 22) 632.

[27] See especially *Barton v Commonwealth* (1974) 131 CLR 477, 488 (Barwick CJ), 491 (McTiernan and Menzies JJ), 501 (Mason J), 506–08 (Jacobs J); *Ling v Commonwealth* (1994) 51 FCR 88, 94, 97 (Gummow, Lee and Hill JJ); *Tampa case* (n 10) 544–46 [199]–[204] (French J, Beaumont J agreeing

the High Court has not been prepared to accept that inherent executive power has survived the enactment of a detailed statutory regime that places conditions and limits on the exercise of equivalent executive powers.[28]

Finally, it was argued that the majority decision in the *Tampa case* should not detract from the weight of authority that suggests that there are limitations to the depth of the nationhood power. The authorities examined in this book do not support the finding that the nationhood power is capable of supporting executive action that is capable of affecting the legal rights, duties and status of individuals, in the absence of statutory authorisation. The judgments of the dissenting justices of the High Court in *CPCF* and Gageler J's recognition of an inherent constitutional incapacity of the Executive Government to 'authorise or enforce a deprivation of liberty' in *Plaintiff M68* support this contention.

In the *AAP case* Mason J stated:

> [T]he executive power to engage in activities appropriate to a national government, arising as it does from an implication drawn from the Constitution and having no counterpart apart from the incidental power, in the expressed heads of legislative power, is limited in scope. It would be inconsistent with the broad division of responsibilities between the Commonwealth and the States achieved by the distribution of legislative powers to concede to this aspect of the executive power a wide operation effecting a radical transformation in what has hitherto been through to be the Commonwealth's area of responsibility under the Constitution, thereby enabling the Commonwealth to carry out within Australia programmes standing outside the acknowledged heads of legislative power merely because these programmes can be conveniently formulated and administered by the national government.[29]

The cases that have been examined in this book lend support to this contention. Australian courts have imposed limitations on the scope of the nationhood power so that it cannot be exercised by the Commonwealth to take executive action in relation to any matter that it regards as being of national interest or concern or which 'befits' its status as the national government.[30]

at 514 [95]); *Oates v Attorney-General (Cth)* (2003) 214 CLR 496, 511 [37]–[40], 512–13 [45]–[46] (Gleeson CJ, McHugh, Gummow, Kirby, Hayne and Heydon JJ).

[28] See *CPCF* (n 16) 538 [41] (French CJ), 564–65 [141] (Hayne and Bell JJ), 601–02 [283] (Kiefel J).

[29] *AAP case* (n 2) 398 (Mason J).

[30] *Williams v Commonwealth [No 2]* (n 6) 466–67 [72] (French CJ, Hayne, Kiefel, Bell and Keane JJ). See also Twomey (n 13) 54.

# BIBLIOGRAPHY


Anderson, R, 'Australian Communist Party v The Commonwealth' (1951) 1 *University of Queensland Law Journal* 34

Appleby, G, 'There Must be Limits: The Commonwealth Spending Power' (2009) 37 *Federal Law Review* 93

Appleby, G and McDonald, S, 'Looking at the Executive Power through the High Court's New Spectacles' (2013) 35 *Sydney Law Review* 253

Appleby, G and McDonald, S, 'The Ramifications of *Pape v Federal Commissioner of Taxation* for the Spending Power and Legislative Powers of the Commonwealth' (2011) 37 *Monash University Law Review* 162

Aroney, N, 'A Power "Singular and Eccentrical": Royal Commissions and Executive Power after Williams' (2014) 25 *Public Law Review* 99

Aroney, N, 'A Seductive Plausibility: Freedom of Speech in the Constitution' (1995) 18 *University of Queensland Law Journal* 249

Aroney, N, '*R (Miller) v Secretary of State for Exiting the European Union*: Three Competing Syllogisms' (2017) 80 *Modern Law Review* 726

Aroney, N, 'Towards the "Best Explanation" of the Constitution: Text, Structure, History and Principle in *Roach v Electoral Commissioner*' (2011) 30 *University of Queensland Law Journal* 145

Aroney, N, *The Constitution of a Federal Commonwealth: The Making and Meaning of the Australian Constitution* (Cambridge, Cambridge University Press, 2009)

Aroney, N, Gerangelos, P, Stellios, J and Murray, SL, *The Constitution of the Commonwealth of Australia: History, Principle and Interpretation* (Port Melbourne, Cambridge University Press, 2015)

Australian Department of Defence, *Defence Assistance to the Civil Community Manual* (17 August 2020)

Australian Department of Defence, *Defence Assistance to the Civil Community Policy* (17 August 2020)

Australian Department of Defence, 'Defence Support to firefighting effort' (Media release of Senator Hon Linda Reynolds CSC, 11 November 2019)

Australian Department of Defence, 'Defence Support to Mandatory Quarantine Measures Commences' (Media release of Senator Hon Linda Reynolds CSC, 29 March 2020)

Australian Department of Defence, 'Expansion of ADF support to COVID-19 Assist' (Media release of Senator Hon Linda Reynolds CSC, 1 April 2020)

Australian Department of Defence, 'Operation Bushfire Assist concludes' (Joint Media Release of Prime Minister of Australia Hon Scott Morrison MP and Senator Hon Linda Reynolds CSC, 26 March 2020)

Australian Department of Defence, 'Operation COVID-19 Assist' (Web page, 25 March 2022)

Australian Department of Defence, 'The Hon Malcolm Turnbull Prime Minister & Senator the Hon Marise Payne Minister for Defence joint media release – Defence Support to domestic Counter-Terrorism arrangements' (Joint Media Release of Prime Minister of Australia Hon Malcolm Turnbull MP and Senator Hon Marise Payne, 17 July 2017)

Australian Department of Health, 'Defence support the vaccine rollout in aged care' (Media Release of Hon Greg Hunt MP, 3 March 2021)

Australian Government, *COMDISPLAN 2020: Australian Government Disaster Response Plan* (Department of Home Affairs, 2020)

Bateman, S, 'Constitutional Dimensions of State Executive Power: An Analysis of the Power to Contract and Spend' (2015) 26 *Public Law Review* 255

Bateman, W, *Public Finance and Parliamentary Constitutionalism* (Cambridge, Cambridge University Press, 2020)

Bernays, CA, *Queensland Politics During Sixty (1859–1919) Years* (Brisbane, Queensland Government Printer, 1919)

Beynon, HJ, 'Prerogative to Supply Plastic Baton Rounds and CS to the Police' [1987] (Summer) *Public Law* 146

Billings, P, 'Operation Sovereign Borders and Interdiction at Sea: *CPCF v Minister for Immigration and Border Protection*' (2016) 23 *Australian Journal of Administrative Law* 76

Black, HC, *Handbook of American Constitutional Law*, 3rd edn (Saint Paul, West Publishing Co, 1910)

Blackshield, AR, 'The Siege of Bowral – The Legal Issues' (1978) 4 *Pacific Defence Reporter* 6

Blackstone, W, *Commentaries on the Laws of England*, Book I, 1st edn (Oxford, Oxford University Press, 2016)

Boughey, J and Burton-Crawford, L, 'Executive Power in an Age of Statutes' in J Boughey and L Burton-Crawford (eds), *Interpreting Executive Power* (Alexandria, Federation Press, 2020)

Bradley, AW, 'Police Powers and the Prerogative' [1988] (Autumn) *Public Law* 298

Brennan, G, 'A Tribute to The Hon Sir Anthony Mason' in C Saunders (ed), *Courts of Final Jurisdiction – The Mason Court in Australia* (Alexandria, Federation Press, 1996)

Burton-Crawford, L, *The Rule of Law and the Australian Constitution* (Annandale, The Federation Press, 2017)

Byers, M, 'Commentaries' in G Evans (ed), *Labor and the Constitution 1972–1975: The Whitlam Years in Australian Government* (Richmond, Heinemann Educational Australia, 1977)

Campbell, E, 'Commonwealth Contracts' (1970) 44 *Australian Law Journal* 14

Campbell, E, 'Parliament and the Executive' in L Zines (ed), *Commentaries on the Australian Constitution* (Sydney, Butterworths, 1977)

Chitty, J, *A Treatise on the Law of the Prerogatives of the Crown and the Relative Duties and Rights of the Subject* (London, J Butterworth, 1820)

Chordia, S, Lynch, A and Williams, G, '*Williams v Commonwealth*: Commonwealth Executive Power and Australian Federalism' (2013) 37 *Melbourne University Law Review* 189

Clarke, J, Keyzer, P and Stellios, J, *Hanks' Australian Constitutional Law*, 9th edn (Chatswood, LexisNexis Butterworths, 2013)

Cohn, M, 'Medieval Chains, Invisible Inks: On Non-Statutory Powers of the Executive' (2005) 25 *Oxford Journal of Legal Studies* 97

Commonwealth, *Parliamentary Debates*, House of Representatives, 29 August 2001, 30517–8, 30569–70 (John Howard, Prime Minister)

Commonwealth, *Parliamentary Debates*, House of Representatives, 29 August 2001, 30570 (John Howard, Prime Minister)

Commonwealth, *Parliamentary Debates*, House of Representatives, 30 August 2001, 30729 (Anthony Albanese)

Commonwealth, *Parliamentary Debates*, Senate, 30 August 2001, 27095 (Robert Hill, Minister for Defence)

Commonwealth, *Parliamentary Debates*, House of Representatives, 18 September 2001, 30869 (Philip Ruddock, Minister for Immigration and Multicultural Affairs)

Commonwealth, *Parliamentary Debates*, House of Representatives, 19 September 2001, 30968 (De-Anne Kelly)

Condylis, N, 'Debating the Nature and Ambit of the Commonwealth's Non-Statutory Executive Power' (2015) 39 *Melbourne University Law Review* 385

*Convention on the Prevention and Punishment of Crimes against Internationally Protected Persons, including Diplomatic Agents*, opened for signature 14 December 1973, Australian Treaty Series 1977 No 18 (entered into force 20 February 1977)

Cooray, LJM, *Conventions, the Australian Constitution and the Future* (Sydney, Legal Books, 1979)

Crock, M, Saul, B and Dastyari, A, *Future Seekers II: Refugees and Irregular Migration in Australia* (Annandale, Federation Press, 2006)

Crommelin, M, 'The Executive' in G Craven (ed), *The Convention Debates 1891–1898: Commentaries, Indices and Guide*, vol 6 (Sydney, Legal Books, 1986)
Crowe, J, *Legal Theory*, 2nd edn (Pyrmont, Thomson Reuters, 2013)
Crowe, J, 'The Role of Contextual Meaning in Judicial Interpretation' (2013) 41 *Federal Law Review* 417
Crowe, J and Stephenson, P, 'Reimagining Fiscal Federalism: Section 96 as a Transitional Provision' (2014) 33 *University of Queensland Law Journal* 221
Deakin, A, 'Channel of Communication with Imperial Government: Position of Consuls: Executive Power of Commonwealth Constitution' in P Brazil and B Mitchell (eds), *Opinions of Attorneys-General of the Commonwealth of Australia*, vol 1 (Canberra, Australian Government Publishing Service, 1981)
Department of the Prime Minister and Cabinet, 'Joint Press Conference with the Minister for Immigration the Hon Philip Ruddock MP' (Transcript 11753, Sydney, 1 September 2001)
Detmold, M, 'The New Constitutional Law' (1994) 16 *Sydney Law Review* 228
Dicey, AV, *An Introduction to the Study of the Law of the Constitution*, 10th edn (London, Macmillan, 1959)
Donaghue, S, 'The Clamour of Silent Constitutional Principles' (1996) 24 *Federal Law Review* 133
Doogan, CM, 'Defence Powers under the Constitution' (1981) 31 *Defence Force Journal* 31
Duke, G, 'Popular Sovereignty and the Nationhood Power' (2017) 45 *Federal Law Review* 415
Emerton, P, 'Political Freedoms and Entitlements in the *Australian Constitution* – An Example of Referential Intentions Yielding Unintended Legal Consequences' (2010) 38 *Federal Law Review* 169
Evans, S, 'The Rule of Law, Constitutionalism and the MV Tampa' (2002) 13 *Public Law Review* 94
Evatt, HV, *The Royal Prerogative* (North Ryde, Law Book Co, 1987)
Foley, K, 'What Is the Relevance of *Williams* and *Plaintiff M61* for the Exercise of State Executive Power?' (2012) 36 *University of Western Australia Law Review* 234
French, R, 'The Executive Power' (Speech delivered at the Inaugural George Winterton Lecture, The University of Sydney, 18 February 2010)
Garran, RR, *Prosper the Commonwealth* (Sydney, Angus & Robertson, 1958)
Gerangelos, P, 'Executive Power' in N Aroney, P Gerangelos, J Stellios and SL Murray (eds), *The Constitution of the Commonwealth of Australia: History, Principle and Interpretation* (Port Melbourne, Cambridge University Press, 2015)
Gerangelos, P, 'Parliament, the Executive, the Governor-General and the Republic: The George Winterton Thesis' in HP Lee and P Gerangelos (eds), *Constitutional Advancement in a Frozen Continent: Essays in Honour of George Winterton* (Annandale, Federation Press, 2009)
Gerangelos, P, 'Reflections on the Executive Power of the Commonwealth: Recent Developments, Interpretational Methodology and Constitutional Symmetry' (2018) 37 *University of Queensland Law Journal* 191
Gerangelos, P, 'Section 61 of the *Commonwealth Constitution* and an "Historical Constitutional Approach": An Excursus on Justice Gageler's Reasoning in the *M68* Case' (2018) 43 *University of Western Australia Law Review* 103
Gerangelos, P, 'Sir Owen Dixon and the Concept of "Nationhood" as a Source of Commonwealth Power' in J Eldridge and T Pilkington (eds), *Sir Owen Dixon's Legacy* (Alexandria, Federation Press, 2019) 56
Gerangelos, P, 'The Executive' in N Aroney, P Gerangelos, J Stellios and SL Murray (eds), *The Constitution of the Commonwealth of Australia: History, Principle and Interpretation* (Port Melbourne, Cambridge University Press, 2015)
Gerangelos, P, 'The Executive Power of the Commonwealth of Australia: Section 61 of the Commonwealth Constitution, "Nationhood" and the Future of the Prerogative' (2012) 12 *Oxford University Commonwealth Law Journal* 97
Gerangelos, P, Lee, HP, Aroney, N, Murray, S, Evans, S and Emerton, P, *Winterton's Australian Federal Constitutional Law: Commentary and Materials*, 3rd edn (Pyrmont, Thomson Reuters, 2013)
Gerard, G, 'A Reply to the A.A.P. Case' (1978) 2 *University of New South Wales Law Journal* 105
Goldring, J, 'The Impact of Statutes on the Royal Prerogative: Australasian Attitudes as to the Rule in Attorney-General v De Keyser's Royal Hotel Ltd' (1974) 48 *Australian Law Journal* 434

Goldsworthy, J, 'Constitutional Implications and Freedom of Political Speech: A Reply to Stephen Donaghue' (1997) 32 *Monash University Law Review* 362

Goldsworthy, J, 'Constitutional Implications Revisited' (2011) 30 *University of Queensland Law Journal* 9

Goldsworthy, J, 'Implications in Language, Law and the Constitution' in G Lindell (ed), *Future Directions in Australian Constitutional Law: Essays in honour of Professor Leslie Zines* (Sydney, Federation Press, 1994)

Goldsworthy, J, 'The High Court, Implied Rights and Constitutional Implications' (1995) 39 *Quadrant* 46

Gordon, M, 'Communist Party Case: Core Themes and Legacy' (Speech delivered at the Centre for Comparative Constitutional Studies Constitutional Law Conference, Melbourne, 23 July 2021)

Gray, A, 'The Australian Government's Use of the Military in an Emergency and the Constitution' (2021) 44(1) *University of New South Wales Law Journal* 355

Gummow, W, 'Unity' in C Saunders and A Stone (eds), *The Oxford Handbook of the Australian Constitution* (Oxford, Oxford University Press, 2018)

Gummow, WMC, 'The *Constitution:* Ultimate Foundation of Australian Law?' (2005) 79 *Australian Law Journal* 167

Hanna, A, 'Nationhood Power and Judicial Review: A Bridge Too Far' (2015) 39 *University of Western Australia Law Review* 327

Harris, BV, 'The "Third Source" of Authority for Government Action Revisited' (2007) 123 *Law Quarterly Review* 225

Hayne, KM, 'Government Contracts and Public Law' (2017) 41 *Melbourne University Law Review* 155

Head, M, 'Another Expansion of Military Call Out Powers in Australia: Some Critical Legal, Constitutional and Political Questions' (2019) 5 *University of New South Wales Law Journal Forum* 1

Head, M, 'Calling out the Troops – Disturbing Trends and Unanswered Questions' (2005) 28 *University of New South Wales Law Journal* 479

Head, M, *Calling Out the Troops: The Australian Military and Civil Unrest* (Annandale, Federation Press, 2009)

Head, M, 'The Military Call-Out Legislation – Some Legal and Constitutional Questions' (2001) 29 *Federal Law Review* 273

Hill, G, '*Austin v Commonwealth:* Discrimination and the *Melbourne Corporation* Doctrine' (2003) 14 *Public Law Review* 80

Hocking, J, *The Dismissal Dossier Updated Edition: Everything You Were Never Meant to Know about November 1975* (Carlton, Melbourne University Press, 2016)

Hocking, J, *The Palace Letters: The Queen, the Governor-General and the Plot to Dismiss Gough Whitlam* (Brunswick, Scribe Publishing, 2020)

Hocking, J, *Gough Whitlam: His Time* (Carlton, Miegunyah Press, 2012)

Hocking, J, *Terror Laws: ASIO, Counter-Terrorism and the Threat to Democracy* (Sydney, University of New South Wales Press, 2004)

Hohfeld, WN, 'Fundamental Legal Conceptions as Applied in Judicial Reasoning' (1917) 26 *Yale Law Journal* 710

Hohfeld, WN, 'Some Fundamental Legal Conceptions as Applied in Judicial Reasoning' (1913) 23 *Yale Law Journal* 16

Hope, RM, *Protective Security Review (unclassified version)* (Parliamentary Paper No 397, 1979)

Horan, C, 'Commentary' in A Stone and G Williams (eds), *The High Court at the Crossroads: Essays in Constitutional Law* (Leichhardt, Federation Press, 2000)

Horan, C, 'Judicial Review of Non-Statutory Executive Powers' (2003) 31 *Federal Law Review* 551

Howard, C and Saunders, C, 'The Blocking of the Budget and Dismissal of the Government' in Gareth Evans (ed), *Labor and the Constitution 1972–1975* (Richmond, Heinemann Educational Australia, 1977)

Hudson, WJ and Sharp, MP, *Australian Independence: Colony to Reluctant Kingdom* (Carlton, Melbourne University Press, 1988)

Hume, D, Lynch, A and Williams, G, 'Heresy in the High Court? Federalism as a Constraint on Commonwealth Power' (2013) 41 *Federal Law Review* 71

Johnston, PW, '*Re Tracey:* Some Implications for the Military-Civil Authority Relationship' (1990) 20(1) *University of Western Australia Law Review* 73

Kalmo, H and Skinner, Q (eds), *Sovereignty in Fragments: The Past, Present and Future of a Contested Concept* (Cambridge, Cambridge University Press, 2010)

Kirby, M, 'Sir Anthony Mason Lecture 1996: A F Mason – From *Trigwell* to *Teoh*' (1996) 20 *Melbourne University Law Review* 1087

Kirby, M, 'Whitlam as Internationalist' (Speech delivered at the University of Western Sydney Whitlam Lecture, Sydney, 25 February 2010)

Kirby, M, 'Whitlam as Law Reformer' (1979) 10 *Federal Law Review* 53

Kirk, J, 'Constitutional Guarantees, Characterisation and the Concept of Proportionality' (1997) 21 *Melbourne University Law Review* 25

Kirk, J, 'Constitutional Implications (I): Nature, Legitimacy, Classification, Examples' (2000) 24 *Melbourne University Law Review* 645

Kirk, J, 'Constitutional Implications (II): Doctrines of Equality and Democracy' (2001) 25 *Melbourne University Law Review* 24

Kirk, J, 'Constitutional Implications from Representative Democracy' (1995) 23 *Federal Law Review* 37

Krasner, SD (ed), *Problematic Sovereignty: Contested Rules and Political Possibilities* (New York, Columbia University Press, 2001)

Krasner, SD, *Sovereignty: Organized Hypocrisy* (Princeton, Princeton University Press, 1999)

La Nauze, JA, *The Making of the Australian Constitution* (Carlton, Melbourne University Press, 1972)

Lane, PH, *Lane's Commentary on the Australian Constitution*, 2nd edn (North Ryde, Law Book, 1997)

Lee, HP, 'A Unifying Constitution for a Diverse Nation' (2001) 24 *University of New South Wales Law Journal* 605

Lee, HP, 'Constitutional Fidelity in Troubled Times' in HP Lee and P Gerangelos (eds), *Constitutional Advancement in a Frozen Continent: Essays in Honour of George Winterton* (Annandale, Federation Press, 2009)

Lee, HP, *Emergency Powers* (Sydney, Law Book Co, 1984)

Lee, HP, 'Legislative Comment – The Australia Act 1986 – Some Legal Conundrums' (1988) 14 *Monash University Law Review* 298

Lee, HP, 'The Australian High Court and Implied Fundamental Guarantees' [1993] *Public Law* 606

Lee, HP, 'The Implied Freedom of Political Communication' in HP Lee and G Winterton (eds), *Australian Constitutional Landmarks* (Cambridge, Cambridge University Press, 2003)

Lee, HP, Adams, MWR, Campbell, C and Emerton, P, *Emergency Powers in Australia*, 2nd edn (Cambridge, Cambridge University Press, 2019)

Lee, HP, and Paterson, J, 'Australian Nationhood in the Constitutional Interpretation of Section 117' (2000) 8 *Asia Pacific Law Review* 169

Letts, D and McLaughlin, R, 'Call-Out Powers for the Australian Defence Force in an Age of Terrorism: Some Legal Implications' (2016) 85 *Australian Institute of Administrative Law Forum* 63

Letts, D and McLaughlin, R, 'Military Aid to the Civil Power' in R Creyke, D Stephens and P Sutherland (eds), *Military Law in Australia* (Alexandria, Federation Press, 2019)

Lindell, G, 'Further Reflections on the Date of the Acquisition of Australia's Independence' in R French, G Lindell and C Saunders (eds), *Reflections on the Australian Constitution* (Annandale, Federation Press, 2003)

Lindell, G, 'Introduction: The Vision in Hindsight Explained' in G Lindell and R Bennett (eds), *Parliament: The Vision in Hindsight* (Annandale, Federation Press, 2001)

Lindell, G, 'Responsible Government' in PD Finn (ed), *Essays on Law and Government*, vol 1 (North Ryde, Law Book Co, 1995)

Lindell, G, 'The Changed Landscape of the Executive Power of the Commonwealth after the *Williams* Case' (2013) 39 *Monash University Law Review* 348

Lindell, G, 'Why Is Australia's Constitution Binding? – The Reasons in 1900 and Now, and the Effect of Independence' (1986) 16 *Federal Law Review* 29

Mason, A, 'The Australian Constitution 1901–1988' (1988) 62 *Australian Law Journal* 752

Mason, A, 'Trends in Constitutional Interpretation' (1995) 18 *University of New South Wales Law Journal* 237
Mathew, P, 'Australian Refugee Protection in the Wake of the Tampa' (2002) 96 *American Journal of International Law* 661
McHugh, M, 'The Constitutional Jurisprudence of the High Court: 1989–2004' (Inaugural Sir Anthony Mason Lecture, Sydney, 26 November 2004)
Mitchell, N, Interview with John Howard, Prime Minister of Australia (Radio 3AW, Melbourne, 31 August 2001)
Moore, C, *Crown and Sword – Executive Power and the Use of Force by the Australian Defence Force* (Canberra, ANU Press, 2017)
Moore, WH, *The Constitution of the Commonwealth of Australia*, 2nd edn (London, Sweet & Maxwell Ltd, 1910)
Myers, AJ, 'The Grants Power: Key to Commonwealth-State Financial Relations' (1970) 7 *Melbourne University Law Review* 549
*Official Report of the National Australasian Convention Debates*, Sydney, 4 March 1891
Oppenheimer, M, 'Voluntary Action, Social Welfare and the Australian Assistance Plan in the 1970s' (2008) 39 *Australian Historical Studies* 167
Pearce, D, Campbell E and Harding, D, *Australian Law Schools: A Discipline Assessment for the Commonwealth Tertiary Education Commission* (Canberra, Australian Government Publishing Service, 1987)
Pierce, J, *Inside the Mason Court Revolution: The High Court of Australia Transformed* (Durham, Carolina Academic Press, 2006)
Pintos-Lopez, H and Williams, G, '"Enemies Foreign and Domestic": *Thomas v Mowbray* and the New Scope of the Defence Power' (2008) 27 *University of Tasmania Law Review* 83
Poole, T, 'Devotion to Legalism: On the Brexit Case' (2017) 80 *Modern Law Review* 696
Poole, T, 'Judicial Review at the Margins: Law, Power, and Prerogative' (2010) 60 *University of Toronto Law Journal* 81
Poole, T, 'The Law of Emergency and Reason of State' in E Criddle (ed), *Human Rights in Emergencies* (New York, Cambridge University Press, 2016)
Poole, T, 'United Kingdom: The Royal Prerogative' (2010) 8 *International Journal of Constitutional Law* 146
Prime Minister of Australia, 'National Royal Commission into Black Summer Bushfires established' (Media release of Prime Minister of Australia Hon Scott Morrison MP, 20 February 2020)
Pringle, H and Thompson, E, 'The Tampa Affair and the Role of the Australian Parliament' (2002) 13 *Public Law Review* 128
Quick, J and Garran, RR, *The Annotated Constitution of the Australian Commonwealth* (Sydney, Angus & Robertson, 1901)
Ratnapala, S, *Jurisprudence*, 2nd edn (Port Melbourne, Cambridge University Press, 2013)
Ratnapala, S and Crowe, J, *Australian Constitutional Law: Foundations and Theory*, 3rd edn (South Melbourne, Oxford University Press, 2012)
Renfree, HE, *The Executive Power of the Commonwealth of Australia* (Sydney, Legal Books, 1984)
Richardson, JE, 'The Executive Power of the Commonwealth' in L Zines (ed), *Commentaries on the Australian Constitution: A Tribute to Geoffrey Sawer* (Sydney, Butterworths, 1977)
Rothwell, D, 'The Law of the Sea and the MV Tampa Incident: Reconciling Maritime Principles with Coastal State Sovereignty' (2002) 13 *Public Law Review* 118
Royal Commission into National Natural Disaster Arrangements, *Royal Commission into National Natural Disaster Arrangements Report* (28 October 2020)
Sapienza, A, 'Interpreting the Limits of Non-Statutory Executive Action: What Role for Grounds of Judicial Review?' in J Boughey and L Burton Crawford (eds), *Interpreting Executive Power* (Alexandria, Federation Press, 2020)
Sapienza, A, *Judicial Review of Non-Statutory Executive Action* (Alexandria, Federation Press, 2020)
Sapienza, A, 'Judicial Review of Non-Statutory Executive Action: Australia and the United Kingdom Reunited?' (2018) 43 *University of Western Australia Law Review* 67

Saunders, B, 'Democracy, Liberty and the Prerogative: The Displacement of Inherent Executive Power by Statute' (2013) 41 *Federal Law Review* 363

Saunders, BB and Kennedy, SP, 'Popular Sovereignty, "the People" and the Australian Constitution: A Historical Reassessment' (2019) 30 *Public Law Review* 36

Saunders, C, 'Intergovernmental Agreements and the Executive Power' (2005) 16 *Public Law Review* 294

Saunders, C, 'The Concept of the Crown' (2015) 38 *Melbourne University Law Review* 873

Saunders, C, 'The Development of the Commonwealth Spending Power' (1978) 11 *Melbourne University Law Review* 369

Saunders, C, 'The National Cabinet Has Worked. Can it Last?' (2020) *Pursuit* (Online journal)

Saunders, C, 'Separation of Legislative and Executive Power' in C Saunders and A Stone (eds), *The Oxford Handbook of the Australian Constitution* (Oxford, Oxford University Press, 2018)

Saunders, C, *The Constitution of Australia: A Contextual Analysis* (Oxford, Hart Publishing, 2011)

Saunders, C, 'The National Implied Power and Implied Restrictions on Commonwealth Power' (1984) 14 *Federal Law Review* 267

Saunders, C, 'The Sources and Scope of Commonwealth Power to Spend' (2009) 20 *Public Law Review* 251

Saunders, C, 'Towards a Theory for Section 96 (Part I)' (1987) 16 *Melbourne University Law Review* 1

Saunders, C, 'Towards a Theory for Section 96 (Part II)' (1988) 16 *Melbourne University Law Review* 699

Saunders, C and Yam, K, 'Government Regulation by Contract: Implications for the Rule of Law' (2004) 15 *Public Law Review* 51

Sawer, G, *Federation Under Strain: Australia 1972–1975* (Carlton, Melbourne University Press, 1977)

Sawyer, G, 'The Executive Power of the Commonwealth and the Whitlam Government' (Speech delivered at the Octagon Lecture, University of Western Australia, 1976)

Selway, B, 'All at Sea – Constitutional Assumptions and "the Executive Power of the Commonwealth"' (2003) 31 *Federal Law Review* 495

Senate Select Committee on a Certain Maritime Incident, 'Inquiry into a Certain Maritime Incident' (Main Report, Parliament of Australia, 23 October 2002)

Simpson, A, 'State Immunity from Commonwealth Laws: *Austin v Commonwealth* and Dilemmas of Doctrinal Design' (2004) 32 *University of Western Australia Law Review* 44

Smith, S, 'The Scope of a Nationhood Power to Respond to COVID-19: Unanswered Questions' (*AUSPUBLAW*, 13 May 2020).

State Coroner of New South Wales, *Inquest into the deaths arising from the Lindt Café Siege: Findings and recommendations* (May 2017)

Stellios, J, *Zines's The High Court and the Constitution*, 6th edn (Annandale, Federation Press, 2015)

Stephen, N, 'The Governor-General as Commander-in-Chief' (1984) 14 *Melbourne University Law Review* 563

Stephenson, P, 'Fertile Ground for Federalism? Internal Security, the States and Section 119 of the *Constitution*' (2015) 43 *Federal Law Review* 289

Stephenson, P, 'Justice Mason in the Australian Assistance Plan Case (1975): Nationhood, Federalism and Commonwealth Executive Power' in A Lynch (ed), *Great Australian dissents* (Cambridge, Cambridge University Press, 2016)

Stephenson, P, 'Nationhood and Section 61 of the Constitution' (2018) 43 *University of Western Australia Law Review* 149

Stephenson, P, 'Statutory Displacement of the Prerogative in Australia' in J Boughey and L Burton Crawford (eds), *Interpreting Executive Power* (Alexandria, Federation Press, 2020) 203

Stephenson, P, 'The Relationship between the Royal Prerogative and Statute in Australia' (2021) 44 *Melbourne University Law Review* 1001

Stephenson, P, Bennett, B and Freckelton, I, 'Public Health Emergencies in Australia' in B Bennett and I Freckelton (eds), *Pandemics, Public Health Emergencies and Government Powers: Perspectives on Australian Law* (Annandale, Federation Press, 2021)

Thomson, J, 'Drafting the Australian Constitution: The Neglected Documents' (1986) 15 *Melbourne University Law Review* 533

Twomey, A, 'Executive Power Following the *Williams* Cases' in J Griffiths and J Stellios (eds), *Current Issue in Australian Constitutional Law: Tributes to Professor Leslie Zines* (Alexandria, Federation Press, 2020)

Twomey, A, 'Federal Limitations on the Legislative Power of the States and the Commonwealth to Bind One Another' (2003) 31 *Federal Law Review* 507

Twomey, A, 'Federal and State Powers to Deal with Pandemics: Cooperation, Conflict and Confusion' in B Bennett and I Freckelton (eds), *Pandemics, Public Health Emergencies and Government Powers: Perspectives on Australian Law* (Annandale, Federation Press, 2021)

Twomey, A, 'Independence' in C Saunders and A Stone (eds), *The Oxford Handbook of the Australian Constitution* (Oxford, Oxford University Press, 2018)

Twomey, A, '*Miller* and the Prerogative' in M Elliott, J Williams and AL Young (eds), *The UK Constitution after Miller: Brexit and Beyond* (Oxford, Hart Publishing, 2018)

Twomey, A, 'Post-*Williams* Expenditure – When Can the Commonwealth and States Spend Public Money Without Parliamentary Authorisation?' (2014) 33 *University of Queensland Law Journal* 9

Twomey, A, 'Pushing the Boundaries of Executive Power: *Pape*, the Prerogative and Nationhood Powers' (2010) 34 *Melbourne University Law Review* 313

Twomey, A, 'Relevance to Australia of the UK Supreme Court's Brexit Decision' (2017) 91 *Australian Law Journal* 177

Twomey, A, '*Sue v Hill* – The Evolution of Australian Independence' in A Stone and G Williams (eds), *The High Court at the Crossroads: Essays in Constitutional Law* (Leichhardt, Federation Press, 2000)

Twomey, A, *The Australia Acts 1986: Australia's Statutes of Independence* (Annandale, Federation Press, 2010)

Twomey, A, *The Chameleon Crown: The Queen and Her Australian Governors* (Annandale, Federation Press, 2006)

Twomey, A, *The Constitution of New South Wales* (Annandale, Federation Press, 2004)

Twomey, A, 'The French Court, the Nature of the Executive Power and its Reconciliation with the Expenditure Power' in H Jackson (ed), *Essays in Honour of Chief Justice French* (Alexandria, Federation Press, 2019)

Twomey, A, 'The Prerogative and the Courts in Australia' (2021) 3 *Journal of Commonwealth Law* 55

Twomey, A, *The Veiled Sceptre: Reserve Powers of Heads of State in Westminster Systems* (Port Melbourne, Cambridge University Press, 2018)

Ward, R, 'Baton Rounds and Circulars' (1988) 1 *Cambridge Law Journal* 155

Wheeler, F, 'Judicial Review of Prerogative Power in Australia: Issues and Prospects' (1992) 14 *Sydney Law Review* 432

White, M, 'The Executive and the Military' (2005) 28 *University of New South Wales Law Journal* 438

Whitlam, EG, 'A New Federalism' (1971) 43 *Australian Quarterly* 6

Whitlam, EG, 'People and Power – Community Participation in Federal Government' (1975) 47 *Australian Quarterly* 36

Whitlam, EG, 'The Labor Government and the Constitution' in G Evans (ed), *Labor and the Constitution 1972–1975: Essays and Commentaries on the Constitutional Controversies of the Whitlam years* (Richmond, Heinemann Educational Australia, 1977)

Whitlam, EG, *The Whitlam Government 1972–1975* (Ringwood, Penguin, 1985)

Willheim, E, 'MV Tampa: The Australian Response' (2003) 15 *International Journal of Refugee Law* 159

Williams, G, Brennan, S and Lynch, A, *Blackshield and Williams Australian Constitutional Law and Theory: Commentary and Materials*, 7th edn (Annandale, Federation Press, 2018)

Williams, J, *The Australian Constitution: A Documentary History* (Carlton, Melbourne University Press, 2005)

Windeyer, V, 'Responsible Government – Highlights, Sidelights and Reflections' (1957) 41 *Royal Australian Historical Society Journal and Proceedings* 257

Winterton, G, '1975: The Dismissal of the Whitlam Government' in HP Lee and G Winterton (eds), *Australian Constitutional Landmarks* (Port Melbourne, Cambridge University Press, 2003)

Winterton, G, *Parliament, the Executive and the Governor-General: A Constitutional Analysis* (Melbourne, Melbourne University Press, 1983)

Winterton, G, 'The Acquisition of Independence' in R French, G Lindell and C Saunders (eds), *Reflections on the Australian Constitution* (Annandale, Federation Press, 2003)
Winterton, G, 'The *Communist Party Case*' in HP Lee and G Winterton (eds), *Australian Constitutional Landmarks* (Cambridge, Cambridge University Press, 2003)
Winterton, G, 'The Evolution of a Separate Australian Crown' (1993) 19 *Monash University Law Review* 1
Winterton, G, 'The Limits and Use of Executive Power by Government' (2003) 31 *Federal Law Review* 421
Winterton, G, 'The Prerogative in Novel Situations' (1983) 99 *Law Quarterly Review* 407
Winterton, G, 'The Relationship between Commonwealth Legislative and Executive Power' (2004) 25 *Adelaide Law Review* 21
Winterton, G, 'The Significance of the *Communist Party Case*' (1992) 18 *Melbourne University Law Review* 630
Wood, GA, 'Introduction' in K Cramp, *The State and Federal Constitutions of Australia* (Sydney, Angus & Robertson, 1913)
Zines, L, 'Commentary' in HV Evatt, *The Royal Prerogative* (North Ryde, Law Book Co, 1987)
Zines, L, 'Sir Anthony Mason' (2008) 28 *Federal Law Review* 171
Zines, L, 'The Inherent Executive Power of the Commonwealth' (2005) 16 *Public Law Review* 279
Zines, L, 'The Growth of Australian Nationhood and its Effect on the Powers of the Commonwealth' in L Zines (ed), *Commentaries on the Australian Constitution: A Tribute to Geoffrey Sawer* (Sydney, Butterworths, 1977)
Zines, L, *The High Court and the Constitution* (Sydney, Butterworths, 1981)
Zines, L, *The High Court and the Constitution*, 5th edn (Annandale, Federation Press, 2008)

# INDEX

www.ingramcontent.com/pod-product-compliance
Ingram Content Group UK Ltd.
Pitfield, Milton Keynes, MK11 3LW, UK
UKHW020818290926
15470UKWH00003B/1238